THE HEART OF THE MATTER

On the heat-drenched fever coast of Africa,
a searching man fights a lonely battle—
torn between a wife he no longer loves and a beautiful
stranger ... torn between his God and a
forbidden passion ...

Books by Graham Greene

Novels

- THE MAN WITHIN
- IT'S A BATTLEFIELD
- THE SHIPWRECKED
- BRIGHTON ROCK
- THE HEART OF THE MATTER
- THE END OF THE AFFAIR
- THE QUIET AMERICAN
- A BURNT-OUT CASE
- THE POWER AND THE GLORY
- THE COMEDIANS

Short Stories

- TWENTY-ONE STORIES
- A SENSE OF REALITY

Entertainments

- ORIENT EXPRESS
- THIS GUN FOR HIRE
- THE CONFIDENTIAL AGENT
- THE THIRD MAN
- LOSER TAKES ALL
- OUR MAN IN HAVANA
- THE MINISTRY OF FEAR

Plays

THE LIVING ROOM
THE COMPLAISANT LOVER
THE POTTING SHED

Travel

JOURNEY WITHOUT MAPS
ANOTHER MEXICO
IN SEARCH OF A CHARACTER

Essays

THE LOST CHILDHOOD

Published by Bantam Books, Inc.

the heart of the matter

by

Graham Greene

BANTAM BOOKS · TORONTO · NEW YORK · LONDON

*This low-priced Bantam Book
has been completely reset in a type face
designed for easy reading, and was printed
from new plates. It contains the complete
text of the original hard-cover edition.*
NOT ONE WORD HAS BEEN OMITTED.

THE HEART OF THE MATTER

*A Bantam Book / published by arrangement with
The Viking Press, Inc.*

PRINTING HISTORY

Viking edition published July 1948

2nd printing .... July 1948	4th printing .... July 1948
3rd printing .... July 1948	5th printing ... November 1948

Book-of-the-Month Club selection published midsummer 1948

Garden City edition published March 1951

Omnibook edition published December 1948

Bantam edition published February 1956
2nd printing ...... October 1957
3rd printing ... December 1967
4th printing

Published simultaneously in the United States and Canada

Bantam Books are published by Bantam Books, Inc., a subsidiary of Grosset & Dunlap, Inc. Its trade-mark, consisting of the words "Bantam Books" and the portrayal of a bantam, is registered in the United States Patent Office and in other countries. Marca Registrada. Bantam Books, Inc., 271 Madison Avenue, New York, N.Y. 10016.

*Le pécheur est au cœur même de chrétienté.
. . . Nul n'est aussi compétent que le pécheur
en matière de chrétienté. Nul, si ce n'est le saint.*

Péguy

N<small>O CHARACTER IN THIS BOOK IS BASED ON</small> that of a living person. The geographical background of the story is drawn from that part of West Africa of which I have had personal experience—that is inevitable—but I want to make it absolutely clear that no inhabitant, past or present, of that particular colony appears in my book. Even an imaginary colony must have its officials—a commissioner of police and a colonial secretary, for example; I have a special reason for not wanting such characters in my book to be identified with real people, for I remember with very great gratitude the courtesy and consideration I received from the Commissioner of Police and the Colonial Secretary in the colony where I worked in 1942-43.

The poem quoted on page 236 is from *Selected Poems* of *Rainer Maria Rilke*, translated by J. D. Leishmann (London: Hogarth Press, 1941).

Book 1

Part One

I. WILSON SAT ON THE BALCONY OF THE BEDFORD Hotel with his bald pink knees thrust against the ironwork. It was Sunday and the Cathedral bell clanged for matins. On the other side of Bond Street, in the windows of the High School, sat the young Negresses in dark blue gym smocks engaged on the interminable task of trying to wave their wirespring hair. Wilson stroked his very young moustache and dreamed, waiting for his gin-and-bitters.

Sitting there, facing Bond Street, he had his face turned to the sea. His pallor showed how recently he had emerged from it into the port: so did his lack of interest in the schoolgirls opposite. He was like the lagging finger of the barometer, still pointing to Fair long after its companion had moved to Stormy. Below him the black clerks moved churchward, but their wives in brilliant afternoon dresses of blue and cerise aroused no interest in Wilson. He was alone on the balcony except for one bearded Indian in a turban who had already tried to tell his fortune: this was not the hour or the day for white men—they would be at the beach five miles away, but Wilson had no car. He felt almost intolerably lonely. On either side of the school the tin roofs sloped towards the sea, and the corrugated iron above his head clanged and clattered as a vulture alighted.

Three merchant officers from the convoy in the harbour came into view, walking up from the quay. They were surrounded immediately by small boys wearing school caps. The boys' refrain came faintly up to Wilson like a nursery rhyme: "Captain want jig jig, my sister pretty girl schoolteacher, captain want jig jig." The bearded Indian frowned over intricate calculations on the back of an envelope—a

3

horoscope, the cost of living? When Wilson looked down into the street again the officers had fought their way free, and the schoolboys had swarmed again round a single able-seaman; they led him triumphantly away towards the brothel near the police station, as though to the nursery.

A black boy brought Wilson's gin and he sipped it very slowly because he had nothing else to do except to return to his hot and squalid room and read a novel—or a poem. Wilson liked poetry, but he absorbed it secretly like a drug. *The Golden Treasury* accompanied him wherever he went, but it was taken at night in small doses—a finger of Longfellow, Macaulay, Mangan: *Go on to tell how, with genius wasted, Betrayed in friendship, befooled in love* . . . His taste was romantic. For public exhibition he had his Wallace. He wanted passionately to be indistinguishable on the surface from other men; he wore his moustache like a club tie—it was his highest common factor: but his eyes betrayed him—brown dog's eyes, a setter's eyes, pointing mournfully towards Bond Street.

"Excuse me," a voice said, "aren't you Wilson?"

He looked up at a middle-aged man in the inevitable khaki shorts with a drawn face the colour of hay.

"Yes, that's me."

"May I join you? My name's Harris."

"Delighted, Mr. Harris."

"You're the new accountant at the U.A.C."

"That's me. Have a drink?"

"I'll have a lemon squash if you don't mind. Can't drink in the middle of the day."

The Indian rose from his table and approached with deference. "You remember me, Mr. Harris. Perhaps you would tell your friend, Mr. Harris, of my talents. Perhaps he would like to read my letters of recommendation . . ." The grubby sheaf of envelopes was always in his hand. "The leaders of society."

"Go off. Beat it, you old scoundrel," Harris said.

"How did you know my name?" Wilson asked.

"Saw it on a cable. I'm a cable censor," Harris said. "What a job. What a place."

"I can see from here, Mr. Harris, that your fortune has changed considerably. If you would step with me for a moment into the bathroom . . ."

4

"Beat it, Gunga Din."

"Why the bathroom?" Wilson asked.

"He always tells fortunes there. I suppose it's the only private room available. I never thought of asking why."

"Been here long?"

"Eighteen bloody months."

"Going home soon?"

Harris stared over the tin roofs towards the harbour. He said, "The ships all go the wrong way. But when I do get home you'll never see me here again." He lowered his voice and said with venom over his lemon squash, "I hate the place. I hate the people. I hate the bloody niggers. Mustn't call 'em that, you know."

"My boy seems all right."

"A man's boy's always all right. He's a real nigger—but these, look at 'em, look at that one with a feather boa down there. They aren't even real niggers. Just West Indians, and they rule the coast. Clerks in the stores, city council, magistrates, lawyers—my God. It's all right up in the Protectorate. I haven't anything to say against a real nigger. God made our colours. But these—my God. The Government's afraid of them. The police are afraid of them. Look down there," Harris said, "look at Scobie."

A vulture flapped and shifted on the iron roof and Wilson looked at Scobie. He looked without interest in obedience to a stranger's direction, and it seemed to him that no particular interest attached to the squat grey-haired man walking alone up Bond Street. He couldn't tell that this was one of those occasions a man never forgets: a small cicatrice had been made on the memory, a wound that would ache whenever certain things combined—the taste of gin at midday, the smell of flowers under a balcony, the clang of corrugated iron, an ugly bird flopping from perch to perch.

"He loves 'em so much," Harris said, " he sleeps with 'em."

"Is that the police uniform?"

"It is. Our great police force. A lost thing will they never find—you know the poem."

"I don't read poetry," Wilson said. His eyes followed Scobie up the sun-drowned street. Scobie stopped and had a word with a black man in a white panama: a black policeman passed by, saluting smartly. Scobie went on.

5

"Probably in the pay of the Syrians too, if the truth were known."

"The Syrians?

"This is the original Tower of Babel," Harris said. "West Indians, Africans, real Indians, Syrians, Englishmen, Scotsmen in the Office of Works. Irish priests, French priests, Alsatian priests."

"What do the Syrians do?"

"Make money. They run all the stores up-country and most of the stores here. Run diamonds too."

"I suppose there's a lot of that."

"The Germans pay a high price."

"Hasn't he got a wife here?"

"Who? Oh, Scobie. Rather. He's got a wife. Perhaps if I had a wife like that, I'd sleep with niggers too. You'll meet her soon. She's the city intellectual. She likes art, poetry. Got up an exhibition of arts for the shipwrecked seamen. You know the kind of thing—poems on exile by aircraftsmen, water-colours by stokers, poker-work from the mission schools. Poor old Scobie. Have another gin?"

"I think I will," said Wilson.

2

Scobie turned up James Street past the Secretariat. With its long balconies it had always reminded him of a hospital. For fifteen years he had watched the arrival of a succession of patients: periodically at the end of eighteen months certain patients were sent home, yellow and nervy, and others took their place—colonial secretaries, secretaries of agriculture, treasurers and directors of public works. He watched their temperature charts every one—the first outbreak of unreasonable temper, the drink too many, the sudden stand for principle after a year of acquiescence. The black clerks carried their bedside manner like doctors down the corridors; cheerful and respectful, they put up with any insult. The patient was always right.

Round the corner, in front of the cotton tree, where the earliest settlers had gathered their first day on the unfriendly shore, stood the law courts and police station, a great stone building like the grandiloquent boast of weak men. Inside that massive frame the human being rattled in the corridors like a dry kernel. No one could have been adequate to so rhetorical a conception. But the idea in any case was only one room deep. In the dark narrow passage behind, in the charge-room and the cells, Scobie could always detect the odour of human meanness and injustice —it was the smell of a zoo, of sawdust, excrement, ammonia, and lack of liberty. The place was scrubbed daily, but you could never eliminate the smell. Prisoners and policemen carried it in their clothing like cigarette smoke.

Scobie climbed the great steps and turned to his right along the shaded outside corridor to his room: a table, two kitchen chairs, a cupboard, some rusty handcuffs hanging on a nail like an old hat, a filing cabinet: to a stranger it would have appeared a bare uncomfortable room but to Scobie it was home. Other men slowly build up the sense of home by accumulation—a new picture, more and more books, an odd-shaped paper-weight, the ash-tray bought for a forgotten reason on a forgotten holiday; Scobie built his home by a process of reduction. He had started out fifteen years ago with far more than this. There had been a photograph of his wife, bright leather cushions from the market, an easy chair, a large coloured map of the port on the wall. The map had been borrowed by younger men: it was of no more use to him: he carried the whole coastline of the colony in his mind's eye: from Kufa Bay to Medley was his beat. As for the cushions and the easy chair, he had soon discovered how comfort of that kind down in the airless town meant heat. Where the body was touched or enclosed it sweated. Last of all, his wife's photograph had been made unnecessary by her presence. She had joined him the first year of the phony war and now she couldn't get away: the danger of submarines had made her as much a fixture as the handcuffs on the nail. Besides, it had been a very early photograph, and he no longer cared to be reminded of the unformed face, the expression calm and gentle with lack of knowledge, the lips parted obediently in the smile the photographer had demanded. Fifteen years form a face, gentleness ebbs with experience, and he was always aware of his own responsibility. He had led the way: the experience that had come to her was the experience selected by himself. He had formed her face.

He sat down at his bare table and almost immediately his Mende sergeant clicked his heels in the doorway. "Sah?"

7

"Anything to report?"

"The Commissioner want to see you, sah."

"Anything on the charge sheet?"

"Two black men fight in the market, sah."

"Mammy trouble?"

"Yes, sah."

"Anything else?"

"Miss Wilberforce want to see you, sah. I tell her you was at church and she got to come back by an' by, but she stick. She say she no budge."

"Which Miss Wilberforce is that, sergeant?"

"I don't know, sah. She come from Sharp Town, sah."

"Well, I'll see her after the Commissioner. But no one else, mind."

"Very good, sah."

Scobie, passing down the passage to the Commissioner's room, saw the girl sitting alone on a bench against the wall: he didn't look twice: he caught only the vague impression of a young black African face, a bright cotton frock, and then she was already out of his mind, and he was wondering what he should say to the Commissioner. It had been on his mind all that week.

"Sit down, Scobie." The Commissioner was an old man of fifty-three—one counted age by the years a man had served in the colony. The Commissioner with twenty-two years' service was the oldest man there, just as the Governor was a stripling of sixty-five compared with any district officer who had five years' knowledge behind him.

"I'm retiring, Scobie," the Commissioner said, "after this tour."

"I know."

"I suppose everyone knows."

"I've heard the men talking about it."

"And yet you are the second man I've told. Do they say who's taking my place?"

Scobie said, "They know who isn't."

"It's damned unfair," the Commissioner said. "I can do nothing more than I have done, Scobie. You are a wonderful man for picking up enemies. Like Aristides the Just."

"I don't think I'm as just as all that."

"The question is, what do you want to do? They are sending a man called Baker from Gambia. He's younger

8

than you are. Do you want to resign, retire, transfer, Scobie?"

"I want to stay," Scobie said.

"Your wife won't like it."

"I've been here too long to go." He thought to himself: Poor Louise, if I had left it to her, where should we be now? and he admitted straightaway that they wouldn't be here—somewhere far better, better climate, better pay, better position. She would have taken every opening for improvement: she would have steered agilely up the ladders and left the snakes alone. I've landed her here, he thought, with the odd premonitory sense of guilt he always felt, as though he were responsible for something in the future he couldn't even foresee. He said aloud, "You know I like the place."

"I believe you do. I wonder why."

"It's pretty in the evening," Scobie said vaguely.

"Do you know the latest story they are using against you at the Secretariat?"

"I suppose I'm in the Syrians' pay?"

"They haven't got that far yet. That's the next stage. No, you sleep with black girls. You know what it is, Scobie, you ought to have flirted with one of their wives. They feel insulted."

"Perhaps I ought to sleep with a black girl. Then they won't have to think up anything else."

"The man before you slept with dozens," the Commissioner said, "but it never bothered anyone. They thought up something different for him. They said he drank secretly. It made them feel better drinking publicly. What a lot of swine they are, Scobie."

"The Chief Assistant Colonial Secretary's not a bad chap."

"No, the Chief Assistant Colonial Secretary's all right." The Commissioner laughed. "You're a terrible fellow, Scobie. Scobie the Just."

Scobie returned down the passage: the girl sat in the dusk: her feet were bare: they stood side by side like casts in a museum: they didn't belong to the bright smart cotton frock. "Are you Miss Wilberforce?" Scobie asked.

"Yes, sir."

"You don't live here, do you?"

9

"No! I live in Sharp Town, sir."

"Well, come in." He led the way into his office and sat down at his desk. There was no pencil laid out and he opened his drawer. Here and here only had objects accumulated: letters, india-rubbers, a broken rosary—no pencil. "What's the trouble, Miss Wilberforce?" His eye caught a snapshot of a bathing party at Medley Beach: his wife, the Colonial Secretary's wife, the Director of Education holding up what looked like a dead fish, the Colonial Treasurer's wife. The expanse of white flesh made them look like a gathering of albinos, and all the mouths gaped with laughter.

The girl said, "My landlady—she broke up my home last night. She come in when it was dark, and she pull down all the partition, an' she thieve my chest with all my belongings."

"You got plenty lodgers?"

"Only three, sir."

He knew exactly how it all was: a lodger would take a one-roomed shack for five shillings a week, stick up a few thin partitions, and let the so-called rooms for half a crown apiece—a horizontal tenement. Each room would be furnished with a box containing a little china and glass, "dashed" by an employer or stolen from an employer, a bed made out of old packing cases, and a hurricane lamp. The glass of these lamps did not long survive, and the little open flames were always ready to catch some spilt paraffin; they licked at the plywood partitions and caused innumerable fires. Sometimes a landlady would thrust her way into her house and pull down the dangerous partitions, sometimes she would steal the lamps of her tenants, and the ripple of her theft would go out in widening rings of lamp thefts until they touched the European quarter, and became a subject of gossip at the club. "Can't keep a lamp for love or money."

"Your landlady," Scobie told the girl sharply, "she say you make plenty trouble: too many lodgers: too many lamps."

"No, sir. No lamp palaver."

"Mammy palaver, eh? You bad girl?"

"No, sir."

"Why you come here? Why you not call Corporal Laminah in Sharp Town?"

"He my landlady's brother, sir."

"He is, is he? Same father, same mother?"

"No, sir. Same father."

The interview was like a ritual between priest and server: he knew exactly what would happen when one of his men investigated the affair. The landlady would say that she had told her tenant to pull down the partitions and when that failed she had taken action herself. She would deny that there had ever been a chest of china. The corporal would confirm this. He would turn out not to be the landlady's brother, but some other unspecified relation—probably disreputable. Bribes—which were known respectably as dashes—would pass to and fro: the storm of indignation and anger that had sounded so genuine would subside: the partitions would go up again: nobody would hear any more about the chest, and several policemen would be a shilling or two the richer. At the beginning of his service Scobie had flung himself into these investigations: he had found himself over and over again in the position of a partisan, supporting as he believed the poor and innocent tenant against the wealthy and guilty house-owner. But he soon discovered that the guilt and innocence were as relative as the wealth. The wronged tenant turned out to be also the wealthy capitalist, making a profit of five shillings a week on a single room, living rent-free herself. After that he had tried to kill these cases at birth: he would reason with the complainant and point out that the investigation would do no good and undoubtedly cost her time and money: he would sometimes even refuse to investigate. The result of that inaction had been stones flung at his car window, slashed tires, the nickname of the Bad Man that had stuck to him through all one long sad tour—it worried him unreasonably in the heat and damp: he couldn't take it lightly. Already he had begun to desire these people's trust and affection. That year he had black-water fever and was nearly invalided from the service altogether.

The girl waited patiently for his decision: they had an infinite capacity for patience when patience was required—just as their impatience knew no bounds of propriety when they had anything to gain by it. They would sit quietly all day in a white man's back yard in order to beg for something he hadn't the power to grant, or they would shriek

11

and fight and abuse to get served in a store before their neighbour. He thought: How beautiful she is. It was strange to think that fifteen years ago he would not have noticed her beauty—the small high breasts, the tiny wrists, the thrust of the young buttocks; she would have been indistinguishable from her fellows—a black. In those days he had thought his wife beautiful. A white skin had not then reminded him of an albino. Poor Louise. He said, "Give this chit to the sergeant at the desk."

"Thank you, sir."

"That's all right." He smiled. "Try to tell him the truth."

He watched her go out of the dark office like fifteen wasted years.

3

Scobie had been outmanœuvred in the interminable war over housing. During his last leave he had lost his bungalow in Cape Station, the main European quarter, to a senior sanitary inspector called Fellowes, and had found himself relegated to a square two-storied house, built originally for a Syrian trader, on the flats below—a piece of reclaimed swamp which would return to swamp as soon as the rains set in. From the windows he looked directly out to sea over a line of Creole houses: on the other side of the road lorries backed and churned in a military transport camp and vultures strolled like domestic turkeys in the regimental refuse. On the low ridge of hills behind him the bungalows of the station lay among the low clouds; lamps burned all day in the cupboards, mould gathered on the boots—nervertheless these were the houses for men of his rank. Women depended so much on pride, pride in themselves, their husbands, their surroundings. They were seldom proud, it seemed to him, of the invisible.

"Louise," he called, "Louise." There was no reason to call: if she wasn't in the living-room there was nowhere else for her to be but the bedroom (the kitchen was simply a shed in the yard opposite the back door); yet it was his habit to cry her name, a habit he had formed in the days of anxiety and love. The less he needed Louise the more conscious he became of his responsibility for her happiness. When he called her name he was crying like Canute against

12

a tide—the tide of her melancholy, dissatisfaction, and disappointment.

In the old days she had replied, but she was not such a creature of habit as he was—nor so false, he sometimes told himself. Kindness and pity had no power with her: she would never have pretended an emotion she didn't feel, and like an animal she gave way completely to the momentary sickness and recovered as suddenly. When he found her in the bedroom under the mosquito net she reminded him of a dog or a cat, she was so completely "out." Her hair was matted, her eyes closed. He stood very still like a spy in foreign territory, and indeed he was in foreign territory now. If home for him meant the reduction of things to a firm, friendly, unchanging minimum, home to her was accumulation. The dressing table was crammed with pots and photographs—himself as a young man in the curiously dated officer's uniform of the last war: the Chief Justice's wife whom for the moment she counted as her friend: their only child, who had died at school in England three years ago—a little pious nine-year-old girl's face in the white muslin of first communion: innumerable photographs of Louise herself, in groups with nursing sisters, with the Admiral's party at Medley Beach, on a Yorkshire moor with Teddy Bromley and his wife. It was as if she were accumulating evidence that she had friends like other people. He watched her through the muslin net. Her face had the yellow-ivory tinge of atabrine: her hair, which had once been the colour of bottled honey, was dark and stringy with sweat. These were the times of ugliness when he loved her, when pity and responsibility reached the intensity of a passion. It was pity that told him to go: he wouldn't have woken his worst enemy from sleep—leave alone Louise. He tiptoed out and down the stairs. (The inside stairs could be found nowhere else in this bungalow city except in Government House, and she had tried to make them an object of pride with stair carpets and pictures on the wall.) In the living-room there was a bookcase full of her books, rugs on the floor, a native mask from Nigeria, more photographs. The books had to be wiped daily to remove the damp, and she had not succeeded very well in disguising with flowery curtains the food-safe, which stood with each foot in a little enamel basin of water to keep the ants out. The boy was laying a single place for lunch.

13

The boy was short and squat with the broad ugly pleasant face of a Temne. His bare feet flapped like empty gloves across the floor.

"What's wrong with Missus?" Scobie asked.

"Belly humbug," Ali said.

Scobie took a Mende grammar from the bookcase: it was tucked away in the bottom shelf where its old untidy cover was least conspicuous. In the upper shelves were the flimsy rows of Louise's authors—not-quite-so-young modern poets and the novels of Virginia Woolf. He couldn't concentrate: it was too hot and his wife's absence was like a garrulous companion in the room reminding him of his responsibility. A fork fell on the floor and he watched Ali surreptitiously wipe it on his sleeve, watched him with affection: they had been together fifteen years—a year longer than his marriage—a long time to keep a servant. He had been "small boy" first, then assistant steward in the days when one kept four servants, now he was plain steward. After each leave Ali would be on the landing-stage waiting to organize his luggage with three or four ragged carriers. In the intervals of leave many people tried to steal Ali's services, but he had never yet failed to be waiting —except once when he had been in prison. There was no disgrace about prison; it was an obstacle that no one could avoid for ever.

"Ticki," a voice wailed, and Scobie rose at once. "Ticki." He went upstairs.

His wife was sitting up under the mosquito net, and for a moment he had the impression of a joint under a meat cover. But pity trod on the heels of the cruel image and hustled it away. "Are you feeling better, darling?"

Louise said, "Mrs. Castle's been in."

"Enough to make anyone ill," Scobie said.

"She's been telling me about you."

"What about me?" He gave her a bright fake smile; so much of life was a putting off of unhappiness for another time. Nothing was ever lost by delay. He had a dim idea that perhaps if one delayed long enough, things were taken out of one's hands altogether by death.

"She says the Commissioner's retiring, and they've passed you over."

"Her husband talks too much in his sleep."

"Is it true?"

"Yes. I've known it for weeks. It doesn't matter, dear, really."

Louise said, "I'll never be able to show my face at the Club again."

"It's not as bad as that. These things happen, you know."

"You'll resign, won't you, Ticki?"

"I don't think I can do that, dear."

"Mrs. Castle's on our side. She's furious. She says everyone's talking about it and saying things. Darling, you aren't in the pay of the Syrians, are you?"

"No, dear."

"I was so upset I came out of Mass before the end. It's so mean of them, Ticki. You can't take it lying down. You've got to think of me."

"Yes, I do. All the time." He sat down on the bed and put his hand under the net and touched hers. Little beads of sweat started where their skins touched. He said, "I do think of you, dear. But I've been fifteen years in this place. I'd be lost anywhere else even if they gave me another job. It isn't much of a recommendation, you know, being passed over."

"We could retire."

"The pension isn't much to live on."

"I'm sure I could make a little money writing. Mrs. Castle says I ought to be a professional. With all this experience," Louise said, gazing through the white muslin tent as far as her dressing table: there another face in white muslin stared back and she looked away. She said, "If only we could go to South Africa. I can't bear the people here."

"Perhaps I could arrange a passage for you. There haven't been many sinkings that way lately. You ought to have a holiday."

"There was a time when you wanted to retire too. You used to count the years. You made plans—for all of us."

"Oh well, one changes," he said evasively.

She said mercilessly, "You didn't think you'd be alone with me then."

He pressed his sweating hand against hers. "What nonsense you talk, dear. You must get up and have some food. . . ."

"Do you love anyone, Ticki, except yourself?"

"No, I just love myself, that's all. And Ali. I forgot Ali. Of course I love him too. But not you," he ran on with

15

worn mechanical raillery, stroking her hand, smiling, soothing. . . .

"And Ali's sister?"

"Has he got a sister?"

"They've all got sisters, haven't they? Why didn't you go
to Mass today?"

"It was my morning on duty, dear. You know that."

"You could have changed it. You haven't got much faith,
have you, Ticki?"

"You've got enough for both of us, dear. Come and have
some food."

"Ticki, I sometimes think you just became a Catholic to
marry me. It doesn't mean a thing to you, does it?"

"Listen, darling, you want to come down and eat a bit.
Then you want to take the car along to the Beach and have
some fresh air."

"How different the whole day would have been," she
said, staring out of her net, "if you'd come home and said,
'Darling, I'm going to be the Commissioner.'"

Scobie said slowly, "You know, dear, in a place like this
in war-time—an important harbour—the Vichy French just
across the border—all this diamond smuggling from the
Protectorate—they need a younger man." He didn't believe
a word he was saying.

"I hadn't thought of that."

"That's the only reason. You can't blame anyone. It's the
war."

"The war does spoil everything, doesn't it?"

"It gives the younger men a chance."

"Darling, perhaps I'll come down and just pick at a little
cold meat."

"That's right, dear." He withdrew his hand: it was dripping with sweat. "I'll tell Ali."

Downstairs he shouted "Ali" out of the back door.

"Massa?"

"Lay two places. Missus better."

The first faint breeze of the day came off the sea, blowing
up over the bushes and between the Creole huts. A vulture
flapped heavily upwards from the iron roof and down
again in the yard next door. Scobie drew a deep breath:
he felt exhausted and victorious: he had persuaded Louise
to pick a little meat. It had always been his responsibility

16

to maintain happiness in those he loved. One was safe now, for ever, and the other was going to eat her lunch.

4

In the evening the port became beautiful for perhaps five minutes. The laterite roads that were so ugly and clay-heavy by day became a delicate flowerlike pink. It was the hour of content. Men who had left the port for ever would sometimes remember on a grey wet London evening the bloom and glow that faded almost as soon as it was seen: they would wonder why they had hated the coast and for a space of a drink they would long to return.

Scobie stopped his Morris at one of the great loops of the climbing road and looked back. He was just too late. The flower had withered upwards from the town: the white stones that marked the edge of the precipitous hill shone like candles in the new dusk.

"I wonder if anybody will be there, Ticki."

"Sure to be. It's library night."

"Do hurry up, dear. It's so hot in the car. I'll be glad when the rains come."

"Will you?"

"If only they just went on for a month or two and then stopped."

Scobie made the right reply. He never listened while his wife talked. He worked steadily to the even current of sound; but if a note of distress were struck he was aware of it at once. Like a wireless operator with a novel open in front of him, he could disregard every signal except the ship's symbol and the S.O.S. He could even work better while she talked than when she was silent, for so long as his ear-drum registered those tranquil sounds—the gossip of the Club, comments on the sermons preached by Father Rank, the plot of a new novel, even complaints about the weather—he knew that all was well. It was silence that stopped him working—silence in which he might look up and see tears waiting in the eyes for his attention.

"There's a rumour going round that the refrigerators were all sunk last week."

He considered while she talked his line of action with

the Portuguese ship that was due in as soon as the boom opened in the morning. The fortnightly arrival of a neutral ship provided an outing for the junior officers: a change of food, a few glasses of real wine, even the opportunity of buying some small decorative object in the ship's store for a girl. In return they had only to help the Field Security Police in the examination of passports, the searching of the suspects' cabins: all the hard and disagreeable work was done by the F.S.P., in the hold, sifting sacks of rice for commercial diamonds, or in the heat of the kitchen, plunging the hand into tins of lard, disembowelling the stuffed turkeys. To try to find a few diamonds in a liner of fifteen thousand tons was absurd: no malign tyrant in a fairy story had ever set a goose girl a more impossible task, and yet as regularly as the ships called the cipher telegrams came in—"So-and-so travelling first class suspected of carrying diamonds. The following members of the ship's crew suspected . . ." Nobody ever found anything. He thought: It's Harris's turn to go on board, and Fraser can go with him. I'm too old for these excursions. Let the boys have a little fun.

"Last time half the books arrived damaged."

"Did they?"

Judging from the number of cars, he thought, there were not many people at the Club yet. He switched off his lights and waited for Louise to move, but she just sat there with a clenched fist showing in the switchboard light. "Well, dear, here we are," he said in the hearty voice that strangers took as a mark of stupidity. Louise said, "Do you think they all know by this time?"

"Know what?"

"That you've been passed over."

"My dear, I thought we'd finished with all that. Look at all the generals who've been passed over since 1940. They won't bother about a deputy commissioner."

She said, "But they don't like me."

Poor Louise, he thought, it is terrible not to be liked, and his mind went back to his own experience in that early tour when the blacks had slashed his tires and written insults on his car. "My dear, how absurd you are. I've never known anyone with so many friends." He ran unconvincingly on. "Mrs. Halifax, Mrs. Castle . . ." and then decided it was better after all not to list them.

18

"They'll all be waiting there," she said, "just waiting for me to walk in. . . . I never wanted to come to the Club tonight. Let's go home."

"We can't. Here's Mrs. Castle's car arriving." He tried to laugh. "We're trapped, Louise." He saw the fist open and close, the damp inefficient powder lying like snow in the ridges of the knuckles. "Oh, Ticki, Ticki," she said, "you won't leave me ever, will you? I haven't got any friends—not since the Tom Barlows went away." He lifted the moist hand and kissed the palm: he was bound by the pathos of her unattractiveness.

They walked side by side like a couple of policemen on duty into the lounge where Mrs. Halifax was dealing out the library books. It is seldom that anything is quite so bad as one fears: there was no reason to believe that they had been the subject of conversation. "Goody, goody," Mrs. Halifax called to them, "the new Clemence Dane's arrived." She was the most inoffensive woman in the station: she had long untidy hair, and one found hairpins inside the library books where she had marked her place. Scobie felt it quite safe to leave his wife in her company, for Mrs. Halifax had no malice and no capacity for gossip: her memory was too bad for anything to lodge there for long: she read the same novels over and over again without knowing it.

Scobie joined a group on the verandah. Fellowes, the Sanitary Inspector, was talking fiercely to Reith, the Chief Assistant Colonial Secretary, and a naval officer called Brigstock. "After all this is a club," he was saying, "not a railway refreshment room." Ever since Fellowes had snatched his house, Scobie had done his best to like the man—it was one of the rules by which he set his life, to be a good loser. But sometimes he found it very hard to like Fellowes. The hot evening had not been good to him: the thin damp ginger hair, the small prickly moustache, the goosegog eyes, the scarlet cheeks, and the old Lancing tie. "Quite," said Brigstock, swaying slightly.

"What's the trouble?" Scobie asked.

Reith said, "He thinks we are not exclusive enough." He spoke with the comfortable irony of a man who had in his time been completely exclusive, who had in fact excluded from his solitary table in the Protectorate every one but

19

himself. Fellowes said hotly, "There are limits," fingering for confidence the Lancing tie.

"Tha's so," said Brigstock.

"I knew it would happen," Fellowes said, "as soon as we made every officer in the place an honorary member. Sooner or later they would begin to bring in undesirables. I'm not a snob, but in a place like this you've got to draw lines —for the sake of the women. It's not like it is at home."

"But what's the trouble?" Scobie asked.

"Honorary members," Fellowes said, "should not be allowed to introduce guests. Only the other day we had a private brought in. The army can be democratic if it likes, but not at our expense. That's another thing, there's not enough drink to go round as it is without these fellows."

"Tha's a point," Brigstock said, swaying more violently.

"I wish I knew what it was all about," Scobie said.

"The dentist from the Forty-ninth has brought in a civilian called Wilson, and this man Wilson wants to join the Club. It puts everybody in a very embarrassing position."

"What's wrong with him?"

"He's one of the U.A.C. clerks. He can join the club in Sharp Town. What does he want to come up here for?"

"That club's not functioning," Reith said.

"Well, that's their fault, isn't it?" Over the Sanitary Inspector's shoulder Scobie could see the enormous range of the night. The fireflies signalled to and fro along the edge of the hill and the lamp of a patrol boat moving on the bay could be distinguished only by its steadiness. "Blackout time," Reith said. "We'd better go in."

"Which is Wilson?" Scobie asked him.

"That's him over there. The poor devil looks lonely. He's only been out a few days."

Wilson stood uncomfortably alone in a wilderness of arm-chairs, pretending to look at a map on the wall. His pale face shone and trickled like plaster. He had obviously bought his tropical suit from a shipper who had worked off on him an unwanted line: it was oddly striped and liverish in colour. "You're Wilson, aren't you?" Reith said. "I saw your name in the Col. Sec.'s book today."

"Yes, that's me," Wilson said.

"My name's Reith. I'm Chief Assistant Col. Sec. This is Scobie, the Deputy Commissioner."

"I saw you this morning outside the Bedford Hotel, sir," Wilson said. There was something defenceless, it seemed to Scobie, in his whole attitude: he stood there waiting for people to be friendly or unfriendly—he didn't seem to expect one reaction more than another. He was like a dog. Nobody had yet drawn on his face the lines that make a human being.

"Have a drink, Wilson."

"I don't mind if I do, sir."

"Here's my wife," Scobie said. "Louise, this is Mr. Wilson."

"I've heard a lot about Mr. Wilson already," Louise said stiffly.

"You see, you're famous, Wilson," Scobie said. "You're a man from the town and you've gate-crashed Cape Station Club."

"I didn't know I was doing anything wrong. Major Cooper invited me."

"That reminds me," Reith said, "I must make an appointment with Cooper. I think I've got an abscess." He slid away.

"Cooper was telling me about the library," Wilson said, "and I thought perhaps . . ."

"Do you like reading?" Louise asked, and Scobie realized with relief that she was going to be kind to the poor devil. It was always a bit of a toss-up with Louise. Sometimes she could be the worst snob in the station, and it occurred to him with pity that perhaps now she believed she couldn't afford to be snobbish. Any new face that didn't 'know' was welcome.

"Well," Wilson said, and fingered desperately at his thin moustache, "well . . ." It was as if he were gathering strength for a great confession or a great evasion.

"Detective stories?" Louise asked.

"I don't mind detective stories," Wilson said uneasily. "Some detective stories."

"Personally," Louise said, "I like poetry."

"Poetry," Wilson said, "yes." He took his fingers reluctantly away from his moustache, and something in his dog-like look of gratitude and hope made Scobie think with happiness: Have I really found her a friend?

"I like poetry myself," Wilson said.

Scobie moved away towards the bar: once again a load

was lifted from his mind. The evening was not spoilt: she would come home happy, go to bed happy. During one night a mood did not change, and happiness would survive until he left to go on duty. He could sleep. . . .

He saw a gathering of his junior officers in the bar. Fraser was there and Tod and a new man from Palestine with the extraordinary name of Thimblerigg. Scobie hesitated to go in. They were enjoying themselves, and they would not want a senior officer with them. "Infernal cheek," Tod was saying. They were probably talking about poor Wilson. Then before he could move away he heard Fraser's voice. "He's punished for it. Literary Louise has got him." Thimblerigg gave a small gurgling laugh, a bubble of gin forming on a plump lip.

Scobie walked rapidly back into the lounge. He went full tilt into an arm-chair, and came to a halt. His vision moved jerkily back into focus, but sweat dripped into his right eye. The fingers that wiped it free shook like a drunkard's. He told himself: Be careful. This isn't a climate for emotion. It's a climate for meanness, malice, snobbery, but anything like hate or love drives a man off his head. He remembered Bowers sent home for punching the Governor's A.D.C. at a party, Makin the missionary who ended in an asylum at Chislehurst.

"It's damned hot," he said to someone who loomed vaguely beside him.

"You look bad, Scobie. Have a drink."

"No, thank you. Got to drive round on inspection."

Beside the bookshelves Louise was talking happily to Wilson, but he could feel the malice and snobbery of the world padding up like wolves about her. They wouldn't even let her enjoy her books, he thought, and his hand began to shake again. Approaching, he heard her say in her kindly Lady Bountiful manner, "You must come and have dinner with us one day. I've got a lot of books that might interest you."

"I'd love to," Wilson said.

"Just ring us up and take pot luck." Scobie thought: What are those others worth that they have the nerve to sneer at any human being? He knew every one of her faults. How often he had winced at her patronage of strangers. He knew each phrase, each intonation that alienated others. Sometimes he longed to warn her—don't wear that dress, don't say that again—as a mother might teach a daughter, but he had to remain silent, aching with the fore-knowledge of her loss of friends. The worst was when he detected in his colleagues an extra warmth of friendliness towards himself, as though they pitied him. What right have you, he longed to exclaim, to criticize her? This is my doing. This is what I've made of her. She wasn't always like this.

He came abruptly up to them and said, "My dear, I've got to go round the beats."

"Already?"

"I'm sorry."

"I'll stay, dear. Mrs. Halifax will run me home."

"I wish you'd come with me."

"What? Round the beats? It's ages since I've been."

"That's why I'd like you to come." He lifted her hand and kissed it: it was a challenge. He proclaimed to the whole Club that he was not to be pitied, that he loved his wife, that they were happy. But nobody that mattered saw—Mrs. Halifax was busy with the books, Reith had gone long ago, Brigstock was in the bar, Fellowes talked too busily to Mrs. Castle to notice anything—nobody saw except Wilson.

Louise said, "I'll come another time, dear. But Mrs. Halifax has just promised to run Mr. Wilson home by our house. There's a book I want to lend him."

Scobie felt an immense gratitude to Wilson. "That's fine," he said, "fine. But stay and have a drink till I get back. I'll run you home to the Bedford. I shan't be late." He put a hand on Wilson's shoulder and prayed silently: Don't let her patronize him too far: don't let her be absurd: let her keep this friend at least. "I won't say good night," he said, "I'll expect to see you when I get back."

"It's very kind of you, sir."

"You mustn't sir me. You're not a policeman, Wilson. Thank your stars for that."

5

Scobie was later than he expected. It was the encounter with Yusef that delayed him. Halfway down the hill he found Yusef's car stuck by the roadside, with Yusef sleeping quietly in the back: the light from Scobie's car lit up the large pasty face, the lick of his white hair falling over the forehead, just touched the beginning of the huge thighs in their tight white drill. Yusef's shirt was open at the neck and tendrils of black breast-hair coiled around the buttons.

"Can I help you?" Scobie unwillingly asked and Yusef opened his eyes: the gold teeth fitted by his brother, the dentist, flashed instantaneously like a torch. If Fellowes drives by now, what a story he will have for the Secretariat in the morning, Scobie thought. The Deputy Commissioner meeting Yusef, the storekeeper, clandestinely at night. To give help to a Syrian was only a degree less dangerous than to receive help.

"Ah, Major Scobie," Yusef said, "a friend in need is a friend indeed."

"Can I do anything for you?"

"We have been stranded a half an hour," Yusef said. "The cars have gone by, and I have thought: When will a Good Samaritan appear?"

"I haven't any spare oil to pour into your wounds, Yusef."

"Ha, ha, Major Scobie. That is very good. But if you would just give me a lift into town . . ."

Yusef settled himself into the Morris, easing a large thigh against the brakes.

"Your boy had better get in at the back."

"Let him stay here," Yusef said. "He will mend the car if he knows it is the only way he can get to bed." He folded his large fat hands over his knee and said, "You have a very fine car, Major Scobie. You must have paid four hundred pounds for it."

"One hundred and fifty," Scobie said.

"I would pay you four hundred."

"It isn't for sale, Yusef. Where would I get another?"

"Not now, but maybe when you leave."

"I'm not leaving."

"Oh, I had heard that you were resigning, Major Scobie."

"No."

"We shopkeepers hear so much—but all of it is unreliable gossip."

"How's business?"

"Oh, not bad. Not good."

24

"What I hear is that you've made several fortunes since the war. Unreliable gossip, of course."

"Well, Major Scobie, you know how it is. My store in Sharp Town, that does fine because I am there to keep an eye on it. My store in Macaulay Street—that does not bad because my sister is there. But my stores in Durban Street and Bond Street, they do badly. I am cheated all the time. Like all my countrymen, I cannot read or write, and everyone cheats me."

"Gossip says you can keep all your stocks in all your stores in your head."

Yusef chuckled and beamed. "My memory is not bad. But it keeps me awake at night, Major Scobie. Unless I take a lot of whisky I keep thinking about Durban Street and Bond Street and Macaulay Street."

"Which shall I drop you at now?"

"Oh, now I go home to bed, Major Scobie. My house in Sharp Town, if you please. Won't you come in and have a little whisky?"

"Sorry. I'm on duty, Yusef."

"It is very kind of you, Major Scobie, to give me this lift. Would you let me show my gratitude by sending Mrs. Scobie a roll of silk?"

"Just what I wouldn't like, Yusef."

"Yes, yes, I know. It's very hard, all this gossip. Just because there are some Syrians like Tallit."

"You would like Tallit out of your way, wouldn't you, Yusef?"

"Yes, Major Scobie. It would be for my good, but it would also be for your good."

"You sold him some of those fake diamonds last year, didn't you?"

"Oh, Major Scobie, you don't really believe I'd get the better of anyone like that. Some of the poor Syrians suffered a great deal over those diamonds, Major Scobie. It would be a shame to deceive your own people like that."

"They shouldn't have broken the law by buying diamonds. Some of them even had the nerve to complain to the police."

"They are very ignorant, poor fellows."

"You weren't as ignorant as all that, were you, Yusef?"

"If you ask me, Major Scobie, it was Tallit. Otherwise, why does he pretend I sold him the diamonds?"

25

Scobie drove slowly. The rough street was crowded. Thin black bodies weaved like daddy-long-legs in the dimmed head-lights. "How long will the rice shortage go on, Yusef?"

"You know as much about that as I do, Major Scobie."

"I know these poor devils can't get rice at the controlled price."

"I've heard, Major Scobie, that they can't get their share of the free distribution unless they tip the policemen at the gate."

It was quite true. There was a retort in this colony to every accusation. There was always a blacker corruption elsewhere to be pointed at. The scandalmongers of the Secretariat fulfilled a useful purpose—they kept alive the idea that no one was to be trusted. That was better than complacence. Why, he wondered, swerving the car to avoid a dead pye-dog, do I love this place so much? Is it because here human nature hasn't had time to disguise itself? Nobody here could ever talk about a heaven on earth. Heaven remained rigidly in its proper place on the other side of death, and on this side flourished the injustices, the cruelties, the meannesses, that elsewhere people so cleverly hushed up. Here you could love human beings nearly as God loved them, knowing the worst: you didn't love a pose, a pretty dress, a sentiment artfully assumed. He felt a sudden affection for Yusef. He said, "Two wrongs don't make a right. One day, Yusef, you'll find my foot under your fat arse."

"Maybe, Major Scobie," Yusef said, "or maybe we'll be friends together. That is what I should like more than anything in the world."

They drew up outside the Sharp Town house and Yusef's steward ran out with a torch to light him in. "Major Scobie," Yusef said, "it would give me such pleasure to give you a glass of whisky. I think I could help you a lot. I am very patriotic, Major Scobie."

"That's why you are hoarding your cottons against a Vichy invasion, isn't it? They will be worth more than English pounds."

"The Esperança is in tomorrow, isn't she?"

"Probably."

"What a waste of time it is searching a big ship like that

26

for diamonds. Unless you know beforehand exactly where they are. You know that when the ship returns to Angola a seaman reports where you looked. You will sift all the sugar in the hold. You will search the lard in the kitchens because someone once told Captain Druce that a diamond can be heated and dropped in the middle of a tin of lard Of course the cabins and the ventilators and the lockers. Tubes of toothpaste. Do you think one day you will find one little diamond?"

"No."

"I don't either."

6

A hurricane lamp burned at each corner of the wooden pyramids of crates. Across the black slow water he could just make out the naval depôt ship, a disused liner, where she lay, so it was believed, on a reef of empty whisky bottles. He stood quietly for a while breathing in the heavy smell of the sea: within half a mile of him a whole convoy lay at anchor, but all he could detect were the long shadow of the depôt ship and a scatter of small red lights as though a street were up: he could hear nothing from the water but the water itself, slapping against the jetties. The magic of this place never failed him: here he kept his foothold on the very edge of a strange continent.

Somewhere in the darkness two rats scuffled. These waterside rats were the size of rabbits: the natives called them pigs and ate them roasted: the name helped to distinguish them from the wharf rats, who were a human breed. Walking along a light railway line Scobie made in the direction of the markets. At the corner of a warehouse he came on two policemen.

"Anything to report?"

"No, sah."

"Been along this way?"

"Oh yes, sah, we just come from there."

He knew that they were lying: they would never go alone to that end of the wharf, the playground of the human rats, unless they had a white officer to guard them. The rats were cowards but dangerous—boys of sixteen or so, armed with

27

razors or bits of broken bottle, they swarmed in groups around the warehouses, pilfering if they found an easily opened case, settling like flies around any drunken sailor who stumbled their way, occasionally slashing a policeman who had made himself unpopular with one of their innumerable relatives. Gates couldn't keep them off the wharf: they swam round from Kru Town or the fishing beaches.

"Come on," Scobie, said, "we'll have another look."

With weary patience the policemen trailed behind him, half a mile one way, half a mile the other. Only the pigs moved on the wharf, and the water slapped. One of the policemen said self-righteously, "Quiet night, sah." They shone their torches with self-conscious assiduity from one side to another, lighting the abandoned chassis of a car, an empty truck, the corner of a tarpaulin, a bottle standing at the corner of a warehouse with palm leaves stuffed in for a cork. Scobie said, "What's that?" One of his official nightmares was an incendiary bomb: it was so easy to prepare: every day men from Vichy territory came into town with smuggled cattle—they were encouraged to come in for the sake of the meat supply. On this side of the border native saboteurs were being trained in case of invasion: why not on the other side?

"Let me see it," he said, but neither of the policemen moved to touch it.

"Only native medicine, sah," one of them said with a skin-deep sneer.

Scobie picked the bottle up. It was a dimpled Haig, and when he drew out the palm leaves the stench of dog's pizzle and nameless decay blew out like a gas escape. A nerve in his head beat with sudden irritation. For no reason at all he remembered Fraser's flushed face and Thimblerigg's giggle. The stench from the bottle moved him with nausea, and he felt his fingers polluted by the palm leaves. He threw the bottle over the wharf, and the hungry mouth of the water received it with a single belch, but the contents were scattered on the air, and the whole windless place smelt sour and ammoniac. The policemen were silent: Scobie was aware of their mute disapproval. He should have left the bottle where it stood: it had been placed there for one purpose, directed at one person, but now that its

28

contents had been released it was as if the evil thought were left to wander blindly through the air, to settle maybe on the innocent.

"Good night," Scobie said, and turned abruptly on his heel. He had not gone twenty yards before he heard their boots scuffling rapidly away from the dangerous area.

Scobie drove up to the police station by way of Pitt Street. Outside the brothel on the left-hand side the girls were sitting along the pavement taking a bit of air. Within the police station behind the black-out blinds the scent of a monkey house thickened for the night. The sergeant on duty took his legs off the table in the charge room and stood to attention.

"Anything to report?"

"Five drunk and disorderly, sah. I lock them in the big cell."

"Anything else?"

"Two Frenchmen, sah, with no passes."

"Black?"

"Yes, sah."

"Where were they found?"

"In Pitt Street, sah."

"I'll see them in the morning. What about the launch? Is it running all right? I shall want to go out to the Esperança."

"It's broken, sah. Mr. Fraser he try to mend it, sah, but it humbug all the time."

"What time does Mr. Fraser come on duty?"

"Seven, sah."

"Tell him I shan't want him to go out to the Esperança. I'm going out myself. If the launch isn't ready, I'll go with the F.S.P."

"Yes, sah."

Climbing again into his car, pushing at the sluggish starter, Scobie thought that a man was surely entitled to that much revenge. Revenge was good for the character: out of revenge grew forgiveness. He began to whistle, driving back through Kru Town. He was almost happy: he only needed to be quite certain that nothing had happened at the Club after he left, that at this moment, ten fifty-five P.M., Louise was at ease, content. He could face the next hour when the next hour arrived.

29

Before he went indoors he walked round to the seaward side of the house to check the black-out. He could hear the murmur of Louise's voice inside: she was probably reading poetry. He thought: By God, what right has that young fool Fraser to despise her for that? and then his anger moved away again, like a shabby man, when he thought of Fraser's disappointment in the morning—no Portuguese visit, no present for his best girl, only the hot humdrum office day. Feeling for the handle of the back door to avoid flashing his torch, he tore his right hand on a splinter.

He came into the lighted room and saw that his hand was dripping with blood. "Oh, darling," Louise said, "what have you done?" and covered her face. She couldn't bear the sight of blood. "Can I help you, sir?" Wilson asked. He tried to rise, but he was sitting in a low chair at Louise's feet and his knees were piled with books.

"It's all right," Scobie said. "It's only a scratch. I can see to it myself. Just tell Ali to bring a bottle of water." Half-way upstairs he heard the voice resume: Louise said, "A lovely poem about a pylon." Scobie walked into the bathroom, disturbing a rat that had been couched on the cool rim of the bath, like a cat on a gravestone.

Scobie sat down on the edge of the bath and let his hand drip into the lavatory pail among the wood shavings. Just as in his own office, the sense of home surrounded him. Louise's ingenuity had been able to do little with this room: the bath of scratched enamel with a single tap which always ceased to work before the end of the dry season: the tin bucket under the lavatory seat emptied once a day: the fixed basin with another useless tap: bare floorboards: drab green black-out curtains. The only improvements Louise had been able to impose were the cork mat by the bath, the bright white medicine cabinet.

The rest of the room was all his own. It was like a relic of his youth carried from house to house. It had been like this years ago in his first house before he married. This was the room in which he had always been alone.

Ali came in, his pink soles flapping on the floorboards, carrying a bottle of water from the filter. "The back door humbug me," Scobie explained. He held his hand out over the wash-basin, while Ali poured the water over the wound. The boy made gentle chuckling sounds of commiseration: his hands were as gentle as a girl's. When Scobie said impatiently, "That's enough," Ali paid him no attention. "Too much dirt," he said.

"Now iodine." The smallest scratch in this country turned green if it were neglected for an hour. "Again," he said, "pour it over," wincing at the sting. Down below out of the swing of voices the word "beauty" detached itself and sank back into the trough. "Now the elastoplast."

"No," Ali said, "no. Bandage better."

"All right. Bandage then." Years ago he had taught Ali to bandage: now he could tie one as expertly as a doctor.

"Good night, Ali. Go to bed. I shan't want you again."

"Missus want drinks."

"No. I'll attend to the drinks. You can go to bed." Alone, he sat down again on the edge of the bath. The wound had jarred him a little, and anyway he was unwilling to join the two downstairs, for his presence would embarrass Wilson. A man couldn't listen to a woman reading poetry in the presence of an outsider. "I had rather be a kitten and cry mew . . ." but that wasn't really his attitude. He did not despise: he just couldn't understand such bare relations of intimate feeling. And besides he was happy here, sitting where the rat had sat, in his own world. He began to think of the Esperança and of the next day's work.

"Darling," Louise called up the stairs, "are you all right? Can you drive Mr. Wilson home?"

"I can walk, Mrs. Scobie."

"Nonsense."

"Yes, really."

"Coming," Scobie called. "Of course I'll drive you back." When he joined them Louise took the bandaged hand tenderly in hers. "Oh, the poor hand," she said. "Does it hurt?" She was not afraid of the clean white bandage: it was like a patient in a hospital with the sheets drawn tidily up to the chin. One could bring grapes and never know the details of the scalpel wound out of sight. She put her lips to the bandage and left a little smear of orange lipstick.

"It's quite all right," Scobie said.

"Really, sir. I can walk."

"Of course you won't walk. Come along, get in."

The light from the dashboard lit up a patch of Wilson's

extraordinary suit. He leant out of the car and cried, "Good night, Mrs. Scobie. It's been lovely. I can't thank you enough." The words vibrated with sincerity: it gave them the sound of a foreign language—the sound of English spoken in England. Here intonations changed in the course of a few months: became high-pitched and insincere, or flat and guarded. You could tell that Wilson was fresh from home.

"You must come again soon," Scobie said, remembering Louise's happy face, as they drove down the Burnside road towards the Bedford Hotel.

8

The smart of his wounded hand woke Scobie at two in the morning. He lay coiled like a watch-spring on the outside of the bed, trying to keep his body away from Louise's: wherever they touched—if it were only a finger lying against a finger—sweat started. Even when they were separated the heat trembled between them. The moonlight lay on the dressing-table like coolness and lit the bottles of lotion, the little pots of cream, the edge of a photograph frame. At once he began to listen for Louise's breathing.

It came irregularly in jerks. She was awake. He put his hand up and touched the hot moist hair: she lay stiffly as though she were guarding a secret. Sick at heart, knowing what he would find, he moved his fingers down until they touched her lids. She was crying. He felt an enormous tiredness, bracing himself to comfort her. "Darling," he said, "I love you." It was how he always began. Comfort, like the act of sex, developed a routine.

"I know," she said, "I know." It was how she always answered. He blamed himself for being heartless because the idea occurred to him that it was two o'clock: this might go on for hours, and at six the day's work began. He moved the hair away from her forehead and said, "The rains will soon be here. You'll feel better then."

"I feel all right," she said, and began to sob.

"What is it, darling? Tell me." He swallowed. "Tell Ticki." He hated the name she had given him, but it always worked. She said, "Oh, Ticki, Ticki. I can't go on."

"I thought you were happy tonight."

32

"I was—but think of being happy because a U.A.C. clerk was nice to me. Ticki, why won't they like me?"

"Don't be silly, darling. It's just the heat: it makes you fancy things. They all like you."

"Only Wilson," she repeated with despair and shame, and began to sob again.

"Wilson's all right."

"They won't have him at the Club. He gate-crashed with the dentist. They'll be laughing about him and me. Oh, Ticki, Ticki, please let me go away and begin again."

"Of course, darling," he said, "of course," staring out through the net and through the window to the quiet flat infested sea. "Where to?"

"I could go to South Africa and wait until you have leave. Ticki, you'll be retiring soon. I'll get a home ready for you, Ticki."

He flinched a little away from her, and then hurriedly in case she had noticed lifted her damp hand and kissed the palm. "It will cost a lot, darling." The thought of retirement set his nerves twitching and straining: he always prayed that death would come first. He had prepared his life insurance in that hope: it was payable only on death. He thought of a home, a permanent home: the gay artistic curtains, the bookshelves full of Louise's books, a pretty tiled bathroom, no office anywhere—a home for two until death, no change any more before eternity settled in.

"Ticki, I can't bear it any longer here."

"I'll have to figure it out, darling."

"Ethel Maybury's in South Africa, and the Collinses. We've got friends in South Africa."

"Prices are high."

"You could drop some of your silly old life insurances, Ticki. And, Ticki, you could economize here without me. You could have your meals at the mess and do without the cook."

"He doesn't cost much."

"Every little helps, Ticki."

"I'd miss you," he said.

"No, Ticki, you wouldn't," she said, and surprised him by the range of her sad spasmodic understanding. "After all," she said, "there's nobody to save for."

He said gently, "I'll try and work something out. You know if it's possible I'd do anything for you—anything."

33

"This isn't just two-in-the-morning comfort, Ticki, is it? You will do something?"

"Yes, dear. I'll manage somehow." He was surprised how quickly she went to sleep: she was like a tired carrier who has slipped his load. She was asleep before he had finished his sentence, clutching one of his fingers like a child, breathing as easily. The load lay beside him now, and he prepared to lift it.

II.

EIGHT IN THE MORNING ON HIS WAY TO THE jetty Scobie called at the bank. The manager's office was shaded and cool: a glass of iced water stood on top of a safe. "Good morning, Robinson."

Robinson was tall and hollow-chested and bitter because he hadn't been posted to Nigeria. He said, "When will this filthy weather break? The rains are late."

"They've started in the Protectorate."

"In Nigeria," Robinson said, "one always knew where one was. What can I do for you, Scobie?"

"Do you mind if I sit down?"

"Of course. I never sit down before ten myself. Standing up keeps the digestion in order." He rambled restlessly across his office on legs like stilts: he took a sip of the iced water with distaste as though it were medicine. On his desk Scobie saw a book called *Diseases of the Urinary Tract* open at a coloured illustration. "What can I do for you?" Robinson repeated.

"Give me two hundred and fifty pounds," Scobie said with a nervous attempt at jocularity.

"You people always think a bank's made of money," Robinson mechanically jested. "How much do you really want?"

"Three fifty."

"What's your balance at the moment?"

"I think about thirty pounds. It's the end of the month."

"We'd better check up on that." He called a clerk and

while they waited Robinson paced the little room—six paces to the wall and round again. "There and back a hundred and seventy-six times," he said, "makes a mile. I try and put in three miles before lunch. It keeps one healthy. In Nigeria I used to walk a mile and a half to breakfast at the Club, and then a mile and a half back to the office. Nowhere fit to walk here," he said, pivoting on the carpet. A clerk laid a slip of paper on the desk. Robinson held it close to his eyes as though he wanted to smell it. "Twenty-eight pounds fifteen and sevenpence," he said.

"I want to send my wife to South Africa."

"Oh, yes. Yes."

"I daresay," Scobie said, "I might do it on a bit less. I shan't be able to allow her very much on my salary, though."

"I really don't see how . . ."

"I thought perhaps I could get an overdraft," he said vaguely. "Lots of people have them, don't they? Do you know, I believe I only had one once—for a few weeks— for about fifteen pounds. I didn't like it. It scared me. I always felt I owed the bank manager the money."

"The trouble is, Scobie," Robinson said, "we've had orders to be very strict about overdrafts. It's the war, you know. There's one valuable security nobody can offer now, his life."

"Yes, I see that, of course. But my life's pretty good, and I'm not stirring from here. No submarines for me. And the job's secure, Robinson," he went on with the same ineffectual attempt at flippancy.

"The Commissioner's retiring, isn't he?" Robinson said, reaching the safe at the end of the room and turning.

"Yes, but I'm not."

"I'm glad to hear that, Scobie. There've been rumours . . ."

"I suppose I'll have to retire one day, but that's a long way off. I'd much rather die in my boots. There's always my life insurance policy, Robinson. What about that for security?"

"You know you dropped one insurance three years ago."

"That was the year Louise went home for an operation."

"I don't think the paid-up value of the other two amounts to much, Scobie."

"Still, they protect you in case of death, don't they?"

35

"If you go on paying the premiums. We haven't any guarantee, you know."

"Of course not," Scobie said, "I see that."

"I'm very sorry, Scobie. This isn't personal. It's the policy of the bank. If you'd wanted fifty pounds, I'd have lent it you myself."

"Forget it, Robinson," Scobie said. "It's not important." He gave his embarrassed laugh. "The boys at the Secretariat would say I can always pick it up in bribes. How's Molly?"

"She's very well, thank you. Wish I were the same."

"You read too many of those medical books, Robinson."

"A man's got to know what's wrong with him. Going to be at the Club tonight?"

"I don't think so. Louise is tired. You know how it is before the rains. Sorry to have kept you, Robinson. I must be getting along to the wharf."

He walked rapidly downhill from the bank with his head bent. He felt as though he had been detected in a mean action—he had asked for money and had been refused. Louise had deserved better of him. It seemed to him that he must have failed in some way in manhood.

2

Druce had come out himself to the Esperança with his squad of F.S.P. men. At the gangway a steward awaited them with an invitation to join the captain for drinks in his cabin. The officer in charge of the naval guard was already there before them. This was a regular part of the fortnightly routine—the establishment of friendly relations; by accepting his hospitality they tried to ease down for the neutral the bitter pill of search; below the bridge the search party would proceed smoothly without them. While the first-class passengers had their passports examined, their cabins would be ransacked by a squad of the F.S.P. Already others were going through the hold—the dreary hopeless business of sifting rice. What had Yusef said, "Have you ever found one little diamond? Do you think you ever will?" In a few minutes, when relations had become sufficiently smooth after the drinks, Scobie would have the unpleasant task of searching the captain's own

36

cabin. The stiff disjointed conversation was carried on mainly by the naval lieutenant.

The captain wiped his fat yellow face and said, "Of course for the English I feel in the heart an enormous admiration."

"We don't like doing it, you know," the lieutenant said. "Hard luck being a neutral."

"My heart," the Portuguese captain said, "is full of admiration for your great struggle. There is no room for resentment. Some of my people feel resentment. Me, none." The face streamed with sweat, and the eyeballs were contused. The man kept on speaking of his heart, but it seemed to Scobie that a long deep surgical operation would have been required to find it.

"Very good of you," the lieutenant said. "Appreciate your attitude."

"Another glass of port, gentlemen?"

"Don't mind if I do. Nothing like this on shore, you know. You, Scobie?"

"No, thanks."

"I hope you won't find it necessary to keep us here tonight, Major?"

Scobie said, "I don't think there's any possibility of your getting away before midday tomorrow."

"Will do our best, of course," the lieutenant said.

"On my honour, gentlemen, my hand upon my heart, you will find no bad hats among my passengers. And the crew—I know them all."

Druce said, "It's a formality, Captain, which we have to go through."

"Have a cigar, Captain. Throw away that cigarette. Here is a very special box."

Druce lit the cigar, which began to spark and crackle. The captain giggled. "Only my joke, gentlemen. Quite harmless. I keep the box for my friends. The English have a wonderful sense of humour. I know you will not be angry. A German, yes, an Englishman, no. It is quite cricket, eh?"

"Very funny," Druce said sourly, laying the cigar down on the ash-try the captain held out to him. The ash-tray, presumably set off by the captain's finger, began to play a little tinkly tune. Druce jerked again: he was overdue for leave and his nerves were unsteady. The captain smiled

37

and sweated. "Swiss," he said. "A wonderful people. Neutral too."

One of the Field Security men came in and gave Druce a note. He passed it to Scobie, who read, *Steward, who is under notice of dismissal, says the captain has letters concealed in his bathroom.*

Druce said, "I think I'd better go and make them hustle down below. Coming, Evans? Many thanks for the port, Captain."

Scobie was left alone with the captain. This was the part of the job he always hated: these men were not criminals: they were merely breaking regulations enforced on the shipping companies by the navicert system. You never knew in a search what you would find. A man's bedroom was his private life: prying in drawers you came on humiliations; little petty vices were tucked out of sight like a soiled handkerchief; under a pile of linen you might come on a grief he was trying to forget. Scobie said gently, "I'm afraid, Captain, I'll have to look around. You know it's a formality."

"You must do your duty, Major," the Portuguese said.

Scobie went quickly and neatly through the cabin: he never moved a thing without replacing it exactly: he was like a careful housewife. The captain stood with his back to Scobie looking out onto the bridge: it was as if he preferred not to embarrass his guest in the odious task. Scobie came to an end, closing the box of French letters and putting them carefully back in the top drawer of the locker with the handkerchiefs, the gaudy ties, and the little bundle of dirty photographs. "All finished?" the captain asked politely, turning his head.

"That door," Scobie said, "what would be through there?"

"That is only the bathroom, the w.c."

"I think I'd better take a look."

"Of course, Major, but there is not much cover there to conceal anything."

"If you don't mind . . ."

"Of course not. It is your duty."

The bathroom was bare and extraordinarily dirty. The bath was rimmed with dry grey soap, and the tiles slopped under the feet. The problem was to find the right place quickly. He couldn't linger here without disclosing the fact that he had special information. The search had got to have all the appearances of formality—neither too lax nor too thorough. "This won't take long," he said cheerily, and caught sight of the fat calm face in the shaving mirror. The information, of course, might be false, given by the steward simply in order to cause trouble.

Scobie opened the medicine cabinet and went rapidly through the contents: unscrewing the toothpaste, opening the razor box, dipping his finger into the shaving cream. He did not expect to find anything there. But the search gave him time to think. He went next to the taps, turned the water on, felt up each funnel with his finger. The floor engaged his attention: there were no possibilities of concealment there. The porthole: he examined the big screws and swung the inner mask to and fro. Every time he turned he caught sight of the captain's face in the mirror, calm, patient, complacent. It said "Cold, cold" to him all the while, as in a children's game.

Finally, the lavatory: he lifted up the wooden seat: nothing had been laid between the porcelain and the wood. He put his hand on the lavatory chain, and in the mirror became aware for the first time of a tension: the brown eyes were no longer on his face, they were fixed on something else, and following that gaze home, he saw his own hand tighten on the chain.

Is the cistern empty of water? he wondered, and pulled. Gurgling and pounding in the pipes, the water flushed down. He turned away and the Portuguese said with a smugness he was unable to conceal, "You see, Major." And at that moment Scobie did see. I'm becoming careless, he thought. He lifted the cap of the cistern. Fixed in the cap with adhesive tape and clear of the water lay a letter.

He looked at the address—a Frau Groener in Friedrich-strasse, Leipzig. He repeated, "I'm sorry, Captain," and, because the man didn't answer, he looked up and saw the tears beginning to pursue the sweat down the hot fat cheeks. "I'll have to take it away," Scobie said, "and report . . ."

"Oh, this war," the captain burst out, "how I hate this war."

"We've got cause to hate it too, you know," Scobie said.

39

"A man is ruined because he writes to his daughter."

"Your daughter?"

"Yes. She is Frau Groener. Open it and read. You will see."

"I can't do that. I must leave it to the censorship. Why didn't you wait to write till you got to Lisbon, Captain?"

The man had lowered his bulk onto the edge of the bath as though it were a heavy sack his shoulders could no longer bear. He kept on wiping his eyes with the back of his hand like a child—an unattractive child, the fat boy of the school. Against the beautiful and the clever and the successful one can wage a pitiless war, but not against the unattractive: then the millstone weighs on the breast. Scobie knew he should have taken the letter and gone; he could do no good with his sympathy.

The captain moaned, "If you had a daughter you'd understand. You haven't got one," he accused, as though there were a crime in sterility.

"No."

"She is anxious about me. She loves me," he said, raising his tear-drenched face as though he must drive the unlikely statement home. "She loves me," he repeated mournfully.

"But why not write from Lisbon?" Scobie asked again. "Why run this risk?"

"I am alone. I have no wife," the captain said. "One cannot always wait to speak. And in Lisbon—you know how things go—friends, wine. I have a little woman there too who is jealous even of my daughter. There are rows, the time passes. In a week I must be off again. It was always so easy before this voyage."

Scobie believed him. The story was sufficiently irrational to be true. Even in war-time one must sometimes exercise the faculty of belief if it is not to atrophy. He said, "I'm sorry. There's nothing I can do about it. Perhaps nothing will happen."

"Your authorities," the captain said, "will blacklist me. You know what that means. The consul will not give a navicert to any ship with me as captain. I shall starve on shore."

"There are so many slips," Scobie said, "in these matters. Files get mislaid. You may hear no more about it."

"I shall pray," the man said without hope.

"Why not?" Scobie said.

40

"You are an Englishman. You wouldn't believe in prayer."

"I'm a Catholic, too," Scobie said.

The fat face looked quickly up at him. "A Catholic?" he exclaimed with hope. For the first time he began to plead. He was like a man who meets a fellow countryman in a strange continent. He began to talk rapidly of his daughter in Leipzig; he produced a battered pocket-book and a yellowing snapshot of a stout young Portuguese woman as graceless as himself. The little bathroom was stifling hot and the captain repeated again and again: "You will understand." He had discovered suddenly how much they had in common: the plaster statues with the swords in the bleeding heart: the whisper behind the confessional curtains: the holy coats and the liquefaction of blood: the dark side chapels and the intricate movements, and somewhere behind it all the love of God. "And in Lisbon," he said, "she will be waiting, she will take me home, she will take away my trousers so that I cannot go out alone: every day it will be drink and quarrels until we go to bed. You will understand. I cannot write to my daughter from Lisbon. She loves me so much and she waits." He shifted his fat thigh and said, "The pureness of that love," and wept. They had in common all the wide region of repentance and longing.

Their kinship gave the captain courage to try another angle. He said, "I am a poor man, but I have enough money to spare . . ." He would never have attempted to bribe an Englishman: it was the most sincere compliment he could pay to their common religion.

"I'm sorry," Scobie said.

"I have English pounds. I will give you twenty English pounds . . . fifty." He implored. "A hundred . . . that is all I have saved."

"It can't be done," Scobie said. He put the letter quickly in his pocket and turned away. The last time he saw the captain as he looked back from the door of the cabin, he was beating his head against the cistern, the tears catching in the folds of his cheeks. As he went down to join Druce in the saloon he could feel the millstone weighing on his breast. How I hate this war, he thought, in the very words the captain had used.

41

The letter to the daughter in Leipzig, and a small bundle of correspondence found in the kitchens, was the sole result of eight hours' search by fifteen men. It could be counted an average day. When Scobie reached the police station he looked in to see the Commissioner, but his office was empty, so he sat down in his own room under the hand-cuffs and began to write his report. *A special search was made of the cabins and effects of the passengers named in your telegrams . . . with no results.* The letter to the daughter in Leipzig lay on the desk beside him. Outside it was dark. The smell of the cells seeped in under the door, and in the next office Fraser was singing to himself the same tune he had sung every evening since his last leave:

> *What will we care for*
> *The why and the wherefore*
> *When you and I*
> *Are pushing up the daisies?*

It seemed to Scobie that life was immeasurably long. Couldn't the test of man have been carried out in fewer years? Couldn't we have committed our first major sin at seven, have ruined ourselves for love or hate at ten, have clutched at redemption on a fifteen-year-old death bed? He wrote: *A steward who had been dismissed for incompetence reported that the captain had correspondence concealed in his bathroom. I made a search and found the enclosed letter addressed to Frau Groener in Leipzig concealed in the lid of the lavatory cistern. An instruction on this hiding place might well be circulated, as it has not been encountered before at this station. The letter was fixed by tape above the water line. . . .*

He sat there staring at the paper, his brain confused with the conflict that had really been decided hours ago when Druce said to him in the saloon, "Anything?" and he had shrugged his shoulders in a gesture he left Druce to interpret. Had he ever intended it to mean: "The usual private correspondence we are always finding"? Druce had taken it for "No." Scobie put his hand against his forehead and shivered: the sweat seeped between his fingers, and he thought: Am I in for a touch of fever? Perhaps it was because his temperature had risen that it seemed to him he was on the verge of a new life. One felt this way before a proposal of marriage or a first crime.

Scobie took the letter and opened it. The act was irrevocable, for no one in this city had the right to open clandestine mail. A microphotograph might be concealed in the gum of an envelope. Even a simple word code would be beyond him; his knowledge of Portuguese would take him no further than the most surface meaning. Every letter found—however obviously innocent—must be sent to the London censors unopened. Scobie against the strictest orders was exercising his own imperfect judgment. He thought to himself: If the letter is suspicious, I will send my report. I can explain the torn envelope. The captain insisted on opening the letter to show me the contents. But if he wrote that, he would be unjustly blackening the case against the captain, for what better way could he have found for destroying a microphotograph? There must be some lie to be told, Scobie thought, but he was unaccustomed to lies. With the letter in his hand, held carefully over the white blotting pad, so that he could detect anything that might fall from between the leaves, he resolved to tell no lie. If the letter were suspicious, he would write a full report on all the circumstances including his own act.

Dear little money spider, the letter began, *your father who loves you more than anything upon earth will try to send you a little more money this time. I know how hard things are for you, and my heart bleeds. Little money spider, if only I could feel your fingers running across my cheek. How is it that a great fat father like I am should have so tiny and beautiful a daughter? Now, little money spider, I will tell you everything that has happened to me. We left Lobito a week ago after only four days in port. I stayed one night with Señor Aranjuez and I drank more wine than was good for me, but all my talk was of you. I was good all the time I was in port because I had promised my little money spider, and I went to Confession and Communion, so that if anything should happen to me on the way to Lisbon—for who knows in these terrible days? —I should not have to live my eternity away from my little*

43

spider. Since we left Lobito we have had good weather. Even the passengers are not seasick. Tomorrow night, because Africa will be at last behind us, we shall have a ship's concert, and I shall perform on my whistle. All the time I perform I shall remember the days when my little money spider sat on my knee and listened. My dear, I am growing old, and after every voyage I am fatter: I am not a good man, and sometimes I fear that my soul in all this bulk of flesh is no larger than a pea. You do not know how easy it is for a man like me to commit the unforgivable despair. Then I think of my daughter. There was just enough good in me once for you to be fashioned. A wife shares too much of a man's sin for perfect love. But a daughter may save him at the last. Pray for me, little spider. Your father who loves you more than life.

Mais que a vida. Scobie felt no doubt at all of the sincerity of this letter. This was not written to conceal a photograph of the Cape Town defences or a microphotograph report on troop movements at Durban. It should, he knew, be tested for secret ink, examined under a microscope, and the inner lining of the envelope exposed. Nothing should be left to chance with a clandestine letter. But he had committed himself to a belief. He tore the letter up, and his own report with it, and carried the scraps out to the incinerator in the yard—a petrol tin standing upon two bricks with its sides punctured to make a draught. As he struck a match to light the papers, Fraser joined him in the yard. What will we care for The why and the wherefore? On the top of the scraps lay unmistakably half a foreign envelope: one could even read part of the address —Friedrichstrasse. He quickly held the match to the uppermost scrap as Fraser crossed the yard, striding with unbearable youth. The scrap went up in flame, and in the heat of the fire another scrap uncurled the name of Groener. Fraser said cheerfully, "Burning the evidence?" and looked down into the tin. The name had blackened: there was nothing there surely that Fraser could see—except a brown triangle of envelope that seemed to Scobie obviously foreign. He ground it out of existence with a stick and looked up at Fraser to see whether he could detect any surprise or suspicion. There was nothing to be read in the vacuous face, blank as a school notice-board out of term. Only his own heart-beats told him he was guilty—

that he had joined the ranks of the corrupt police officers
—Bailey who had kept a safe deposit in another city, Cray-
shaw who had been found with diamonds, Boyston against
whom nothing had been definitely proved and who had
been invalided out. They had been corrupted by money,
and he had been corrupted by sentiment. Sentiment was
the more dangerous, because you couldn't name its price.
A man open to bribes was to be relied upon below a certain
figure, but sentiment might uncoil in the heart at a name,
a photograph, even a smell remembered.

"What sort of day, sir?" Fraser asked, staring at the small
pile of ash. Perhaps he was thinking that it should have
been his day.

"The usual kind of a day," Scobie said.

"How about the captain?" Fraser asked, looking down
into the petrol tin, beginning to hum again his languid
tune.

"The captain?" Scobie said.

"Oh, Druce told me some fellow informed on him."

"Just the usual thing," Scobie said. "A dismissed steward
with a grudge. Didn't Druce tell you we found nothing?"

"No," Fraser said, "he didn't seem to be sure. Good
night, sir. I must be pushing off to mess."

"Thimblerigg on duty?"

"Yes, sir."

Scobie watched him go. The back was as vacuous as the
face: one could read nothing there. Scobie thought: What
a fool I have been. What a fool. He owed his duty to
Louise, not to a fat sentimental Portuguese skipper who
had broken the rules of his own company for the sake of a
daughter equally unattractive. That had been the turning-
point, the daughter. And now, Scobie thought, I must
return home: I shall put the car away in the garage, and
Ali will come forward with his torch to light me to the
door. She will be sitting there between two draughts for
coolness, and I shall read on her face the story of what she
has been thinking all day. She will have been hoping that
everything is fixed, that I shall say, "I've put your name
down at the agent's for South Africa," but she'll be afraid
that nothing so good as that will ever happen to us. She'll
wait for me to speak, and I shall try to talk about anything
under the sun to postpone seeing her misery. (It would
be waiting at the corners of her mouth to take possession

of her whole face.) He knew exactly how things would go:
it had happened so often before. He rehearsed every word,
going back into his office, locking his desk, going down to
his car. People talk about the courage of condemned men
walking to the place of execution: sometimes it needs as
much courage to walk with any kind of bearing towards
another person's habitual misery. He forgot Fraser: he forgot everything but the scene ahead: I shall go in and I'll
say, "Good evening, sweetheart," and she'll say, "Good evening, darling. What kind of a day?" and I'll talk and talk,
but all the time I shall know I'm coming nearer to the
moment when I shall say, "What about you, darling?" and
let the misery in.

4

"What about you, darling?" He turned quickly away
from her and began to fix two more pink gins. There was
a tacit understanding between them that "liquor helped":
growing more miserable with every glass, one hoped for
the moment of relief.

"You don't really want to know about me."

"Of course I do, darling. What sort of a day have you
had?"

"Ticki, why are you such a coward? Why don't you tell
me it's all off?"

"All off?"

"You know what I mean—the passage. You've been talking and talking since you came in about the *Esperança*.
There's a Portuguese ship in once a fortnight. You don't
talk that way every time. I'm not a child, Ticki. Why don't
you say straight out—'you can't go'?"

He grinned miserably at his glass, twisting it round and
round to let the angostura cling along the curve. He said,
"That wouldn't be true. I'll find some way." Reluctantly
he had recourse to the hated nickname. If that failed, the
misery would deepen and go right on through the short
night he needed for sleep. "Trust Ticki," he said. It was
as if a ligament tightened in his brain with the suspense.
If only I could postpone the misery, he thought, until
daylight. Misery is worse in the darkness: there's nothing
to look at except the green black-out curtains, the Gov-

ernment furniture, the flying ants scattering their wings over the table: a hundred yards away the Creoles' pye-dogs yapped and wailed. "Look at that little beggar," he said, pointing at the house lizard that always came out upon the wall about this time to hunt for moths and cockroaches. He said, "We only got the idea last night. These things take time to fix. Ways and means, ways and means," he said with strained humour.

"Have you been to the bank?"

"Yes," he admitted.

"And you couldn't get the money?"

"No. They couldn't manage it. Have another pink gin, darling?"

She held the glass out to him, crying dumbly: her face reddened when she cried—she looked ten years older, a middle-aged and abandoned woman—it was like the terrible breath of the future on his cheek. He went down on one knee beside her and held the pink gin to her lips as though it were medicine. "My dear," he said, "I'll find a way. Have a drink."

"Ticki, I can't bear this place any longer. I know I've said it before, but I mean it this time. I shall go mad. Ticki, I'm so lonely. I haven't a friend, Ticki."

"Let's have Wilson up tomorrow."

"Ticki, for God's sake don't always mention Wilson. Please, please do something."

"Of course, I will. Just be patient a while, dear. These things take time."

"What will you do, Ticki?"

"I'm full of ideas, darling," he said wearily. (What a day it had been.) "Just let them simmer for a little while."

"Tell me one idea. Just one."

His eyes followed the lizard as it pounced: then he picked an ant wing out of his gin and drank again. He thought to himself: what a fool I really was not to take the hundred pounds. I destroyed the letter for nothing. I took the risk. I might just as well . . . Louise said, "I've known it for years. You don't love me." She spoke with calmness: he knew that calmness—it meant they had reached the quiet centre of the storm: always in this region at about this time they began to speak the truth at each other. The truth, he thought, has never been of any real value to any human being—it is a symbol for mathemati-

47

cians and philosophers to pursue. In human relations kindness and lies are worth a thousand truths. He involved himself in what he always knew was a vain struggle to retain the lies. "Don't be absurd, darling. Who do you think I love if I don't love you?"

"You don't love anybody."

"Is that why I treat you so badly?" He tried to hit a light note, and it sounded hollowly back at him.

"That's your conscience," she said sadly, "your sense of duty. You've never loved anyone since Catherine died."

"Except myself, of course. You always say I love myself."

"No, I don't think you do."

He defended himself by evasions: in this cyclonic centre he was powerless to give the comforting lie. "I try all the time to keep you happy. I work hard for that."

"Ticki, you won't even say you love me. Go on. Say it once."

He eyed her bitterly over the pink gin, the visible sign of his failure: the skin a little yellow with atabrine, the eyes bloodshot with tears. No man could guarantee love for ever, but he had sworn fourteen years ago, at Ealing, silently, during the horrible little elegant ceremony among the lace and candles, that he would at least always see to it that she was happy.

"Ticki, I've got nothing except you, and you've got—nearly everything."

The lizard flicked across the wall and came to rest again, the wing of a moth in his small crocodile jaws. The ants struck tiny muffled blows at the electric globe.

"And yet you want to go away from me," he said accusingly.

"Yes," she said, "I know you aren't happy either. Without me you'll have peace."

This was what he always left out of account—the accuracy of her observation. He had nearly everything, and all he needed was peace. Everything meant work, the daily regular routine in the little bare office, the change of seasons in a place he loved. How often he had been pitied for the austerity of the work, the bareness of the rewards. But Louise knew him better than that. If he had become young again this was the life he would have again chosen to live: only this time he would not have expected any other person to share it with him, the rat upon the bath, the lizard on the wall, the tornado blowing open the windows at one in the morning, and the last pink light upon the laterite roads at sundown.

"You are talking nonsense, dear," he said and went through the doomed motions of mixing another gin and bitters. Again the nerve in his head tightened: unhappiness had uncoiled with its inevitable routine—first her misery and his strained attempts to leave everything unsaid: then her own calm statement of truths much better lied about, and finally the snapping of his own control—truths flung back at her as though she were his enemy. As he embarked on this last stage, crying suddenly and truthfully out at her while the angostura trembled in his hand, "You can't give me peace," he already knew what would succeed it, the reconciliation and the easy lies again until the next scene.

"That's what I say," she said. "If I go away, you'll have your peace."

"You haven't any conception," he accused her angrily, "of what peace means." It was as if she had spoken slightingly of a woman he loved. For he dreamed of peace by day and night. Once in sleep it had appeared to him as the great glowing shoulder of the moon heaving across his window like an iceberg, arctic and destructive in the moment before the world was struck: by day he tried to win a few moments of its company, crouched under the rusting handcuffs in the locked office, reading the reports from the sub-stations. Peace seemed to him the most beautiful word in the language: My peace I give you, my peace I leave with you: O Lamb of God, who takest away the sins of the world, grant us thy peace. In the Mass he pressed his fingers against his eyes to keep the tears of longing in.

Louise said with the old tenderness, "Poor dear, you wish I were dead like Catherine. You want to be alone."

He replied obstinately, "I want you to be happy."

She said wearily, "Just tell me you love me. That helps a little." They were through again, on the other side of the scene: he thought coolly and collectedly, this one wasn't so bad: we shall be able to sleep tonight. He said, "Of course I love you, darling. And I'll fix that passage. You'll see."

He would still have made the promise even if he could have foreseen all that would come of it. He had always been prepared to accept the responsibility for his actions, and he had always been half aware too, from the time he made his terrible private vow that she should be happy, how far *this* action might carry him. Despair is the price one pays for setting oneself an impossible aim. It is, one is told, the unforgiveable sin, but it is a sin the corrupt or evil man never practises. He always has hope. He never reaches the freezing point of knowing absolute failure. Only the man of good will carries always in his heart this capacity for damnation.

Part Two

I. WILSON STOOD GLOOMILY BY HIS BED IN THE
Bedford Hotel and contemplated his cummerbund, which
lay uncoiled and ruffled like an angry snake; the small hotel
room was hot with the conflict between them. Through the
wall he could hear Harris cleaning his teeth for the fifth
time that day. Harris believed in dental hygiene. "It's cleaning my teeth before and after every meal that's kept me
well in this bloody climate," he would say, raising his pale
exhausted face over an orange squash. Now he was gargling:
it sounded like a noise in the pipes.

Wilson sat down on the edge of his bed and rested. He
had left his door open for coolness and across the passage
he could see into the bathroom. The Indian with the turban was sitting on the side of the bath fully dressed: he
stared inscrutably back at Wilson and bowed. "Just a moment, sir," he called. "If you would care to step in here
. . ." Wilson angrily shut the door. Then he had another
try with the cummerbund.

He had once seen a film—was it *Bengal Lancer?*—in
which the cummerbund was superbly disciplined. A tur-
baned native held the coil and an immaculate officer spun
like a top, so that the cummerbund encircled him smoothly, tightly. Another servant stood by with iced drinks, and
a punkah swayed in the background. Apparently these
things were better managed in India. However, with one
more effort Wilson did get the wretched thing wrapped
around him. It was too tight and it was badly creased, and
the tuck-in came too near the front, so that it was not
hidden by the jacket. He contemplated his image with
melancholy in what was left of the mirror. Somebody
tapped on the door.

51

"Who is it?" Wilson shouted, imagining for a moment that the Indian had had the cool impertinence to pursue . . . but when the door opened, it was only Harris: the Indian was still sitting on the bath across the passage shuffling his testimonials.

"Going out, old man?" Harris asked with disappointment.

"Yes."

"Everybody seems to be going out this evening. I shall have the table all to myself." He added with gloom, "It's the curry evening too."

"So it is. I'm sorry to miss it."

"You haven't been having it for two years, old man, every Thursday night." He looked at the cummerbund. "That's not right, old man."

"I know it isn't. It's the best I can do."

"I never wear one. It stands to reason that it's bad for the stomach. They tell you it absorbs sweat, but that's not where I sweat, old man. I'd rather wear braces, only the elastic perishes, so a leather belt's good enough for me. I'm no snob. Where are you dining, old man?"

"At Tallit's."

"How did you meet him?"

"He came in to the office yesterday to pay his account and asked me to dinner."

"You don't have to dress for a Syrian, old man. Take it all off again."

"Are you sure?"

"Of course I am. It wouldn't do at all. Quite wrong." He added, "You'll get a good dinner, but be careful of the sweets. The price of life is eternal vigilance. I wonder what he wants out of you." Wilson began to undress again while Harris talked. He was a good listener. His brain was like a sieve through which the rubbish fell all day long. Sitting on the bed in his pants he heard Harris—"You have to be careful of the fish: I never touch it"—but the words left no impression. Drawing up his white drill trousers over his hairless knees he said to himself:

> the poor sprite is
> Imprisoned for some fault of his
> In a body like a grave.

His belly rumbled and tumbled as it always did a little before the hour of dinner.

> From you he only dares to crave,
> For his service and his sorrow,
> A smile today, a song tomorrow.

Wilson stared into the mirror and passed his fingers over the smooth, too smooth skin. The face looked back at him, pink and healthy, plump and hopeless. Harris went happily on, "I said once to Scobie," and immediately the clot of words lodged in Wilson's sieve. He pondered aloud, "I wonder how he ever came to marry her."

"It's what we all wonder, old man. Scobie's not a bad sort."

"She's wonderful."

"Louise?" Harris exclaimed.

"Of course. Who else?"

"There's no accounting for tastes. Go in and win, old man."

"I must be off."

"Be careful of the sweets." Harris went on with a small spurt of energy, "God knows I wouldn't mind something to be careful of instead of Thursday's curry. It is Thursday, isn't it?"

"Yes."

They came out into the passage and into the focus of the Indian eyes. "You'll have to be done sooner or later, old man," Harris said. "He does everybody once. You'll never have peace till he does you."

"I don't believe in fortune-telling," Wilson lied.

"Nor do I, but he's pretty good. He did me the first week I was here. Told me I'd stay here for more than two and a half years. I thought then I was going to have leave after eighteen months. I know better now."

The Indian watched triumphantly from the bath. He said, "I have a letter from the Director of Agriculture. And one from D. C. Parkes."

"All right," Wilson said. "Do me, but be quick about it."

"I'd better push off, old man, before the revelations begin."

"I'm not afraid," Wilson said.

53

"Will you sit on the bath, sir?" the Indian invited him courteously. He took Wilson's hand in his. "It is a very interesting hand, sir," he said unconvincingly, weighing it up and down.

"What are your charges?"

"According to rank, sir. One like yourself, sir, I should charge ten shillings."

"That's a bit steep."

"Junior officers are five shillings."

"I'm in the five-shilling class," Wilson said.

"Oh, no, sir. The Director of Agriculture gave me a pound."

"I'm only an accountant."

"That's as you say, sir. A.D.C. and Major Scobie gave me ten shillings."

"Oh, well," Wilson said. "Here's ten bob. Go ahead."

"You have been here one, two weeks," the Indian said. "You are sometimes at night an impatient man. You think you do not make enough progress."

"Who with?" Harris asked, lolling in the doorway.

"You are very ambitious. You are a dreamer. You read much poetry."

Harris giggled and Wilson, raising his eyes from the finger which traced the lines upon his palm, watched the fortune-teller with apprehension.

The Indian went inflexibly on. His turban was bowed under Wilson's nose and bore the smell of stale food—he probably secreted stray pieces from the larder in its folds. He said, "You are a secret man. You do not tell your friends about your poetry—except one. One," he repeated. "You are very shy. You should take courage. You have a great line of success."

"Go in and win, old man," Harris repeated.

Of course the whole thing was Couéism: if one believed in it enough, it would come true. Diffidence would be conquered. The mistake in a reading would be covered up.

"You haven't told me ten bobs' worth," Wilson said. "This is a five-bob fortune. Tell me something definite, something that's going to happen." He shifted his seat uncomfortably on the sharp edge of the bath and watched a cockroach like a large blood-blister flattened on the wall. The Indian bent forward over the two hands. He said, "I see great success. The Government will be very pleased with you."

Harris said, "*Il pense* that you are *un bureaucrat*."

"Why will the Government be pleased with me?" Wilson asked.

"You will capture your man."

"Why," Harris said, "I believe he thinks you are a new policeman."

"It looks like it," Wilson said. "Not much use wasting any more time."

"And your private life, that will be a great success too. You will win the lady of your heart. You will sail away. Everything is going to be fine. For you," he added.

"A real ten-bob fortune."

"Good night, old fellow," Wilson said. "I won't write you a recommendation on that." He got up from the bath, and the cockroach flashed into hiding. "I can't bear those things," Wilson said, sidling through the door. He turned in the passage and repeated, "Good night."

"I couldn't when I first came, old man. But I evolved a system. Just step into my room and I'll show you."

"I ought to be off."

"Nobody will be punctual at Tallit's." Harris opened his door and Wilson turned his eyes with a kind of shame from the first sight of its disorder. In his own room he would never have exposed himself quite like this—the dirty tooth-glass, the towel on the bed.

"Look here, old man."

With relief he fixed his eyes on some symbols pencilled on the wall inside: the letter H, and under it a row of figures lined against dates as in a cash-book. Then the letters D.D. and under them more figures. "It's my score in cockroaches, old man. Yesterday was an average day—four. My record's nine. It makes you welcome the little brutes."

"What does D.D. stand for?"

"Down the drain, old man. That's when I knock them into the wash-basin and they go down the waste-pipe. It wouldn't be fair to count them as dead, would it?"

"No."

"And it wouldn't do to cheat yourself either. You'd lose interest at once. The only thing is, it gets dull sometimes,

55

playing against yourself. Why shouldn't we make a match of it, old man? It needs skill, you know. They positively hear you coming, and they move like greased lightning. I do a stalk every evening with a torch."

"I wouldn't mind having a try, but I've got to be off now."

"I tell you what—I won't start hunting till you come back from Tallit's. We'll have five minutes before bed. Just five minutes."

"If you like."

"I'll come down with you, old man. I can smell the curry. You know I could have laughed when the old fool mixed you up with the new police officer."

"He got most of it wrong, didn't he?" Wilson said. "I mean the poetry."

2

Tallit's living-room, to Wilson, seeing it for the first time, had the appearance of a country dance-hall. The furniture all lined the walls: hard chairs with tall uncomfortable backs, and in the corners the chaperons sitting out: old women in black silk dresses, yards and yards of silk, and a very old man in a smoking-cap. They watched him intently in complete silence, and evading their gaze he saw only bare walls except that at each corner sentimental French postcards were nailed up in a montage of ribbons and bows; young men smelling mauve flowers, a glossy cherry shoulder, an impassioned kiss.

Wilson found there was only one other guest besides himself: Father Rank, a Catholic priest, wearing his long soutane. They sat in opposite corners of the room among the chaperons, whom Father Rank explained were Tallit's grandparents and parents, two uncles, what might have been a great-great aunt, a cousin. Somewhere out of sight Tallit's wife was preparing little dishes, which were handed to the two guests by his younger brother and his sister. None of them spoke English except Tallit, and Wilson was embarrassed by the way Father Rank discussed his host and his host's family resoundingly across the room. "Thank you, no," Father Rank would say, declining a sweet by shaking his grey tousled head. "I'd advise you to

56

be careful of those, Mr. Wilson. Tallit's a good fellow, but he won't learn what a Western stomach will take. These old people have stomachs like ostriches."

"This is very interesting to me," Wilson said, catching the eye of a grandmother across the room and nodding and smiling at her. The grandmother obviously thought he wanted more sweets, and called angrily out for her granddaughter. "No, no," Wilson said vainly, shaking his head and smiling at the centenarian. The centenarian lifted her lip from a toothless gum and signalled with ferocity to Tallit's younger brother, who hurried forward with yet another dish. "That's quite safe," Father Rank shouted. "Just sugar and glycerine and a little flour." All the time their glasses were charged and recharged with whisky.

"Wish you'd confess to me where you get this whisky from, Tallit," Father Rank called out with the roguery of an old elephant, and Tallit beamed and slid agilely from end to end of the room, a word to Wilson, a word to Father Rank. He reminded Wilson of a young ballet dancer in his white trousers, his plaster of black hair, and his grey polished alien face, one glass eye like a puppet's.

"So the Esperança's gone out," Father Rank shouted across the room. "Did they find anything, do you think?"

"There was a rumour in the office," Wilson said, "about some diamonds."

"Diamonds, my eye," Father Rank said. "They'll never find any diamonds. They don't know where to look, do they, Tallit?" He explained to Wilson. "Diamonds are a sore subject with Tallit. He was taken in by the false ones last year. Yusef humbugged you, eh, Tallit, you young rogue? Not so smart, eh? You, a Catholic, humbugged by a Mahometan. I could have wrung your neck."

"It was a bad thing to do," Tallit said, standing midway between Wilson and the priest.

"I've only been here a few weeks," Wilson said, "and every one talks to me about Yusef. They say he passes false diamonds, smuggles real ones, sells bad liquor, hoards cottons against a French invasion, seduces the nursing sisters from the military hospital."

"He's a dirty dog," Father Rank said, with a kind of relish. "Not that you can believe a single thing you hear in this place. Otherwise everybody would be living with
57

someone else's wife, every police officer who wasn't in Yusef's pay would be bribed by Tallit here."

Tallit said, "Yusef is a very bad man."

"Why don't the authorities run him in?"

"I've been here for twenty-two years," Father Rank said, "and I've never known anything proved against a Syrian yet. Oh, often I've seen the police as pleased as Punch, carrying their happy morning faces around, just going to pounce—and I think to myself, why bother to ask them what it's about? they'll just pounce on air."

"You ought to have been a policeman, Father."

"Ah," Father Rank said, "who knows? There are more policemen in this town than meet the eye—or so they say."

"Who say?"

"Careful of those sweets," Father Rank said, "they are harmless in moderation, but you've taken four already. Look here, Tallit, Mr. Wilson looks hungry. Can't you bring on the bakemeats?"

"Bakemeats?"

"The feast," Father Rank said. His joviality filled the room with hollow sound. For twenty-two years that voice had been laughing, joking, urging people humorously on through the rainy and dry months. Could its cheeriness ever have comforted a single soul? Wilson wondered: had it comforted even itself? It was like the noise one heard rebounding from the tiles in a public bath: the laughs and the splashes of strangers in the steam-heating.

"Of course, Father Rank. Immediately, Father Rank." Father Rank without being invited rose from his chair and sat himself down at a table which like the chairs hugged the wall. There were only a few places laid and Wilson hesitated. "Come on. Sit down, Mr. Wilson. Only the old folks will be eating with us—and Tallit of course."

"You were saying something about a rumour?" Wilson asked.

"My head is a hive of rumours," Father Rank said, making a humorous hopeless gesture. "If a man tells me anything I assume he wants me to pass it on. It's a useful function, you know, at a time like this, when everything is an official secret, to remind people that their tongues were made to talk with and that the truth is meant to be spoken about. Look at Tallit now," Father Rank went on. Tallit was raising the corner of his black-out curtain and gazing into the dark street. "How's Yusef, you young rogue?" he asked. "Yusef's got a big house across the street and Tallit wants it, don't you, Tallit? What about dinner, Tallit? We're hungry."

"It is here, Father, it is here," he said, coming away from the window. He sat down silently beside the centenarian, and his sister served the dishes. "You always get a good meal in Tallit's house," Father Rank said.

"Yusef too is entertaining tonight."

"It doesn't do for a priest to be choosy," Father Rank said, "but I find your dinner more digestible." His hollow laugh swung through the room.

"Is it as bad as all that, being seen at Yusef's?"

"It is, Mr. Wilson. If I saw you there, I'd say to myself, 'Yusef wants some information badly about cottons—what the imports are going to be next month, say—what's on the way by sea—and he'll pay for his information.' If I saw a girl go in, I'd think it was a pity, a great pity." He took a stab at his plate and laughed again. "But if Tallit went in, I'd wait to hear the screams for help."

"If you saw a police officer?" Tallit asked.

"I wouldn't believe my eyes," the priest said. "None of them are such fools after what happened to Bailey."

"The other night a police car brought Yusef home," Tallit said. "I saw it from here plainly."

"One of the drivers earning a bit on the side," Father Rank said.

"I thought I saw Major Scobie. He was careful not to get out. Of course I am not perfectly sure. It looked like Major Scobie."

"My tongue runs away with me," the priest said. "What a garrulous fool I am. Why, if it was Scobie, I wouldn't think twice about it." His eyes roamed the room. "Not twice," he said. "I'd lay next Sunday's collection that everything was all right, absolutely all right," and he swung his great empty-sounding bell to and fro, Ho, ho ho, like a leper proclaiming his misery.

3

The light was still on in Harris's room when Wilson returned to the hotel. He was tired and worried and he tried to tiptoe by, but Harris heard him. "I've been listening for you, old man," he said, waving an electric torch. He wore his mosquito boots outside his pyjamas and looked like a harassed air-raid warden.

"It's late. I thought you'd be asleep."

"I couldn't sleep until we'd had our hunt. The idea's grown on me, old man. We might have a monthly prize. I can see the time coming when other people will want to join in."

Wilson said with irony, "There might be a silver cup."

"Stranger things have happened, old man. The Cockroach Championship."

He led the way, walking softly on the boards, to the middle of his room: the iron bed stood under its greying net, the arm-chair with collapsible back, the dressing-table littered with old *Picture Posts*. It shocked Wilson once again to realize that a room could be a degree more cheerless than his own.

"We'll draw our rooms alternate nights, old man."

"What weapon shall I use?"

"You can borrow one of my slippers." A board squeaked under Wilson's feet and Harris turned warningly. "They have ears like rats," he said.

"I'm a bit tired. Don't you think that tonight . . . ?"

"Just five minutes, old man. I couldn't sleep without a hunt. Look, there's one—over the dressing-table. You can have first shot," but as the shadow of the slipper fell upon the plaster wall the insect shot away.

"No use doing it like that, old man. Watch me." Harris stalked his prey: the cockroach was halfway up the wall, and Harris, as he moved on tiptoe across the creaking floor, began to weave the light of his torch backwards and forwards over the cockroach. Then suddenly he struck, and left a smear of blood. "One up," he said. "You have to mesmerize them."

To and fro across the room they padded, weaving their lights, smashing down their shoes, occasionally losing their heads and pursuing wildly into corners: the lust of the hunt touched Wilson's imagination. At first their manner to each other was "sporting": they would call out, "Good shot," or "Hard luck," but once they met together against the wainscot over the same cockroach when the score was even, and their tempers became frayed.

60

"No point in going after the same bird, old man," Harris said.

"I started him."

"You lost your one, old man. This was mine."

"It was the same. He did a double turn."

"Oh, no."

"Anyway, there's no reason why I shouldn't go for the same one. You drove it towards me. Bad play on your part."

"Not allowed in the rules," Harris said shortly.

"Perhaps not in your rules."

"Damn it all," Harris said, "I invented the game."

A cockroach sat upon the brown cake of soap in the washbasin. Wilson spied it and took a long shot with the shoe from six feet away. The shoe landed smartly on the soap and the cockroach span into the basin: Harris turned on the tap and washed it down. "Good shot, old man," he said placatingly. "One D.D."

"D.D. be damned," Wilson said. "It was dead when you turned on the tap."

"You couldn't be sure of that. It might have been just unconscious—concussion. It's D.D. according to the rules."

"Your rules again."

"My rules are the Queensberry rules in this town."

"They won't be for long," Wilson threatened. He slammed the door hard behind him and the walls of his own room vibrated round him from the shock. His heart beat with rage and the hot night: the sweat drained from his arm-pits. But as he stood there beside his own bed, seeing the replica of Harris's room around him, the washbasin, the table, the grey mosquito net, even the cockroach fastened on the wall, anger trickled out of him and loneliness took its place. It was like quarrelling with one's own image in the glass. "I was crazy," he thought. "What made me fly out like that? I've lost a friend."

That night it took him a long while to sleep, and when he slept at last he dreamed that he had committed a crime, so that he woke with the sense of guilt still heavy upon him: on his way down to breakfast he paused outside Harris's door. There was no sound. He knocked, but there was no answer. He opened the door a little way and saw obscurely through the grey net Harris's damp bed. He asked softly, "Are you awake?"

"What is it, old man?"

61

"I'm sorry, Harris, about last night."

"My fault, old man. I've got a touch of fever. I was sickening for it. Touchy."

"No, it's my fault. You are quite right. It was D.D."

"We'll toss up for it, old man."

"I'll come in tonight."

"That's fine."

But after breakfast something took his mind right away from Harris. He had been in to the Commissioner's office on his way downtown and coming out he ran into Scobie.

"Hallo," Scobie said, "what are you doing here?"

"Been in to see the Commissioner about a pass. There are so many passes one has to have in this town, sir. I wanted one for the wharf."

"When are you going to call on us again, Wilson?"

"You don't want to be bothered with strangers, sir."

"Nonsense. Louise would like another chat about books. I don't read them myself, you know, Wilson."

"I don't suppose you have much time."

"Oh, there's an awful lot of time around," Scobie said, "in a country like this. I just don't have a taste for reading, that's all. Come in to my office a moment while I ring up Louise. She'll be glad to see you. Wish you'd call in and take her for a walk. She doesn't get enough exercise."

"I'd love to," Wilson said, and blushed hurriedly in the shadows. He looked around him: this was Scobie's office. He examined it as a general might examine a battleground, and yet it was difficult to regard Scobie as an enemy. The rusty handcuffs jangled on the wall as Scobie leant back from his desk and dialed.

"Free this evening?"

He brought his mind sharply back, aware that Scobie was watching him: the slightly protruding, slightly reddened eyes dwelt on him with a kind of speculation. "I wonder why you came out here," Scobie said. "You aren't the type."

"One drifts into things," Wilson lied.

"I don't," Scobie said, "I've always been a planner. You see, I even plan for other people." He began to talk into the telephone. His intonation changed: it was as if he were reading a part—a part which called for tenderness and patience, a part which had been read so often that the eyes were blank above the mouth. Putting down the receiver he said, "That's fine. That's settled, then."

"It seems a very good plan to me," Wilson said.

"My plans always start out well," Scobie said. "You two go for a walk and when you get back I'll have a drink ready for you. Stay to dinner," he went on, with a hint of anxiety. "We'll be glad of your company."

When Wilson had gone, Scobie went in to the Commissioner. He said, "I was just coming along to see you, sir, when I ran into Wilson."

"Oh, yes, Wilson," the Commissioner said. "He came in to have a word with me about one of their lightermen."

"I see." The shutters were down in the office to cut out the morning sun. A sergeant passed through carrying with him as well as his file a breath of the zoo behind. The day was heavy with unshed rain: already at eight-thirty in the morning the body ran with sweat. Scobie said, "He told me he'd come about a pass."

"Oh, yes," the Commissioner said. "That too." He put a piece of blotting paper under his wrist to absorb the sweat as he wrote. "Yes, there was something about a pass too, Scobie."

II. WHEN LOUISE AND WILSON CROSSED THE river again and came into Burnside it was quite dark. The head-lamps of a police van lit an open door, and figures moved to and fro carrying packages. "What's up now?" Louise exclaimed, and began to run down the road. Wilson panted after her. Ali came from the house carrying on his head a tin bath, a folding chair, and a bundle tied up in an old towel. "What on earth's happened, Ali?"

"Massa go on trek," he said, and grinned happily in the head-lamps.

In the sitting-room Scobie sat with a drink in his hand. "I'm glad you are back," he said. "I thought I'd have to write a note," and Wilson saw that in fact he had already begun one. He had torn a leaf out of his notebook, and his large awkward writing covered a couple of lines.

"What on earth's happening, Henry?"

"I've got to get off to Bamba."

"Can't you wait for the train on Thursday?"

"No."

"Can I come with you?"

"Not this time. I'm sorry, dear. I'll have to take Ali and leave you the small boy."

"What's happened?"

"There's trouble over young Pemberton."

"Serious?"

"Yes."

"He's such a fool. It was madness to leave him there as D.C."

Scobie drank his whisky and said, "I'm sorry, Wilson. Help yourself. Get a bottle of soda out of the ice-box. The boys are busy packing."

"How long will you be, darling?"

"Oh, I'll be back the day after tomorrow, with any luck. Why don't you go and stay with Mrs. Halifax?"

"I shall be all right here, darling."

"I'd take the small boy and leave you Ali, but the small boy can't cook."

"You'll be happier with Ali, dear. It will be like the old days before I came out."

"I think I'll be off, sir," Wilson said. "I'm sorry I kept Mrs. Scobie out so late."

"Oh, I didn't worry, Wilson. Father Rank came by and told me you were sheltering in the old station. Very sensible of you. He got a drenching. He should have stayed too—he doesn't want a dose of fever at his age."

"Can I fill your glass, sir? Then I'll be off."

"Henry never takes more than one."

"All the same, I think I will. But don't go, Wilson. Stay and keep Louise company for a bit. I've got to be off after this glass. I shan't get any sleep tonight."

"Why can't one of the young men go? You're too old, Ticki, for this. Driving all night. Why don't you send Fraser?"

"The Commissioner asked me to go. It's just one of those cases—carefulness, tact, you can't let a young man handle it." He took another drink of whisky and his eyes moved gloomily away as Wilson watched him. "I must be off."

"I'll never forgive Pemberton for this."

Scobie said sharply, "Don't talk nonsense, dear. We'd forgive most things if we knew the facts." He smiled unwillingly at Wilson. "A policeman should be the most forgiving person in the world if he gets the facts right."

"I wish I could be of help, sir."

"You can. Stay and have a few more drinks with Louise and cheer her up. She doesn't often get a chance to talk about books." At the word books Wilson saw her mouth tighten just as a moment ago he had seen Scobie flinch at the name of Ticki, and for the first time he realized the pain inevitable in any human relationship—pain suffered and pain inflicted. How foolish we were to be afraid of loneliness.

"Good-bye, darling."

"Good-bye, Ticki."

"Look after Wilson. See he has enough to drink. Don't mope."

When she kissed Scobie, Wilson stood near the door with a glass in his hand and remembered the disused station on the hill above and the taste of lipstick. For exactly an hour and a half the mark of his mouth had been the last on hers. He felt no jealousy, only the dreariness of a man who tries to write an important letter on a damp sheet and finds the characters blur.

Side by side they watched Scobie cross the road to the police van. He had taken more whisky than he was accustomed to, and perhaps that was what made him stumble. "They should have sent a younger man," Wilson said.

"They never do. He's the only one the Commissioner trusts." They watched him climb laboriously in, and she went sadly on, "Isn't he the typical second man? The man who always does the work."

The black policeman at the wheel started his engine and began to grind into gear before releasing the clutch. "They don't even give him a good driver," she said. "The good driver will have taken Fraser and the rest to the dance at Cape Station." The van bumped and heaved out of the yard. Louise said, "Well, that's that, Wilson."

She picked up the note Scobie had intended to leave for her and read it aloud. *My dear, I have had to leave for*

Bamba. Keep this to yourself. A terrible thing has happened. Poor Pemberton . . .

"Poor Pemberton," she repeated furiously.

"Who's Pemberton?"

"A little puppy of twenty-five. All spots and bounce. He was Assistant D.C. at Bamba, but when Butterworth went sick they left him in charge. Anybody could have told them there'd be trouble. And when trouble comes it's Henry, of course, who has to drive all night. . . ."

"I'd better leave now, hadn't I?" Wilson said. "You'll want to change."

"Oh, yes, you'd better go—before everybody knows he's gone and that we've been alone five minutes in a house with a bed in it. Alone, of course, except for the small boy and the cook and their relations and friends."

"I wish I could be of some use."

"You could be," she said. "Would you go upstairs and see whether there's a rat in the bedroom? I don't want the small boy to know I'm nervous. And shut the window. They come in that way."

"It will be very hot for you."

"I don't mind."

He stood just inside the door and clapped his hands softly, but no rat moved. Then quickly, surreptitiously, as though he had no right to be there, he crossed to the window and closed it. There was a faint smell of face powder in the room—it seemed to him the most memorable scent he had ever known. He stood again by the door taking the whole room in—the child's photograph, the pots of cream, the dress laid out by Ali for the evening. He had been instructed at home how to memorize, pick out the important detail, collect the right evidence, but his employers had never taught him that he would find himself in a country so strange to him as this.

Part Three

THE POLICE VAN TOOK ITS PLACE IN THE LONG
line of army lorries waiting for the ferry: their head-lamps
were like a little village in the night: the trees came down
on either side smelling of heat and rain: and somewhere
at the end of the column a driver sang—the wailing, tone-
less voice rose and fell like a wind through a keyhole.
Scobie slept and woke, slept and woke. When he woke
he thought of Pemberton and wondered how he would
feel if he were his father—that elderly, retired bank manager whose wife had died in giving birth to Pemberton—
but when he slept he went smoothly back into a dream of
perfect happiness and freedom. He was walking through a
wide cool meadow with Ali at his heels: there was nobody
else anywhere in his dream, and Ali never spoke. Birds went
by far overhead, and once when he sat down the grass was
parted by a small green snake which passed onto his hand
and up his arm without fear and before it slid down into the
grass again touched his cheek with a cold friendly remote
tongue.

Once when he opened his eyes Ali was standing beside
him waiting for him to awake. "Massa like bed," he stated
gently, firmly, pointing to the camp bed he had made up
at the edge of the path with the mosquito net tied from
the branches overhead. "Two three hours," Ali said.
"Plenty lorries." Scobie obeyed and lay down and was immediately back in that peaceful meadow, where nothing
ever happened. The next time he woke Ali was still there,
this time with a cup of tea and a plate of biscuits. "One
hour," Ali said.

Then at last it was the turn of the police van. They
moved down the red laterite slope onto the raft, and then

67

edged foot by foot across the dark Styx-like stream towards the woods on the other side. The two ferrymen pulling on the rope wore nothing but girdles, as though they had left their clothes behind on the bank where life ended, and a third man beat time to them, making do for instrument in this between-world with an empty sardine tin. The wailing tireless voice of the living singer shifted backwards.

This was only the first of three ferries that had to be crossed, with the same queue forming each time. Scobie never succeeded in sleeping properly again: his head began to ache from the heave of the van: he ate some aspirin and hoped for the best. He didn't want a dose of fever when he was away from home. It was not Pemberton that worried him now—let the dead bury their dead: it was the promise he had made to Louise. Two hundred pounds was so small a sum: the figures ran their changes in his aching head like a peal of bells: 200 002 020: it worried him that he could not find a fourth combination: 002 200 020.

They had come beyond the range now of the tin-roofed shacks and the decayed wooden settlers' huts: the villages they passed through were bush villages of mud and thatch: no light showed anywhere: doors were closed and shutters were up, and only a few goats' eyes watched the head-lamps of the convoy. 020 002 200 200 002 020. Ali squatting in the body of the van put an arm round his shoulder, holding a mug of hot tea—somehow he had boiled another kettle in the lurching chassis. Louise was right—it was like the old days. If he had felt younger, if there had been no problem of 200 020 002, how happy he would have felt. Poor Pemberton's death would not have disturbed him —that was merely in the way of duty, and he had never liked Pemberton.

"My head humbug me, Ali."

"Massa take plenty aspirin."

"Do you remember, Ali, that two hundred 002 trek we did twelve years ago in ten days, along the border; two of the carriers went sick . . ."

He could see in the driver's mirror Ali nodding and beaming. It seemed to him that this was all he needed of love or friendship. He could be happy with no more in the world than this—the grinding van, the hot tea against his lips, the heavy damp weight of the forest, even the aching head, the loneliness. If I could just arrange for her happiness first, he thought, and in the confusing night he forgot for the while what experience had taught him—that no human being can really understand another and no one can arrange another's happiness.

"One hour more," Ali said, and he noticed that the darkness was thinning. "Another mug of tea, Ali, and put some whisky in it." The convoy had separated from them a quarter of an hour ago, when the police van had turned away from the main road and bumped along a by-road farther into the bush. He shut his eyes and tried to draw his mind away from the broken peal of figures to the distasteful job. There was only a native police sergeant at Bamba and he would like to be clear in his own mind as to what had happened before he received the sergeant's illiterate report. It would be better, he considered reluctantly, to go first to the Mission and see Father Clay.

Father Clay was up and waiting for him in the dismal little mission house which had been built among the mud huts in laterite bricks to look like a Victorian presbytery. A hurricane lamp shone on the priest's short red hair and his young freckled Liverpool face. He couldn't sit still for more than a few minutes at a time, and then he would be up, pacing his tiny room from hideous oleograph to plaster statue and back to oleograph again. "I saw so little of him," he wailed, motioning with his hands as though he were at the altar. "He cared for nothing but cards and drinking. I don't drink and I've never played cards—except demon, you know, except demon, and that's a patience. It's terrible, terrible."

"He hanged himself?"

"Yes. His boy came over to me yesterday. He hadn't seen him since the night before, but that was quite usual after a bout, you know, a bout. I told him to go to the police. That was right, wasn't it? There was nothing I could do. Nothing. He was quite dead."

"Quite right. Would you mind giving me a glass of water and some aspirin?"

"Let me mix the aspirin for you. You know, Major Scobie, for weeks and months nothing happens here at all. I just walk up and down here, up and down, and then suddenly out of the blue . . . it's terrible." His eyes were red and sleepless: he seemed to Scobie one of those who are quite unsuited to loneliness. There were no books to be

69

seen except a little shelf with his breviary and a few religious tracts. He was a man without resources. He began to pace up and down again and suddenly, turning on Scobie, he shot out an excited question. "Mightn't there be a hope that it's murder?"

"Hope?"

"Suicide," Father Clay said. "It's too terrible. It puts a man outside mercy. I've been thinking about it all night."

"He wasn't a Catholic. Perhaps that makes a difference. Invincible ignorance, eh?"

"That's what I try to think." Halfway between oleograph and statuette he suddenly started and stepped aside as though he had encountered another on his tiny parade. Then he looked quickly and slyly at Scobie to see whether his act had been noticed.

"How often do you get down to the port?" Scobie asked.

"I was there for a night nine months ago. Why?"

"Everybody needs a change. Have you many converts here?"

"Fifteen. I try to persuade myself that young Pemberton had time—time, you know, while he died, to realize . . ."

"Difficult to think clearly when you are strangling, Father." He took a swig at the aspirin, and the sour grains stuck in his throat. "If it was murder you'd simple change your mortal sinner, Father," he said with an attempt at humour which wilted between the holy picture and the holy statue.

"A murderer has time . . ." Father Clay said. He added wistfully, with nostalgia, "I used to do duty sometimes at Liverpool Gaol."

"Have you any idea why he did it?"

"I didn't know him well enough. We didn't get on together."

"The only white men here. It seems a pity."

"He offered to lend me some books, but they weren't at all the kind of books I care to read—love stories, novels . . ."

"What do you read, Father?"

"Anything on the saints, Major Scobie. My great devotion is to the Little Flower."

"He drank a lot, didn't he? Where did he get it from?"

"Yusef's store, I suppose."

70

"Yes. He may have been in debt?"

"I don't know. It's terrible, terrible."

Scobie finished his aspirin. "I suppose I'd better go along." It was day now outside, and there was a peculiar innocence about the light, gentle and clear and fresh before the sun climbed.

"I'll come with you, Major Scobie."

The police sergeant sat in a deck chair outside the D.C.'s bungalow. He rose and raggedly saluted, then immediately in his hollow unformed voice began to read his report. "At three-thirty P.M. yesterday, sah, I was woken by D.C.'s boy, who reported that D.C. Pemberton, sah . . ."

"That's all right, sergeant, I'll just go inside and have a look round." The chief clerk waited for him just inside the door.

The living-room of the bungalow had obviously once been the D.C.'s pride—that must have been in Butterworth's day. There was an air of elegance and personal pride in the furniture; it hadn't been supplied by the Government. There were eighteenth-century engravings of the old colony on the wall and in one bookcase were the volumes that Butterworth had left behind him—Scobie noted some titles and authors, Maitland's *Constitutional History*, Sir Henry Maine, Bryce's *Holy Roman Empire*, Hardy's poems, and the *Doomsday Records of Little Withington*, privately printed. But imposed on all this were the traces of Pemberton—a gaudy leather pouf of so-called native work, the marks of cigarette ends on the chairs, a stack of the books Father Clay had disliked—Somerset Maugham, an Edgar Wallace, two Horlers, and, spread-eagled on the settee, *Death Laughs at Locksmiths*. The room was not properly dusted, and Butterworth's books were stained with damp.

"The body is in the bedroom, sah," the sergeant said.

Scobie opened the door and went in: Father Clay followed him. The body had been laid on the bed with a sheet over the face. When Scobie turned the sheet down to the shoulder he had the impression that he was looking at a child in a night-shirt quietly asleep: the pimples were the pimples of puberty and the dead face seemed to bear the trace of no experience beyond the class-room or the football field. "Poor child," he said aloud. The pious ejaculations of Father Clay irritated him. It seemed to him that

71

unquestionably there must be mercy for someone so un-formed. He asked abruptly, "How did he do it?"

The police sergeant pointed to the picture rail that Butterworth had so meticulously fitted—no Government contractor would have thought of it. A picture—an early native king receiving missionaries under a State umbrella—leant against the wall, and a cord remained twisted over the brass picture hanger. Who would have expected the flimsy contrivance not to collapse? He can weigh very little, he thought, and he remembered a child's bones, light and brittle as a bird's. His feet when he hung must have been only fifteen inches from the ground.

"Did he leave any papers?" Scobie asked the clerk. "They usually do." Men who are going to die are apt to become garrulous with self-revelations.

"Yes, sah, in the office."

It needed only a casual inspection to realize how badly the office had been kept. The filing cabinet was unlocked: the trays on the desk were filled by papers dusty with inattention. The native clerk had obviously followed the same ways as his chief. "There, sah, on the pad."

Scobie read, in a handwriting as unformed as the face, a script-writing which hundreds of his school contemporaries must have been turning out all over the world: *Dear Dad. Forgive all this trouble. There doesn't seem anything else to do. It's a pity I'm not in the army because then I might be killed. Don't go and pay the money I owe—the fellow doesn't deserve it. They may try and get it out of you. Otherwise I wouldn't mention it. It's a rotten business for you, but it can't be helped. Your loving son.* The signature was *Dicky.* It was like a letter from school excusing a bad report.

He handed the letter to Father Clay. "You are not going to tell me there's anything unforgivable there, Father. If you or I did it, it would be despair—I grant you anything with us. We'd be damned, all right, because we know, but *he* doesn't know a thing."

"The Church's teaching . . ."

"Even the Church can't teach me that God doesn't pity the young . . ." Scobie broke abruptly off. "Sergeant, see that a grave's dug quickly before the sun gets too hot. And look out for any bills he owed. I want to have a word with someone about this." When he turned towards the window the light dazzled him. He put his hand over his eyes and said, "I wish to God my head . . ." and shivered. "I'm in for a dose if I can't stop it. If you don't mind Ali putting up my bed at your place, Father, I'll try and sweat it out."

He took a heavy dose of quinine and lay naked between the blankets. As the sun climbed it sometimes seemed to him that the stone walls of the small cell-like room sweated with cold and sometimes were baked with heat. The door was open and Ali squatted on the step just outside whittling a piece of wood. Occasionally he chased away villagers who raised their voices within the area of sickroom silence. The *peine forte et dure* weighed on Scobie's forehead: occasionally it pressed him into sleep.

But in this sleep there were no pleasant dreams. Pemberton and Louise were obscurely linked. Over and over again he was reading a letter which consisted only of variations on the figure 200, and the signature at the bottom was sometimes "Dicky" and sometimes "Ticki": he had the sense of time passing and his own immobility between the blankets—there was something he had to do, someone he had to save, Louise or Dicky or Ticki, but he was tied to the bed and they laid weights on his forehead as you lay weights on loose papers. Once the sergeant came to the door and Ali chased him away: once Father Clay tiptoed in and took a tract off a shelf: and once, but that might have been a dream, Yusef came to the door.

About five in the evening he woke feeling dry and cool and weak and called Ali in. "I dreamed I saw Yusef."

"Yusef come for to see you, sah."

"Tell him I'll see him now." He felt tired and beaten about the body: he turned to face the stone wall and was immediately asleep. In his sleep Louise wept silently beside him: he put out his hand and touched the stone wall again—"Everything shall be arranged. Everything. Ticki promises." When he awoke, Yusef was beside him.

"A touch of fever, Major Scobie. I am very sorry to see you poorly."

"I'm sorry to see you at all, Yusef."

"Ah, you always make fun of me."

"Sit down, Yusef. What did you have to do with Pemberton?"

73

Yusef eased his great haunches onto the hard chair and noticing that his flies were open put down a large and hairy hand to deal with them. "Nothing, Major Scobie."

"It's an odd coincidence that you are here just at the moment when he commits suicide."

"I think myself it's Providence."

"He owed you money, I suppose?"

"He owed my store-manager money."

"What sort of pressure were you putting on him, Yusef?"

"Major, you give an evil name to a dog and the dog is finished. If the D.C. wants to buy at my store, how can my manager stop selling to him? If he does that, what will happen? Sooner or later there will be a first-class row. The Provincial Commissioner will find out. The D.C. will be sent home. If he does not stop selling, what happens then? The D.C. runs up more and more bills. My manager becomes afraid of me, he asks the D.C. to pay—there is a row that way. When you have a D.C. like poor young Pemberton there will be a row one day whatever you do. And the Syrian is always wrong."

"There's quite a lot in what you say, Yusef." The pain was beginning again. "Give me that whisky and quinine, Yusef."

"You are not taking too much quinine, Major Scobie? Remember blackwater."

"I don't want to be stuck up here for days. I want to kill this at birth. I've too many things to do."

"Sit up a moment, Major, and let me beat your pillow."

"You aren't a bad chap, Yusef."

Yusef said, "Your sergeant has been looking for bills, but he could not find any. Here are I.O.U.'s, though. From my manager's safe." He flapped his thigh with a little sheaf of papers.

"I see. What are you going to do with them?"

"Burn them," Yusef said. He took out a cigarette lighter and lit the corners. "There," Yusef said. "He has paid, poor boy. There is no reason to trouble his father."

"Why did you come up here?"

"My manager was worried. I was going to propose an arrangement."

"One needs a long spoon to sup with you, Yusef."

"My enemies do. Not my friends. I would do a lot for you, Major Scobie."

74

"Why do you always call me a friend, Yusef?"

"Major Scobie," Yusef said, leaning his great white head forward, reeking of hair oil, "friendship is something in the soul. It is a thing one feels. It is not a return for something. You remember when you put me into court ten years ago?"

"Yes, yes." Scobie turned his head away from the light of the door.

"You nearly caught me, Major Scobie, that time. It was a matter of import duties, you remember. You could have caught me if you had told your policemen to say something a little different. I was quite overcome with astonishment, Major Scobie, to sit in a police court and hear true facts from the mouths of policemen. You must have taken a lot of trouble to find out what was true and to make them say it. I said to myself, Yusef, a Daniel has come to the Colonial Police."

"I wish you wouldn't talk so much, Yusef. I'm not interested in your friendship."

"Your words are harder than your heart, Major Scobie. I want to explain why in my soul I have always felt your friend. You have made me feel secure. You will not frame me. You need facts, and I am sure the facts will always be in my favour." He dusted the ashes from his white trousers, leaving one more grey smear. "These are facts. I have burned all the I.O.U.'s."

"I may yet find traces, Yusef, of what kind of agreement you were intending to make with Pemberton. This station controls one of the main routes across the border from—damnation, I can't think of names with this head."

"Cattle smugglers. I'm not interested in cattle."

"Other things are apt to go back the other way."

"You are still dreaming of diamonds, Major Scobie. Everybody has gone crazy about diamonds since the war."

"Don't feel too certain, Yusef, that I won't find something when I go through Pemberton's office."

"I feel quite certain, Major Scobie. You know I cannot read or write. Nothing is ever on paper. Everything is always in my head." Even while Yusef talked, Scobie dropped asleep—into one of those shallow sleeps that last a few seconds and have time only to reflect a preoccupation. Louise was coming towards him with both hands held out and a smile that he hadn't seen upon her face for years.

She said, "I am so happy, so happy," and he woke again to Yusef's voice going soothingly on. "It is only your friends who do not trust you, Major Scobie. I trust you. Even that scoundrel Tallit trusts you."

It took him a moment to get this other face into focus. His brain adjusted itself achingly from the phrase "so happy" to the phrase "do not trust." He said, "What are you talking about, Yusef?" He could feel the mechanism of his brain creaking, grinding, scraping, cogs failing to connect, all with pain.

"First, there is the commissionership."

"They need a young man," he said mechanically, and thought: If I hadn't fever I would never discuss a matter like this with Yusef.

"Then, the special man they have sent from London . . ."

"You must come back when I'm clearer, Yusef. I don't know what the hell you are talking about."

"They have sent a special man from London to investigate the diamonds—they are crazy about diamonds—only the Commissioner must know about him—none of the other officers, not even you."

"What rubbish you talk, Yusef. There's no such man."

"Everybody guesses but you. It's Wilson."

"Too absurd. You shouldn't listen to rumour, Yusef."

"And a third thing. Tallit says everywhere you visit me."

"Tallit! Who believes what Tallit says?"

"Everybody everywhere believes what is bad."

"Go away, Yusef. Why do you want to worry me now?"

"I just want you to understand, Major Scobie, that you can depend on me. I have friendship for you in my soul. That is true, Major Scobie, it is true." The reek of hair oil came closer as he bent towards the bed: the deep brown eyes were damp with what seemed to be emotion. "Let me pat your pillow, Major Scobie."

"Oh, for goodness' sake, keep away," Scobie said.

"I know how things are, Major Scobie, and if I can help . . . I am a well-off man."

"I'm not looking for bribes, Yusef," he said wearily, and turned his head away to escape the scent.

"I am not offering you a bribe, Major Scobie. A loan at any time on a reasonable rate of interest—four per cent per

76

annum. No conditions. You can arrest me next day if you have facts. I want to be your friend, Major Scobie. You need not be my friend. There is a Syrian poet who wrote, 'Of two hearts one is always warm and one is always cold: the cold heart is more precious than diamonds: the warm heart has no value and is thrown away.'"

"It sounds a very bad poem to me. But I'm no judge."

"It is a happy coincidence for me that we should be here together. In the town there are so many people watching. But here, Major Scobie, I can be of real help to you. May I fetch you more blankets?"

"No, no, just leave me alone."

"I hate to see a man of your characteristics, Major Scobie, treated badly."

"I don't think the time's ever likely to come, Yusef, when I shall need your pity. If you want to do something for me, though, go away and let me sleep."

But when he slept the unhappy dreams returned. Upstairs Louise was crying, and he sat at a table writing his last letter. *It's a rotten business for you, but it can't be helped. Your loving husband, Dicky,* and then, as he turned to look for a weapon or a rope, it suddenly occurred to him that this was an act he could never do. Suicide was for ever out of his power—he couldn't condemn himself for eternity—no cause was important enough. He tore up his letter and ran upstairs to tell Louise that after all everything was all right, but she had stopped crying and the silence welling out from inside the bedroom terrified him. He tried the door and the door was locked. He called out, "Louise, everything's all right. I've booked your passage," but there was no answer. He cried again, "Louise," and then a key turned and the door slowly opened with a sense of irrecoverable disaster, and he saw standing just inside Father Clay, who said to him, "The teaching of the Church . . ." Then he woke again to the small stone room like a tomb.

2

He was away for a week, for it took three days for the fever to run its course and another two days before he was fit to travel. He did not see Yusef again.

It was past midnight when he drove into town. The houses were white as bones in the moonlight; the quiet streets stretched out on either side like the arms of a skeleton, and the faint sweet smell of flowers lay on the air. If he had been returning to an empty house he knew that he would have been contented. He was tired and he didn't want to break the silence—it was too much to hope that Louise would be asleep, too much to hope that things would somehow have become easier in his absence and that he would see her free and happy as she had been in one of his dreams.

The small boy waved his torch from the door: the frogs croaked from the bushes, and the pye-dogs wailed at the moon. He was home. Louise threw her arms round him: the table was laid for a late supper, the boys ran to and fro with his boxes: he smiled and talked and kept the bustle going. He talked of Pemberton and Father Clay and mentioned Yusef, but he knew that sooner or later he would have to ask how things had been with her. He tried to eat, but he was too tired to taste the food.

"Yesterday I cleared up his office and wrote my report— and that was that." He hesitated—"That's all my news"— and went reluctantly on, "How have things been here?" He looked quickly up at her face and away again. There had been one chance in a thousand that she would have smiled and said vaguely, "Not so bad," and then passed on to other things, but he knew from her mouth that he wasn't so lucky as that. Something fresh had happened.

But the outbreak, whatever it was to be, was delayed. She said, "Oh, Wilson's been attentive."

"He's a nice boy."

"He's too intelligent for his job. I can't think why he's out here as just a clerk."

"He told me he drifted."

"I don't think I've spoken to anybody else since you've been away, except the small boy and the cook. Oh, and Mrs. Halifax." Something in her voice told him that the danger point was reached. Always, hopelessly, he tried to evade it. He stretched and said, "My God, I'm tired. The fever's left me limp as a rag. I think I'll go to bed. It's nearly half past one, and I've got to be at the station at eight."

She said, "Ticki, have you done anything at all?"

"How do you mean, dear?"

"About the passage."

"Don't worry. I'll find a way, dear."

"You haven't found one yet?"

"No. I've got several ideas I'm working on. It's just a question of borrowing." 200, 020, 002 rang in his brain.

"Poor dear," she said, "don't worry," and put her hand against his cheek. "You're tired. You've had fever. I'm not going to bait you now." Her hand, her words broke through every defence: he had expected tears, but he found them now in his own eyes. "Go on up to bed, Henry," she said.

"Aren't you coming up?"

"There are just one or two things I want to do."

He lay on his back under the net and waited for her. It occurred to him as it hadn't occurred to him, for years, that she loved him: poor dear, she loved him: she was someone of human stature with her own sense of responsibility, not simply the object of his care and kindness. The sense of failure deepened round him. All the way back from Bamba he had faced one fact—that there was only one man in the city capable of lending him, and willing to lend him, the two hundred pounds, and that was a man he must not borrow from. It would have been safer to accept the Portuguese captain's bribe. Slowly and drearily he had reached the decision to tell her that the money simply could not be found, that for the next six months at any rate, until his leave, she must stay. If he had not felt so tired he would have told her when she asked him and it would have been over now, but he had flinched away and she had been kind, and it would be harder now than it had ever been to disappoint her. There was silence all through the little house, but outside the half-starved pye-dogs yapped and whined. He listened, leaning on his elbow; he felt oddly unmanned, lying in bed alone waiting for Louise to join him. She had always been the one to go first to bed. He felt uneasy, apprehensive, and suddenly his dream came to mind, how he had listened outside the door and knocked, and there was no reply. He struggled out from under the net and ran downstairs barefooted.

Louise was sitting at the table with a pad of note-paper in front of her, but she had written nothing but a name. The winged ants beat against the light and dropped their

79

wings over the table. Where the light touched her head he saw the grey hairs.

"What is it, dear?"

"Everything was so quiet," he said, "I wondered whether something had happened. I had a bad dream about you the other night. Pemberton's suicide upset me."

"How silly, dear. Nothing like that could ever happen with us. We're Catholics."

"Yes, of course. I just wanted to see you," he said, putting his hand on her hair. Over her shoulder he read the only words she had written, "*Dear Mrs. Halifax . . .*"

"You haven't got your shoes on," she said. "You'll be catching jiggers."

"I just wanted to see you," he repeated, and wondered whether the stains on the paper were sweat or tears.

"Listen, dear," she said. "You are not to worry any more. I've baited you and baited you. It's like fever, you know. It comes and goes. Well, now it's gone—for a while. I know you can't raise the money. It's not your fault. If it hadn't been for that stupid operation . . . It's just the way things are, Henry."

"What's it all got to do with Mrs. Halifax?"

"She and another woman have a two-berth cabin in the next ship and the other woman's fallen out. She thought perhaps I could slip in—if her husband spoke to the agent."

"That's in about a fortnight," he said.

"Darling, give up trying. It's better just to give up. Anyway, I had to let Mrs. Halifax know tomorrow. And I'm letting her know that I shan't be going."

He spoke rapidly—he wanted the words out beyond recall. "Write and tell her that you can go."

"Ticki," she said, "what do you mean?" Her face hardened. "Ticki, please don't promise something which can't happen. I know you're tired and afraid of a scene. But there isn't going to be a scene. I mustn't let Mrs. Halifax down."

"You won't. I know where I can borrow the money."

"Why didn't you tell me when you came back?"

"I wanted to give you your ticket. A surprise."

She was not so happy as he would have expected: she always saw a little further than he hoped. "And you are not worrying any more?" she asked.

80

"I'm not worrying any more. Are you happy?"

"Oh, yes," she said in a puzzled voice. "I'm happy, dear."

3

The liner came in on a Saturday evening: from the bedroom window they could see its long grey form steal past the boom, beyond the palms. They watched it with a sinking of the heart—happiness is never really so welcome as changelessness; hand in hand they watched their separation anchor in the bay. "Well," Scobie said, "that means tomorrow afternoon."

"Darling," she said, "when this time is over, I'll be good to you again. I just couldn't stand this life any more."

They could hear a clatter below-stairs as Ali, who had also been watching the sea, brought out the trunks and boxes. It was as if the house were tumbling down around them, and the vultures took off from the roof rattling the corrugated iron as though they felt the tremor in the walls. Scobie said, "While you are sorting your things upstairs, I'll pack your books." It was as if they had been playing these last two weeks at infidelity, and now the process of divorce had them in its grasp: the division of one life into two: the sharing out of the sad spoils.

"Shall I leave you this photograph, Ticki?" He took a quick sideways glance at the first-communion face and said, "No. You have it."

"I'll leave you this one of us with the Ted Bromleys."

"Yes, leave that." He watched her for a moment laying out her clothes and then he went downstairs. One by one he took out the books and wiped them with a cloth: the *Oxford* Verse, the Woolfs, the younger poets. Afterwards the shelves were almost empty: his own books took up so little room.

Next day they went to Mass together early. Kneeling together at the Communion rail they seemed to claim that this was not separation. He thought: I've prayed for peace and now I'm getting it. It's terrible the way prayer is answered. It had better be good, I've paid a high enough price for it. As they walked back he asked anxiously, "You are happy?"

"Yes, Ticki, and you?"

"I'm happy as long as you are happy."

"It will be all right when I've got on board and settled down. I expect I shall drink a bit tonight. Why don't you have someone in, Ticki?"

"Oh, I prefer being alone."

"Write to me every week."

"Of course."

"And, Ticki, you won't be lazy about Mass? You'll go when I'm not there?"

"Of course."

Wilson came up the road: his face shone with sweat and anxiety. He said, "Are you really off? Ali told me at the house that you are going on board this afternoon."

"She's off," Scobie said.

"You never told me it was close like this."

"I forgot," Louise said, "there was so much to do."

"I never thought you'd really go. I wouldn't have known if I hadn't run into Halifax at the agent's."

"Oh, well," Louise said, "you and Henry will have to keep an eye on each other."

"It's incredible," Wilson said, kicking the dusty road. He hung there, between them and the house, not stirring to let them by. He said, "I don't know a soul but you—and Harris, of course."

"You'll have to start making acquaintances," Louise said. "You'll have to excuse us now. There's so much to do."

They walked round him because he didn't move, and Scobie looking back gave him a kindly wave—he looked so lost and unprotected and out of place on the blistered road. "Poor Wilson," he said, "I think he's in love with you."

"He thinks he is."

"It's a good thing for him you are going. People like that become a nuisance in this climate. I'll be kind to him while you are away."

"Ticki," she said, "I shouldn't see too much of him. I wouldn't trust him. There's something phony about him."

"He's young and romantic."

"He's too romantic. He tells lies. Why does he say he doesn't know a soul?"

"I don't think he does."

82

"He knows the Commissioner. I saw him going up there the other night at dinner time."

"It's just a way of talking."

Neither of them had any appetite for lunch, but the cook, who wanted to rise to the occasion, produced an enormous curry which filled a washing-basin in the middle of the table: round it were ranged the too many small dishes that went with it—the fried bananas, red peppers, ground nuts, pawpaw, orange slices, chutney. They seemed to be sitting miles apart separated by a waste of dishes. The food chilled on their plates and there seemed nothing to talk about except "I'm not hungry," "Try and eat a little," "I can't touch a thing," "You ought to start off with a good meal"—an endless friendly bicker about food. Ali came in and out to watch them: he was like a figure on a clock that records the striking of the hours. It seemed horrible to both of them that now they would be glad when the separation was complete: they could settle down when once this ragged leave-taking was over to a different life which again would exclude change.

"Are you sure you've got everything?" This was another variant which enabled them to sit there not eating but occasionally picking at something easily swallowed, going through all the things that might have been forgotten.

"It's lucky there's only one bedroom. They'll have to let you keep the house to yourself."

"They may turn me out for a married couple."

"You'll write every week?"

"Of course."

Sufficient time had elapsed: they could persuade themselves that they had lunched. "If you can't eat any more I may as well drive you down. The sergeant's organized carriers at the wharf." They could say nothing now which wasn't formal: unreality cloaked their movements: although they could touch each other it was as if the whole coast line of a continent was already between them: their words were like the stilted sentences of a bad letter-writer.

It was a relief to be on board and no longer alone together. Halifax, of the Public Works Department, bubbled over with false *bonhomie*. He cracked risky jokes and told the two women to drink plenty of gin. "It's good for the bow-wows," he said. "First thing to go wrong on board ship

83

are the bow-wows. Plenty of gin at night and what will cover a sixpence in the morning." The two women took stock of their cabin: they stood there in the shadow like cave-dwellers: they spoke in undertones that the men couldn't catch: they were no longer wives—they were sisters belonging to a different race. "You and I are not wanted, old man," Halifax said. "They'll be all right now. Me for the shore."

"I'll come with you." Everything had been unreal, but this suddenly was real pain, the moment of death. Like a prisoner he had not believed in the trial: it had been a dream: the condemnation had been a dream and the truck ride, and then suddenly here he was with his back to the blank wall and everything was true. One steeled oneself to end courageously. They went to the end of the passage, leaving the Halifaxes the cabin.

"Good-bye, dear."

"Good-bye. Ticki, you'll write every . . ."

"Yes, dear."

"I'm an awful deserter."

"No, no. This isn't the place for you."

"It would have been different if they'd made you Commissioner."

"I'll come down for my leave. Let me know if you run short of money before then. I can fix things."

"You've always fixed things for me. Ticki, you'll be glad to have no more scenes."

"Nonsense."

"Do you love me, Ticki?"

"What do you think?"

"Say it. One likes to hear it—even if it isn't true."

"I love you, Louise. Of course it's true."

"If I can't bear it down there alone, Ticki, I'll come back."

They kissed and went up on deck. From here the port was always beautiful: the thin layer of houses sparkled in the sun like quartz or lay in the shadow of the great green swollen hills. "You are well escorted," Scobie said: the destroyers and the corvettes sat around like dogs: signal flags rippled and a helio flashed. The fishing boats rested on the broad bay under their brown butterfly sails.

"Look after yourself, Ticki."

Halifax came booming up behind them. "Who's for shore? Got the police launch, Scobie? Mary's down in the cabin, Mrs. Scobie, wiping off the tears and putting on the powder for the passengers."

"Good-bye, dear."

"Good-bye." That was the real good-bye, the handshake with Halifax watching and the passengers from England looking curiously on. As the launch moved away she was almost at once indistinguishable: perhaps she had gone down to the cabin to join Mrs. Halifax. The dream had finished: change was over: life had begun again.

"I hate these good-byes," Halifax said. "Glad when it's all over. Think I'll go up to the Bedford and have a glass of beer. Join me?"

"Sorry. I have to go on duty."

"I wouldn't mind a nice little black girl to look after me now I'm alone," Halifax said. "However, faithful and true, old fidelity, that's me," and, as Scobie knew, it was.

In the shade of a tarpaulined dump Wilson stood, looking out across the bay. Scobie paused. He was touched by the plump sad boyish face. "Sorry we didn't see you," he said, and lied harmlessly: "Louise sent her love."

4

It was nearly one in the morning before he returned: the light was out in the kitchen quarters and Ali was dozing on the step of the house until the head-lamps woke him, passing across his sleeping face. He jumped up and lit the way from the garage with his torch.

"All right, Ali. Go to bed."

He let himself into the empty house—he had forgotten the deep tones of silence. Many a time he had come in late, after Louise was asleep, but there had never then been quite this quality of security and impregnability in the silence: his ears had listened for, even though they could not catch, the faint rustle of another person's breath, the tiny movement. Now there was nothing to listen for. He went upstairs and looked into the bedroom. Everything had been tidied away: there was no sign of Louise's departure or presence: Ali had even removed the photograph and put it in a drawer. He was indeed alone. In the bath-room a rat moved, and once the iron roof crumpled as a late vulture settled for the night.

Scobie sat down in the living-room and put his feet up on another chair. He felt unwilling yet to go to bed, but he was sleepy: it had been a long day. Now that he was alone he could indulge in the most irrational act: sleep in a chair instead of a bed. The sadness was peeling off his mind, leaving contentment. He had done his duty: Louise was happy. He closed his eyes.

The sound of a car driving in off the road, head-lamps moving across the window, woke him. He imagined it was a police car—that night he was the responsible officer and he thought that some urgent and probably unnecessary telegram had come in. He opened the door and found Yusef on the step.

"Forgive me, Major Scobie, I saw your light as I was passing and I thought . . ."

"Come in," he said, "I have whisky, or would you prefer a little beer . . ."

Yusef said with surprise, "This is very hospitable of you, Major Scobie."

"If I know a man well enough to borrow money from him, surely I ought to be hospitable."

"A little beer then, Major Scobie."

"The Prophet doesn't forbid it?"

"The Prophet had no experience of bottled beer or whisky, Major Scobie. We have to interpret his words in a modern light." He watched Scobie take the bottles from the ice chest. "Have you no refrigerator, Major Scobie?"

"No. Mine's waiting for a spare part—it will go on waiting till the end of the war, I imagine."

"I must not allow that. I have several spare refrigerators. Let me send one up to you."

"Oh, I can manage all right, Yusef. I've managed for two years. So you were just passing by."

"Well, not exactly, Major Scobie. That was a way of speaking. As a matter of fact I waited until I knew your boys were asleep, and I borrowed a car from a garage. My own car is so well-known. And I did not bring a chauffeur. I didn't want to embarrass you, Major Scobie."

"I repeat, Yusef, that I shall never deny knowing a man from whom I have borrowed money."

"You do keep harping on that so, Major Scobie. That was just a business transaction. Four per cent is a fair interest. I ask for more only when I have doubt of the security. I wish you would let me send you a refrigerator."

"What did you want to see me about?"

"First, Major Scobie, I wanted to ask after Mrs. Scobie. Has she got a comfortable cabin? Is there anything she requires? The ship calls at Lagos, and I could have anything she needs sent on board there. I would telegraph to my agent."

"I think she's quite comfortable."

"Next, Major Scobie, I wanted to have a few words with you about diamonds."

Scobie put two more bottles of beer on the ice. He said slowly and gently, "Yusef, I don't want you to think I am the kind of man who borrows money one day and insults his creditor the next to reassure his ego."

"Ego?"

"Never mind. Self-esteem. What you like. I'm not going to pretend that we haven't in a way become colleagues in a business, but my duties are strictly confined to paying you four per cent."

"I agree, Major Scobie. You have said all this before and I agree. I say again that I am never dreaming to ask you to do one thing for me. I would rather do things for you."

"What a queer chap you are, Yusef. I believe you do like me."

"Yes, I do like you, Major Scobie." Yusef sat on the edge of his chair, which cut a sharp edge in his great expanding thighs: he was ill at ease in any house but his own. "And now may I talk to you about diamonds, Major Scobie?"

"Fire away, then."

"You know, I think the Government is crazy about diamonds. They waste your time, the time of the Security Police: they send special agents down the coast: we even have one here—you know who, though nobody is supposed to know but the Commissioner: he spends money on every black or poor Syrian who tells him stories. Then he telegraphs it to England and all down the coast. And after all this, do they catch a single diamond?"

"This has got nothing to do with us, Yusef."

"I want to talk to you as a friend, Major Scobie. There are diamonds and diamonds and Syrians and Syrians. You people hunt the wrong men. You want to stop industrial diamonds going to Portugal and then to Germany, or across the border to the Vichy French. But all the time you are chasing people who are not interested in industrial diamonds, people who just want to get a few gem stones in a safe for when peace comes again."

"In other words, you?"

"Six times this month police have been into my stores making everything untidy. They will never find any industrial diamonds that way. Only small men are interested in industrial diamonds. Why, for a whole matchbox full of them you would only get two hundred pounds. I call them gravel collectors," he said with contempt.

Scobie said slowly, "Sooner or later, Yusef, I felt sure that you'd want something out of me. But you are going to get nothing but four per cent. Tomorrow I am giving a full confidential report of our business arrangement to the Commissioner. Of course he may ask for my resignation, but I don't think so. He trusts me." A memory pricked him. "I think he trusts me."

"Is that a wise thing to do, Major Scobie?"

"I think it's very wise. Any kind of secret between us two would go bad in time."

"Just as you like, Major Scobie. But I don't want anything from you, I promise. I would like to give you things always. You will not take a refrigerator, but I thought you would perhaps take advice, information."

"I'm listening, Yusef."

"Tallit's a small man. He is a Christian. Father Rank and other people go to his house. They say, 'If there's such a thing as an honest Syrian, then Tallit's the man.' Tallit's not very successful, and that looks just the same as honesty."

"Go on."

"Tallit's cousin is sailing in the next Portuguese boat. His luggage will be searched, of course, and nothing will be found. He will have a parrot with him in a cage. My advice, Major Scobie, is to let Tallit's cousin go and keep his parrot."

"Why let the cousin go?"

"You do not want to show your hand to Tallit. You can easily say the parrot is suffering from disease and must stay. He will not dare to make a fuss."

"You mean the diamonds are in its crop?"

"Yes."

"Has that trick been used before on the Portuguese boats?"

"Yes."

"It looks to me as if we'll have to buy an aviary."

"Will you act on that information, Major Scobie?"

"You give me information, Yusef. I don't give you information."

Yusef nodded and smiled. Raising his bulk with some care, he touched Scobie's sleeve quickly and shyly. "You are quite right, Major Scobie. Believe me, I never want to do you any harm at all. I shall be careful, and you be careful too, and everything will be all right." It was as if they were in a conspiracy together to do no harm: even innocence in Yusef's hands took on a dubious colour. He said, "If you were to say a good word to Tallit sometimes it would be safer. The agent visits him."

"I don't know of any agent."

"You are quite right, Major Scobie." Yusef hovered like a fat moth on the edge of the light. He said, "Perhaps if you were writing one day to Mrs. Scobie you would give her my best wishes. Oh, no, letters are censored. You cannot do that. You could say, perhaps—no, better not. As long as you know, Major Scobie, that you have my best wishes—"

Stumbling on the narrow path he made for his car. When he had turned on his lights he pressed his face against the glass: it showed up in the illumination of the dashboard, wide, pasty, untrustworthy, sincere: he made a tentative shy sketch of a wave towards Scobie where he stood alone in the doorway of the quiet and empty house.

Book 2

Part One

I. THEY STOOD ON THE VERANDAH OF THE D.C.'S bungalow at Pende and watched the torches move on the other side of the wide passive river. "So that's France," Druce said, using the native term for it.

Mrs. Perrot said, "Before the war we used to picnic in France."

Perrot joined them from the bungalow, a drink in either hand: bandy-legged, he wore his mosquito boots outside his trousers like riding boots, and gave the impression of having only just got off a horse. "Here's yours, Scobie." He said, "Of course ye know I find it hard to think of the French as enemies. My family came over with the Huguenots. It makes a difference, ye know." His lean long yellow face cut in two by a nose like a wound was all the time arrogantly on the defensive: the importance of Perrot was an article of faith with Perrot—doubters would be repelled, persecuted if he had the chance . . . the faith would never cease to be proclaimed.

Scobie said, "If they ever joined the Germans, I suppose this is one of the points where they'd attack."

"Don't I know it," Perrot said, "I was moved here in 1939. The Government had a shrewd idea of what was coming. Everything's prepared, ye know. Where's the doctor?"

"I think he's taking a last look at the beds," Mrs. Perrot said. "You must be thankful your wife's arrived safely, Major Scobie. Those poor people over there. Forty days in the boats. It shakes one up to think of it."

"It's the damned narrow channel between Dakar and Brazil that does it every time," Perrot said.

The doctor came gloomily out onto the verandah.

Everything over the river was still and blank again: the torches were all out. The light burning on the small jetty below the bungalow showed a few feet of dark water sliding by. A piece of wood came out of the dark and floated so slowly through the patch of light that Scobie counted twenty before it went into darkness again.

"The Froggies haven't behaved too badly this time," Druce said gloomily, picking a mosquito out of his glass.

"They've only brought the women, the old men, and the dying," the doctor said, pulling at his beard. "They could hardly have done less."

Suddenly like an invasion of insects the voices whined and burred upon the farther bank. Groups of torches moved like fire-flies here and there: Scobie lifting his binoculars caught a black face momentarily illuminated: a hammock pole: a white arm: an officer's back. "I think they've arrived," he said. A long line of lights was dancing along the water's edge. "Well," Mrs. Perrot said, "we may as well go in now." The mosquitoes whirred steadily around them like sewing-machines: Druce exclaimed and struck his hand.

"Come in," Mrs. Perrot said. "The mosquitoes here are all malarial." The windows of the living-room were netted to keep them out: the stale air was heavy with the coming rains.

"The stretchers will be across at six A.M.," the doctor said. "I think we are all set, Perrot. There's one case of blackwater, and a few cases of fever, but most are just exhaustion—the worst disease of all. It's what most of us die of in the end."

"Scobie and I will see the walking cases," Druce said. "You'll have to tell us how much interrogation they can stand, Doctor. Your police will look after the carriers, Perrot, I suppose—see that they all go back the way they came."

"Of course," Perrot said. "We're stripped for action here. Have another drink?" Mrs. Perrot turned the nob of the radio and the organ of the Orpheum Cinema, Clapham, sailed to them over three thousand miles. From across the river the excited voices of the carriers rose and fell.

Somebody knocked on the verandah door. Scobie shifted uncomfortably in his chair: the music of the Wurlitzer organ moaned and boomed. It seemed to him outrageously immodest. The verandah door opened and Wilson came in.

"Hello, Wilson," Druce said. "I didn't know you were here."

"Mr. Wilson's up to inspect the U.A.C. store," Mrs. Perrot explained. "I hope the rest-house at the store is all right. It's not often used."

"Oh, yes, it's very comfortable," Wilson said. "Why, Major Scobie, I didn't expect to see you."

"I don't know why you didn't," Perrot said. "I told you he'd be here. Sit down and have a drink." Scobie remembered what Louise once had said to him about Wilson—phony, she had called him. He looked across at Wilson and saw the blush at Perrot's betrayal fading from the boyish face, and the little wrinkles that gathered round the eyes and gave the lie to his youth.

"Have you heard from Mrs. Scobie, sir?"

"She arrived safely last week."

"I'm glad. I'm so glad."

"Well," Perrot said, "what are the scandals from the big city?" The words "big city" came out with a sneer—Perrot couldn't bear the thought that there was a place where people considered themselves important and where he was not regarded. Like a Huguenot imagining Rome, he built up a picture of frivolity, viciousness, and corruption. "We bush-folk," Perrot went heavily on, "live very quietly." Scobie felt sorry for Mrs. Perrot: she had heard these phrases so often: she must have forgotten long ago the time of courtship when she had believed in them. Now she sat close up against the radio with the music turned low, listening or pretending to listen to the old Viennese melodies, while her mouth stiffened in the effort to ignore her husband in his familiar part. "Well, Scobie, what are our superiors doing in the city?"

"Oh," said Scobie vaguely, watching Mrs. Perrot with pity, "nothing very much has been happening. People are too busy with the war . . ."

"Oh, yes," Perrot said, "so many files to turn over in the Secretariat. I'd like to see them growing rice down here. They'd know what work was."

"I suppose the greatest excitement recently," Wilson said, "would be the parrot, sir, wouldn't it?"

"Tallit's parrot?" Scobie asked.

"Or Yusef's, according to Tallit," Wilson said. "Isn't that right, sir, or have I got the story wrong?"

"I don't think we'll ever know what's right," Scobie said.

"But what *is* the story? We're out of touch with the great world of affairs here. We have only the French to think about."

"Well, about three weeks ago Tallit's cousin was leaving for Lisbon on one of the Portuguese ships. We searched his baggage and found nothing, but I'd heard rumours that sometimes diamonds had been smuggled in a bird's crop, so I kept the parrot back, and sure enough there were about a hundred pounds' worth of industrial diamonds inside. The ship hadn't sailed, so we fetched Tallit's cousin back on shore. It seemed a perfect case."

"But it wasn't?"

"You can't beat a Syrian," the doctor said.

"Tallit's cousin's boy swore that it wasn't Tallit's cousin's parrot—and so of course did Tallit's cousin. Their story was that the small boy had substituted another bird to frame Tallit."

"On behalf of Yusef, I suppose," the doctor said.

"Of course. The trouble was the small boy disappeared. Of course there are two explanations of that—perhaps Yusef had given him his money and he'd cleared off, or just as possibly Tallit had given him money to throw the blame on Yusef."

"Down here," Perrot said, "I'd have had 'em both in jail."

"Up in town," Scobie said, "we have to think about the law."

Mrs. Perrot turned the nob of the radio and a voice shouted with unexpected vigour, "Kick him in the pants."

"I'm for bed," the doctor said. "Tomorrow's going to be a hard day."

Sitting up in bed under his mosquito net Scobie opened his diary. Night after night for more years than he could remember he had kept a record—the barest possible record —of his days. If anyone argued a date with him he could check up; if he wanted to know which day the rains had begun in any particular year, when the last-but-one Director of Public Works had been transferred to East Africa, the facts were all there, in one of the volumes stored in the tin box under his bed at home. Otherwise he never opened a volume—particularly that volume where the barest fact of all was contained: *C. died*. He couldn't have told himself why he stored up this record—it was certainly not for posterity. Even if posterity were to be interested in the life of an obscure policeman in an unfashionable colony, it would have learned nothing from these cryptic entries. Perhaps the reason was that forty years ago at a preparatory school he had been given a prize—a copy of *Allan Quatermain*—for keeping a diary throughout one summer holiday, and the habit had simply stayed. Even the form the diary took had altered very little. *Had sausages for breakfast. Fine day. Walk in morning. Riding lesson in afternoon. Chicken for lunch. Treacle roll*. Almost imperceptibly this record had changed into *Louise left. Y. called in the evening. First typhoon 2 a.m.* His pen was powerless to convey the importance of any entry: only he himself, if he had cared to read back, could have seen in the last phrase but one the enormous breach pity had blasted through his integrity. *Y., not Yusef*.

Scobie wrote: *May 5. Arrived Pende to meet survivors of s.s. 43*. He used the code number for security. *Druce with me*. He hesitated for a moment and then added, *Wilson here*. He closed the diary and lying flat on his back under the net he began to pray. This also was a habit. He said the Our Father, the Hail Mary, and then, as sleep began to clog his lids, he added an Act of Contrition. It was a formality not because he felt himself free from serious sin but because it had never occurred to him that his life was important enough one way or another. He didn't drink, he didn't fornicate, he didn't even lie, but he never regarded this absence of sin as virtue. When he thought about it at all, he regarded himself as a man in the ranks, the member of an awkward squad, who had no opportunity to break the more serious military rules. "I missed Mass yesterday for insufficient reason. I neglected my evening prayers." This was no more than admitting what every soldier did—that he had avoided a fatigue when the occasion offered. "'O God, bless—" but before he could mention names he was asleep.

They stood on the jetty next morning: the first light lay in cold strips along the eastern sky. The huts in the village were still shuttered with silver. At two that morning there had been a typhoon—a wheeling pillar of black cloud driving up from the coast, and the air was cold yet with the rain. They stood with coat collars turned up watching the French shore, and the carriers squatted on the ground behind them. Mrs. Perrot came down the path from the bungalow wiping the white sleep from her eyes, and from across the water very faintly came the bleating of a goat. "Are they late?" Mrs. Perrot asked.

"No, we are early." Scobie kept his glasses focussed on the opposite shore. He said, "They are stirring."

"Those poor souls," Mrs. Perrot said, and shivered with the morning chill.

"They are alive," the doctor said.

"Yes."

"In my profession we have to consider that important."

"Does one ever get over a shock like that? Forty days in open boats."

"If you survive at all," the doctor said, "you get over it. It's failure people don't get over, and this, you see, is a kind of success."

"They are fetching them out of the huts," Scobie said. "I think I can count six stretchers. The boats are being brought in."

"We were told to prepare for nine stretcher cases, and four walking ones," the doctor said. "I suppose there've been some more deaths."

"I may have counted wrong. They are carrying them down now. I think there are seven stretchers. I can't distinguish the walking cases."

The flat cold light, too feeble to clear the morning haze, made the distance across the river longer than it would seem at noon. A native dugout canoe bearing, one supposed, the walking cases, came blackly out of the haze: it was suddenly very close to them. On the other shore they were having trouble with the motor of a launch: they could hear the irregular putter, like an animal out of breath.

First of the walking cases to come on shore was an elderly

man with an arm in a sling. He wore a dirty white topee, and a native cloth was draped over his shoulders: his free hand tugged and scratched at the white stubble on his face. He said in an unmistakably Scotch accent, "Ah'm Loder, chief engineer."

"Welcome home, Mr. Loder," Scobie said. "Will you step up to the bungalow and the doctor will be with you in a few minutes?"

"Ah have no need of doctors."

"Sit down and rest. I'll be with you soon."

"Ah want to make ma report to a proper official."

"Would you take him up to the house, Perrot?"

"I'm the District Commissioner," Perrot said. "You can make your report to me."

"What are we waitin' for then?" the engineer said. "It's nearly two months since the sinkin'. There's an awful lot of responsibility on me, for the captain's dead." As they moved up the hill to the bungalow, the persistent Scotch voice, as regular as the pulse of a dynamo, came back to them. "Ah'm responsible to the owners."

The other three had come on shore, and across the river the tinkering in the launch went on: the sharp crack of a chisel, the clank of metal, and then again the spasmodic putter. Two of the new arrivals were the cannon fodder of all such occasions: elderly men with the appearance of plumbers who might have been brothers if they had not been called Forbes and Newall, uncomplaining men without authority, to whom things simply happened: one had a crushed foot and walked with a crutch; the other had his hand bound up with shabby strips of tropical shirt. They stood on the jetty with as natural a lack of interest as they would have stood at a Liverpool street corner waiting for the local to open. A stalwart grey-headed woman in mosquito boots followed them out of the canoe.

"Your name, madam?" Druce asked, consulting a list. "Are you Mrs. Rolt?"

"I am not Mrs. Rolt. I am Miss Malcott."

"Will you go up to the house? The Doctor . . ."

"The doctor has far more serious cases than me to attend to."

Mrs. Perrot said, "You'd like to lie down."

"It's the last thing I want to do," Miss Malcott said. "I am not in the least tired." She shut her mouth between every sentence. "I am not hungry. I am not nervous. I want to get on."

"Where to?"

"To Lagos. To the Educational Department."

"I'm afraid there will be a good many delays."

"I've been delayed two months. I can't stand delay. Work won't wait." Suddenly she lifted her face towards the sky and howled like a dog.

The doctor took her gently by the arm and said, "We'll do what we can to get you there right away. Come up to the house and do some telephoning."

"Certainly," Miss Malcott said, "there's nothing that can't be straightened on a telephone."

The doctor said to Scobie, "Send those other two chaps up after us. They are all right. If you want to do some questioning, question them."

Druce said, "I'll take them along. You stay here, Scobie, in case the launch arrives. French isn't my language."

Scobie sat down on the rail of the jetty and looked across the water. Now that the haze was lifting, the other bank came closer: he could make out now with the naked eye the details of the scene: the white warehouse, the mud huts, the brasswork of the launch glittering in the sun: he could see the red fezzes of the native troops. He thought: Just such a scene as this and I might have been waiting for Louise to appear on a stretcher—or perhaps not waiting. Somebody settled himself on the rail beside him, but Scobie didn't turn his head.

"A penny for your thoughts, sir."

"I was just thinking that Louise is safe, Wilson."

"I was thinking that too, sir."

"Why do you always call me sir, Wilson? You are not in the police force. It makes me feel very old."

"I'm sorry, Major Scobie."

"What did Louise call you?"

"Wilson. I don't think she liked my Christian name."

"I believe they've got that launch to start at last, Wilson. Be a good chap and warn the doctor."

A French officer in a stained white uniform stood in the bow: a soldier flung a rope and Scobie caught and fixed it. "Bon jour," he said, and saluted.

The French officer returned his salute—a drained-out figure with a twitch in the left eyelid. He said in English,

100

"Good morning. I have seven stretcher cases for you here."

"My signal says nine."

"One died on the way and one last night. One from blackwater and one from—from, my English is bad, do you say fatigue?"

"Exhaustion."

"That is it."

"If you will let my labourers come on board they will get the stretchers off." Scobie said to the carriers, "Very softly. Go very softly." It was an unnecessary command: no white hospital attendants could lift and carry more gently. "Won't you stretch your legs on shore?" Scobie asked, "or come up to the house and have some coffee?"

"No. No coffee, thank you. I will just see that all is right here." He was courteous and unapproachable, but all the time his left eyelid flickered a message of doubt and distress.

"I have some English papers if you would like to see them."

"No, no thank you. I read English with difficulty."

"You speak it very well."

"That is a different thing."

"Have a cigarette?"

"Thank you, no. I do not like American tobacco."

The first stretcher came on shore—the sheets were drawn up to the man's chin and it was impossible to tell from the stiff vacant face what his age might be. The doctor came down the hill to meet the stretcher and led the carriers away to the Government rest-house where the beds had been prepared.

"I used to come over to your side," Scobie said, "to shoot with your police chief. A nice fellow called Durand—a Norman."

"He is not here any longer," the officer said.

"Gone home?"

"He's in prison at Dakar," the French officer replied, standing like a figure-head in the bows, but the eye twitching and twitching. The stretchers slowly passed Scobie and turned up the hill: a boy who couldn't have been more than ten, with a feverish face and a twiglike arm thrown out from his blanket: an old lady with grey hair falling every way who twisted and turned and whispered: a man with a bottle nose—a nob of scarlet and blue on a yellow

101

face. One by one they turned up the hill, the carriers' feet moving with the certainty of mules. "And Père Brûle?" Scobie said. "He was a good man."

"He died last year of blackwater."

"He was out here twenty years without leave, wasn't he? He'll be hard to replace."

"He has not been replaced," the officer said. He turned and gave a short savage order to one of his men. Scobie looked at the next stretcher load and looked away again. A small girl—she couldn't have been more than six—lay on it. She was deeply and unhealthily asleep; her fair hair was tangled and wet with sweat; her open mouth was dry and cracked, and she shuddered regularly and spasmodically. "It's terrible," Scobie said.

"What is terrible?"

"A child like that."

"Yes. Both parents were lost. But it is all right. She will die."

Scobie watched the bearers go slowly up the hill, their bare feet very gently flapping the ground. He thought: It would need all Father Brûle's ingenuity to explain that. Not that the child would die: that needed no explanation. Even the pagans realized that the love of God might mean an early death, though the reason they ascribed was different; but that the child should have been allowed to survive the forty days and nights in the open boat— that was the mystery, to reconcile that with the love of God.

And yet he could believe in no God who was not human enough to love what he had created. "How on earth did she survive till now?" he wondered aloud.

The officer said gloomily, "Of course they looked after her on the boat. They gave up their own share of the water often. It was foolish, of course, but one cannot always be logical. And it gave them something to think about." It was like the hint of an explanation—too faint to be grasped. He said, "Here is another who makes one angry."

The face was ugly with exhaustion: the skin looked as though it were about to crack over the cheekbones: only the absence of lines showed that it was a young face. The French officer said, "She was just married—before she sailed. Her husband was lost. Her passport says she is nineteen. She may live. You see, she still has some strength." Her arms as thin as a child's lay outside the blanket, and

102

her fingers clasped a book firmly. Scobie could see the wedding-ring loose on her dried-up finger.

"What is it?"

"Timbres," the French officer said. He added bitterly, "When this damned war started, she must have been still at school."

Scobie always remembered how she was carried into his life on a stretcher, grasping a stamp-album, with her eyes fast shut.

3

In the evening they gathered together again for drinks, but they were subdued; even Perrot was no longer trying to impress them. Druce said, "Well, tomorrow I'm off. You coming, Scobie?"

"I suppose so."

Mrs. Perrot said, "You got all you wanted?"

"All I needed. That chief engineer was a good fellow. He had it ready in his head. I could hardly write fast enough. When he stopped he went flat out. That was what was keeping him together—'ma responsibility.' You know, they'd walked—the ones that could walk—five days to get here."

Wilson said, "Were they sailing without an escort?"

"They started out in convoy, but they had some engine trouble—and you know the rule of the road nowadays: no waiting for lame ducks. They were twelve hours behind the convoy and were trying to pick up, when they were sniped. The submarine commander surfaced and gave them direction. He said he would have given them a tow, but there was a naval patrol out looking for him. You see, you can really blame nobody for this sort of thing," and this sort of thing came at once to Scobie's mind's eye—the child with the open mouth, the thin hands holding the stamp-album. He said, "I suppose the doctor will look in when he gets a chance?"

He went restlessly out onto the verandah, closing the netted door carefully behind him, and a mosquito immediately droned towards his ear. The skirring went on all the time, but when they drove to the attack they had the deeper tone of dive-bombers. The lights were showing in

103

the temporary hospital, and the weight of all that misery lay on his shoulders. It was as if he had shed one responsibility only to take on another. This was a responsibility he shared with all human beings, but there was no comfort in that, for it sometimes seemed to him that he was the only one who recognized it. In the Cities of the Plain a single soul might have changed the mind of God.

The doctor came up the steps onto the verandah. "Hallo, Scobie," he said in a voice as bowed as his shoulders, "taking the night air? It's not healthy in this place."

"How are they?" Scobie asked.

"There'll be only two more deaths, I think. Perhaps only one."

"The child?"

"She'll be dead by morning," the doctor said abruptly.

"Is she conscious?"

"Never completely. She asks for her father sometimes: she probably thinks she's in the boat still. They'd kept it from her there—said her parents were in one of the other boats. But of course they'd signalled to check up."

"Won't she take you for her father?"

"No, she won't accept the beard."

Scobie said, "How's the schoolteacher?"

"Miss Malcott? She'll be all right. I've given her enough bromide to put her out of action till morning. That's all she needs—and the sense of getting somewhere. You haven't got room for her in your police van, have you? She'd be better out of here."

"There's only just room for Druce and me with our boys and kit. We'll be sending proper transport as soon as we get back. The walking cases all right?"

"Yes, they'll manage."

"The boy and the old lady?"

"They'll pull through."

"Who is the boy?"

"He was at a prep school in England. His parents in South Africa thought he'd be safer there."

Scobie said reluctantly, "That young woman—with the stamp-album?" It was the stamp-album and not the face that haunted his memory, for no reason that he could understand, and the wedding-ring loose on the finger, as though a child had dressed up.

"I don't know," the doctor said. "If she gets through tonight . . . perhaps . . ."

"You're dead tired, aren't you? Go in and have a drink."

"Yes. I don't want to be eaten by mosquitoes." The doctor opened the verandah door, and a mosquito struck at Scobie's neck. He didn't bother to guard himself. Slowly, hesitatingly, he retraced the route the doctor had taken, down the steps onto the tough rocky ground. The loose stones turned under his boots. He thought of Pemberton. What an absurd thing it was to expect happiness in a world so full of misery. He had cut down his own needs to a minimum, photographs were put away in drawers, the dead were put out of mind: a razor strop, a pair of rusty handcuffs for decoration: but one still has one's eyes, he thought, one's ears. Point me out the happy man and I will point you out either egotism, selfishness, evil—or else an absolute ignorance.

Outside the rest-house he stopped again. The lights inside would have given an extraordinary impression of peace if one hadn't known, just as the stars on this clear night gave also an impression of remoteness, security, freedom. If one knew, he wondered, the facts, would one have to feel pity even for the planets? if one reached what they called the heart of the matter?

"Well, Major Scobie?" It was the wife of the local missionary speaking to him. She was dressed in white like a nurse, and her flint-grey hair lay back from her forehead in ridges like wind erosion. "Have you come to look on?" she asked forbiddingly.

"Yes," he said. He had no other idea of what to say: he couldn't describe to Mrs. Bowles the restlessness, the haunting images, the terrible impotent feeling of responsibility and pity.

"Come inside," Mrs. Bowles said, and he followed her obediently like a boy. There were three rooms in the rest-house. In the first the walking cases had been put: heavily dosed, they slept peacefully, as though they had been taking healthy exercise. In the second room were the stretcher cases for whom there was reasonable hope: the third room was a small one and contained only two beds divided by a screen: the six-year-old girl with the dry mouth, the young woman lying unconscious on her back, still grasping the stamp-album. A night-light burned in a saucer and cast thin shadows between the beds. "If you want to be useful," Mrs. Bowles said, "stay here a moment. I want to go to the dispensary."

"The dispensary?"

"The cook-house. One has to make the best of things."

Scobie felt cold and strange. A shiver moved his shoulders. He said, "Can't I go for you?"

Mrs. Bowles said, "Don't be absurd. Are you qualified to dispense? I'll only be away a few minutes. If the child shows signs of going, call me." If she had given him time, he would have thought of some excuse, but she was already out of the room and he sat heavily down in the only chair. When he looked at the child, he saw a white communion veil over her head: it was a trick of the light on the pillow and a trick of his own mind. He put his head in his hands and wouldn't look. He had been in Africa when his own child died. He had always thanked God that he had missed that. It seemed after all that one never really missed a thing. To be a human being one had to drink the cup. If one were lucky on one day, or cowardly on another, it was presented on a third occasion. He prayed silently into his hands, "O God, don't let anything happen before Mrs. Bowles comes back." He could hear the heavy uneven breathing of the child. It was as if she were carrying a weight with great effort up a long hill: it was an inhuman situation not to be able to carry it for her. He thought: This is what parents feel year in and year out, and I am shrinking from a few minutes of it. They see their children dying slowly every hour they live. He prayed again. "Father, look after her. Give her peace." The breathing broke, choked, began again with terrible effort. Looking between his fingers he could see the six-year-old face convulsed like a navvy's with labour. "Father," he prayed, "give her peace. Take away my peace for ever, but give her peace." The sweat broke out on his hands. "Father . . ."

He heard a small scraping voice repeat, "Father," and looking up he saw the blue and bloodshot eyes watching him. He thought with horror: this is what I thought I'd missed. He would have called Mrs. Bowles, only he hadn't the voice to call with. He could see the breast of the child struggling for breath to repeat the heavy word; he came over to the bed and said, "Yes, dear. Don't speak, I'm here." The nightlight cast the shadow of his clenched fist on the sheet and it caught the child's eye. An effort to laugh convulsed her, and he moved his hand away. "Sleep, dear," he said, "you are sleepy. Sleep." A memory that he had carefully buried returned, and taking out his handkerchief he made the shadow of a rabbit's head fall on the pillow beside her. "There's your rabbit," he said, "to go to sleep with. It will stay until you sleep. Sleep." The sweat poured down his face and tasted in his mouth as salt as tears. "Sleep." He moved the rabbit's ears up and down, up and down. Then he heard Mrs. Bowles' voice, speaking low just behind him. "Stop that," she said harshly, "the child's dead."

4

In the morning he told the doctor that he would stay till proper transport arrived: Miss Malcott could have his place in the police van. It was better to get her moving, for the child's death had upset her again, and it was by no means certain that there would not be other deaths. They buried the child next day, using the only coffin they could get: it had been designed for a tall man. In this climate delay was unwise. Scobie did not attend the funeral service, which was read by Mr. Bowles, but the Perrots were present, Wilson, and some of the court messengers: the doctor was busy in the rest-house. Instead Scobie walked rapidly through the rice fields, talked to the Agricultural Officer about irrigation, kept away. Later, when he had exhausted the possibilities of irrigation, he went into the store and sat in the dark among all the tins, the tinned jams and the tinned soups, the tinned butter, the tinned biscuits, the tinned milk, the tinned potatoes, the tinned chocolates, and waited for Wilson. But Wilson didn't come: perhaps the funeral had been too much for all of them and they had returned to the D.C.'s bungalow for drinks. Scobie went down to the jetty and watched the sailing boats move down towards the sea. Once he found himself saying aloud as though to a man at his elbow, "Why didn't you let her drown?" A court messenger looked at him askance and he moved on, up the hill.

Mrs. Bowles was taking the air outside the rest-house:

taking it literally, in doses like medicine. She stood there with her mouth opening and closing, inhaling and expelling. She said, "Good afternoon," stiffly, and took another dose. "You weren't at the funeral, Major?"

"No."

"Mr. Bowles and I can seldom attend a funeral together. Except when we're on leave."

"Are there going to be any more funerals?"

"One more, I think. The rest will be all right in time."

"Which of them is dying?"

"The old lady. She took a turn for the worse last night. She had been getting on well."

He felt a merciless relief. He said, "The boy's all right?"

"Yes."

"And Mrs. Rolt?"

"She's not out of danger, but I think she'll do. She's conscious now."

"Does she know her husband's dead?"

"Yes." Mrs. Bowles began to swing her arms, up and down, from the shoulder. Then she stood on tiptoe six times. He said, "I wish there was something I could do to help."

"Can you read aloud?" Mrs. Bowles asked, rising on her toes.

"I suppose so. Yes."

"You can read to the boy. He's getting bored, and boredom's bad for him."

"Where shall I find a book?"

"There are plenty at the Mission. Shelves of them."

Anything was better than doing nothing. He walked up to the Mission and found, as Mrs. Bowles said, plenty of books. He wasn't much used to books, but even to his eye these hardly seemed a bright collection for reading to a sick boy. Damp-stained and late Victorian, the bindings bore titles like *Twenty Years in the Mission Field*, *Lost and Found*, *The Narrow Way*, *The Missionary's Warning*. Obviously at some time there had been an appeal for books for the Mission library, and here were the scrapings of many pious shelves at home. *The Poems of John Oxenham*, *Fishers of Men*. He took a book at random out of the shelf and returned to the rest-house. Mrs. Bowles was in her dispensary mixing medicines.

108

"Found something?"

"Yes."

"You are safe with any of those books," Mrs. Bowles said. "They are censored by the committee before they come out. Sometimes people try to send the most unsuitable books. We are not teaching the children here to read in order that they can read—well, novels."

"No, I suppose not."

"Let me see what you've chosen."

He looked at the title himself for the first time: *A Bishop Among the Bantus.*

"That should be interesting," Mrs. Bowles said. He agreed doubtfully.

"You know where to find him. You can read to him for a quarter of an hour—not more."

The old lady had been moved into the innermost room where the child had died, the man with the bottle-nose had been shifted into what Mrs. Bowles now called the convalescent ward, so that the middle room could be given up to the boy and Mrs. Rolt. Mrs. Rolt lay facing the wall with her eyes closed. They had apparently succeeded in removing the album from her clutch, and it lay on a chair beside the bed. The boy watched Scobie come with the bright intelligent gaze of fever.

"My name's Scobie. What's yours?"

"Fisher."

Scobie said nervously, "Mrs. Bowles asked me to read to you."

"What are you? A soldier?"

"No, a policeman."

"Is it a murder story?"

"No. I don't think it is." He opened the book at random and came on a photograph of the bishop sitting in his robes on a hard drawing-room chair outside a little tin-roofed church: he was surrounded by Bantus, who grinned at the camera.

"I'd like a murder story. Have you ever been in a murder?"

"Not what you'd call a real murder, with clues and a chase."

"What sort of a murder then?"

"Well, people get stabbed sometimes fighting." He

109

spoke in a low voice so as not to disturb Mrs. Rolt. She lay with her fist clenched on the sheet—a fist not much bigger than a tennis-ball.

"What's the name of the book you've brought? Perhaps I've read it. I read *Treasure Island* on the boat. I wouldn't mind a pirate story. What's it called?"

Scobie said dubiously, "*A Bishop Among the Bantus.*"

"What does that mean?"

Scobie drew a long breath. "Well, you see, Bishop is the name of the hero."

"But you said 'a bishop.'"

"Yes. His name was Arthur."

"It's a soppy name."

"Yes, but he's a soppy hero." Suddenly, avoiding the boy's eyes, he noticed that Mrs. Rolt was not asleep: she was staring at the wall, listening. He went wildly on, "The real heroes are the Bantus."

"What are Bantus?"

"They are a peculiarly ferocious lot of pirates who haunted the West Indies and preyed on all the shipping in that part of the Atlantic."

"Does Arthur Bishop pursue them?"

"Yes. It's a kind of detective story too because he's a secret agent of the British Government. He dresses up as an ordinary seaman and sails on a merchantman so that he can be captured by the Bantus. You know they always give the ordinary seamen a chance to join them. If he'd been an officer they would have made him walk the plank anyway. Then he discovers all their secret passwords and hiding-places and their plans of raids, of course, so that he can betray them when the time is ripe."

"He sounds a bit of a swine," the boy said.

"Yes, and he falls in love with the daughter of the captain of the Bantus and that's when he turns soppy. But that comes near the end and we won't get as far as that. There are a lot of fights and murders before then."

"It sounds all right. Let's begin."

"Well, you see, Mrs. Bowles told me I was only to stay a short time today, so I've just told you about the book, and we can start it tomorrow."

"You may not be here tomorrow. There may be a murder or something."

"But the book will be here. I'll leave it with Mrs. Bowles. It's her book. Of course it may sound a bit different when she reads it."

"Just begin it," the boy pleaded.

"Yes, begin it," said a low voice from the other bed, so low that he would have discounted it as an illusion if he hadn't looked up and seen her watching him, the eyes large as a child's in the starved face.

Scobie said, "I'm a very bad reader."

"Go on," the boy said impatiently. "Anyone can read aloud."

Scobie found his eyes fixed on an opening paragraph which stated: "I shall never forget my first glimpse of the continent where I was to labour for thirty of the best years of my life." He said slowly, "From the moment that they left Bermuda the low lean rakehelly craft had followed in their wake. The captain was evidently worried, for he watched the strange ship continually through his spy-glass. When night fell it was still on their trail, and at dawn it was the first sight that met their eyes. Can it be, Arthur Bishop wondered, that I am about to meet the object of my quest, Blackbeard, the leader of the Bantus himself, or his bloodthirsty lieutenant . . ." He turned a page and was temporarily put out by a portrait of the bishop in whites with a clerical collar and a topee, standing before a wicket and blocking a ball a Bantu had just bowled him.

"Go on," the boy said.

". . . Batty Davis, so called because of his insane rages when he would send a whole ship's crew to the plank? It was evident that Captain Buller feared the worst, for he crowded on all canvas and it seemed for a time that he would show the strange ship a clean pair of heels. Suddenly over the water came the boom of a gun, and a cannon-ball struck the water twenty yards ahead of them. Captain Buller had his glass to his eye and called down from the bridge to Arthur Bishop, 'The Jolly Roger, by God.' He was the only one of the ship's company who knew the secret of Arthur's strange quest."

Mrs. Bowles came briskly in. "There, that will do. Quite enough for the day. And what's he been reading you, Jimmy?"

"Bishop Among the Bantus."

"I hope you enjoyed it."

"It's wizard."

"You're a very sensible boy," Mrs. Bowles said approvingly.

"Thank you," a voice said from the other bed, and Scobie turned again reluctantly to take in the young devastated face. "Will you read again tomorrow?"

"Don't worry Major Scobie, Helen," Mrs. Bowles rebuked her. "He's got to get back to the port. They'll all be murdering each other without him."

"You a policeman?"

"Yes."

"I knew a policeman once . . . in our town . . ." the voice trailed off into sleep. He stood a minute looking down at her face. Like a fortune-teller's cards it showed unmistakably the past—a voyage, a loss, a sickness. In the next deal perhaps it would be possible to see the future. He took up the stamp-album and opened it at the fly-leaf: it was inscribed: "Helen, from her loving father on her fourteenth birthday." Then it fell open at Paraguay, full of the decorative images of parakeets—the kind of picture stamps a child collects. "We'll have to find her some new stamps," he said sadly.

5

Wilson was waiting for him outside. He said, "I've been looking for you, Major Scobie, ever since the funeral."

"I've been doing good works," Scobie said.

"How's Mrs. Rolt?"

"They think she'll pull through—and the boy too."

"Oh, yes, the boy." Wilson kicked a loose stone in the path and said, "I want your advice, Major Scobie. I'm a bit worried."

"Yes?—"

"You know I've been down here checking up on our store. Well, I find that our manager has been buying military stuff. There's a lot of tinned food that never came from our exporters."

"Isn't the answer fairly simple—sack him?"

"It seems a pity to sack the small thief if he could lead

112

one to the big thief, but of course that's your job. That's why I wanted to talk to you." Wilson paused, and that extraordinary tell-tale blush spread over his face. He said, "You see, he got the stuff from Yusef's man."

"I could have guessed that."

"You could?"

"Yes, but you see Yusef's man is not the same as Yusef. It's easy for him to disown a country storekeeper. In fact, for all we know Yusef may be innocent. It's unlikely, but not impossible. Your own evidence would point to it. After all, you've only just learned yourself what your storekeeper was doing."

"If there were clear evidence," Wilson said, "would the police prosecute?"

Scobie came to a standstill. "What's that?"

Wilson blushed and mumbled. Then with a venom that took Scobie completely by surprise he said, "There are rumours going about that Yusef is protected."

"You've been here long enough to know what rumours are worth."

"They are all round the town."

"Spread by Tallit—or Yusef himself."

"Don't misunderstand me," Wilson said. "You've been very kind to me—and Mrs. Scobie has too. I thought you ought to know what's being said."

"I've been here fifteen years, Wilson."

"Oh, I know," Wilson said, "this is impertinent. But people are worried about Tallit's parrot. They say he was framed because Yusef wants him run out of town."

"Yes, I've heard that."

"They say that you and Yusef are on visiting terms. It's a lie, of course, but . . ."

"It's perfectly true. I'm also on visiting terms with the Sanitary Inspector, but it wouldn't prevent my prosecuting him . . ." He stopped abruptly. He said, "I have no intention of defending myself to you, Wilson."

Wilson repeated, "I just thought you ought to know."

"You are too young for your job, Wilson."

"My job?"

"Whatever it is."

For the second time Wilson took him by surprise, breaking out with a crack in his voice, "Oh, you are unbearable.

113

You are too damned honest to live." His face was aflame, even his knees seemed to blush with rage, shame, self-depreciation.

"You ought to wear a hat, Wilson," was all Scobie said.

They stood facing each other on the stony path between the D.C.'s bungalow and the rest-house: the light lay flat across the rice-fields below them, and Scobie was conscious of how prominently they were silhouetted to the eyes of any watcher. "You sent Louise away," Wilson said, "because you were afraid of me."

Scobie laughed gently. "This is sun, Wilson, just sun. We'll forget about it in the morning."

"She couldn't stand your stupid, unintelligent . . . You don't know what a woman like Louise thinks."

"I don't suppose I do. Nobody wants another person to know that, Wilson."

Wilson said, "I kissed her that evening . . ."

"It's the colonial sport, Wilson." He hadn't meant to madden the young man: he was only anxious to let the occasion pass lightly, so that in the morning they could behave naturally to each other. It was just a touch of sun, he told himself: he had seen this happen times out of mind during fifteen years.

Wilson said, "She's too good for you."

"For both of us."

"How did you get the money to send her away? That's what I'd like to know. You don't earn all that. I know. It's printed in the Colonial Office List." If the young man had been less absurd, Scobie might have been angered and they might have ended friends. It was his serenity that stoked the flames. He said now, "Let's talk about it tomorrow. We've all been upset by that child's death. Come up to the bungalow and have a drink." He made to pass Wilson, but Wilson barred the way: a Wilson scarlet in the face with tears in the eyes. It was as if he had gone so far that he realized the only thing to do was to go further—there was no return the way he had come. He said, "Don't think I haven't got my eye on you."

The absurdity of the phrase took Scobie off his guard.

"You watch your step," Wilson said, "and Mrs. Rolt . . ."

"What on earth has Mrs. Rolt got to do with it?"

"Don't think I don't know why you've stayed behind,

114

haunted the hospital . . . While we were all at the funeral, you slunk down here . . ."

"You really are crazy, Wilson," Scobie said.

Suddenly Wilson sat down: it was as if he had been
folded up by some large invisible hand. He put his head in
his hands and wept.

"It's the sun," Scobie said. "Just the sun. Go and lie
down," and taking off his hat he put it on Wilson's head.
Wilson looked up at him between his fingers—at the man
who had seen his tears—with hatred.

II. THE SIRENS WERE WAILING FOR A TOTAL BLACK-
out, wailing through the rain which fell in interminable
tears; the boys scrambled into the kitchen quarters, and
bolted the door as though to protect themselves from some
devil of the bush. Without pause the hundred and forty-
four inches of water continued its steady and ponderous
descent upon the roofs of the port. It was incredible to
imagine that any human beings, let alone the dispirited
fever-soaked defeated of Vichy territory, would open an
assault at this time of the year, and yet of course one remembered the Heights of Abraham. . . . A single feat of
daring can alter the whole conception of what is possible.

Scobie went out into the dripping darkness holding his
big striped umbrella: a mackintosh was too hot to wear.
He walked all round his quarters; not a light showed, the
shutters of the kitchen were closed, and the Creole houses
were invisible behind the rain. A torch gleamed momentarily in the transport park across the road, but when he
shouted it went out: a coincidence: no one there could
have heard his voice above the hammering of the water
on the roof. Up in Cape Station the officers' mess was shining wetly towards the sea, but that was not his responsibility. The head-lamps of the military lorries ran like a
chain of beads along the edge of the hills, but that too was
someone else's affair.

Up the road behind the transport park a light went suddenly on in one of the Nissen huts where the minor officials lived; it was a hut that had been unoccupied the day before, and presumably some visitor had just moved in. Scobie considered getting his car from the garage, but the hut was only a couple of hundred yards away, and he walked. Except for the sound of the rain, on the road, on the roofs, on the umbrella, there was absolute silence: only the dying moan of the sirens continued for a moment or two to vibrate within the ear. It seemed to Scobie later that this was the ultimate border he had reached in happiness; being in darkness, alone, with the rain falling, without love or pity.

He knocked on the door of the Nissen hut, loudly because of the blows of the rain on the black roof like a tunnel: he had to knock twice before the door opened. The light for a moment blinded him. He said, "I'm sorry to bother you. One of your lights is showing."

A woman's voice said, "Oh, I'm sorry. It was careless. . . ."

His eyes cleared, but for a moment he couldn't put a name to the intensely remembered features. He knew every one in the colony. This was something that had come from outside . . . a river . . . early morning . . . a dying child. "Why," he said, "it's Mrs. Rolt, isn't it? I thought you were in hospital?"

"Yes. Who are you? Do I know you?"

"I'm Major Scobie of the police. I saw you at Pende."

"I'm sorry," she said. "I don't remember a thing that happened there."

"Can I fix your light?"

"Of course. Please." He came in and drew the curtains close and shifted a table lamp. The hut was divided in two by a curtain: on one side a bed, a makeshift dressing-table; on the other a table, a couple of chairs—the few sticks of furniture of the pattern allowed to junior officials with salaries under five hundred pounds a year. He said, "They haven't done you very proud, have they? I wish I'd known. I could have helped." He took her in closely now: the young worn-out face, with the hair gone dead . . . The pyjamas she was wearing were too large for her: the body was lost in them: they fell in ugly folds. He looked to see

116

whether the ring was still loose upon her finger, but it had gone altogether.

"Everybody's been very kind," she said. "Mrs. Carter gave me a lovely pouf."

His eyes wandered: there was nothing personal anywhere: no photographs, no books, no trinkets of any kind, but then he remembered that she had brought nothing out of the sea except herself and a stamp-album.

"Is there any danger?" she asked anxiously.

"Danger?"

"The sirens."

"Oh, none at all. These are just alarms. We get about one a month. Nothing ever happens." He took another long look at her. "They oughtn't to have let you out of hospital so soon. It's not six weeks . . ."

"I wanted to go. I wanted to be alone. People kept on coming to see me."

"Well. I'll be going now myself. Remember if you ever want anything I'm just down the road. The two-storied white house beyond the transport park sitting in a swamp."

"Won't you stay till the rain stops?" she asked.

"I don't think I'd better," he said. "You see, it goes on until September," and won out of her a stiff unused smile.

"The noise is awful."

"You get used to it in a few weeks. Like living beside a railway. But you won't have to. They'll be sending you home very soon. There's a boat in a fortnight."

"Would you like a drink? Mrs. Carter gave me a bottle of gin as well as the pouf."

"I'd better help you to drink it then." He noticed when she produced the bottle that nearly half had gone. "Have you any limes?"

"No."

"They've given you a boy, I suppose?"

"Yes, but I don't know what to ask him for. And he never seems to be around."

"You've been drinking it neat?"

"Oh, no, I haven't touched it. The boy upset it—that was his story."

"I'll talk to your boy in the morning," Scobie said. "Got an ice-box?"

"Yes, but the boy can't get me any ice." She sat weakly

117

down in a chair. "Don't think me a fool. I just don't know where I am. I've never been anywhere like this."

"Where do you come from?"

"Bury St. Edmunds. In Suffolk. I was there eight weeks ago."

"Oh, no, you weren't. You were in that boat."

"Yes. I forgot the boat."

"They oughtn't to have pushed you out of the hospital all alone like this."

"I'm all right. They had to have my bed. Mrs. Carter said she'd find room for me, but I wanted to be alone. The doctor told them to do what I wanted."

Scobie said, "I can understand you wouldn't want to be with Mrs. Carter, and you've only got to say the word and I'll be off too."

"I'd rather you waited till the All Clear. I'm a bit rattled, you know." The stamina of women had always amazed Scobie. This one had survived forty days in an open boat and she talked about being rattled. He remembered the casualties in the report the chief engineer had made: the third officer and two seamen who had died, and the stoker who had gone off his head as a result of drinking sea water and drowned himself. When it came to strain it was always the man who broke. Now she lay back on her weakness as on a pillow.

He said, "Have you thought out things? Shall you go back to Bury?"

"I don't know. Perhaps I'll get a job."

"Have you had any experience?"

"No," she confessed, looking away from him. "You see, I only left school a year ago."

"Did they teach you anything?" It seemed to him that what she needed more than anything else was just talk, silly aimless talk. She thought that she wanted to be alone, but what she was afraid of was the awful responsibility of receiving sympathy. How could a child like that act the part of a woman whose husband had been drowned more or less before her eyes? As well expect her to act Lady Macbeth. Mrs. Carter would have had no sympathy with her inadequacy. Mrs. Carter of course would have known how to behave, having buried one husband and three children.

118

She said, "I was best at netball," breaking in on his thoughts.

"Well," he said, "you haven't quite the figure for a gym instructor. Or have you, when you are well?"

Suddenly and without warning she began to talk: it was as if by the inadvertent use of a password he had induced a door to open: he couldn't tell now which word he had used. Perhaps it was "gym instructor," for she began rapidly to tell him about the netball (Mrs. Carter, he thought, had probably talked about forty days in an open boat and a three-weeks'-old husband). She said, "I was in the school team for two years," leaning forward excitedly with her chin on her hand and one bony elbow upon a bony knee. With her white skin—unyellowed yet by atabrine or sunlight—he was reminded of a bone the sea has washed and cast up. "A year before that I was in the second team. I would have been captain if I'd stayed another year. In 1940 we beat Roedean and tied with Cheltenham."

He listened with the intense interest one feels in a stranger's life, the interest the young mistake for love. He felt the security of his age sitting there listening with a glass of gin in his hand and the rain coming down. She told him her school was on the downs just behind Seaport: they had a French mistress called Mlle. Dupont who had a vile temper. The headmistress could read Greek just like English—Virgil . . .

"I always thought Virgil was Latin."

"Oh, yes. I meant Homer. I wasn't any good at Classics."

"Were you good at anything besides netball?"

"I think I was next best at Maths, but I was never any good at trigonometry." In summer they went into Seaport and bathed, and every Saturday they had a picnic on the downs—sometimes a paper chase on ponies, and once a disastrous affair on bicycles which spread out over the whole country, and two girls didn't return till one in the morning. He listened fascinated, revolving the heavy gin in his glass without drinking. The sirens squealed the All Clear through the rain, but neither of them paid any attention. He said, "And then in the holidays you went back to Bury?"

Apparently her mother had died ten years ago, and her father was a clergyman attached in some way to the Cathe-

119

dral. They had a very small house on Angel Hill. Perhaps she had not been as happy at Bury as at school, for she tacked back at the first opportunity to discuss the games mistress, whose name was the same as her own—Helen, and for whom the whole of her year had an enormous *schwärmerei*. She laughed now at this passion in a superior way: it was the only indication she gave him that she was grown up, that she was—or rather had been—a married woman.

She broke suddenly off and said, "What nonsense it is telling you all this."

"I like it."

"You haven't once asked me about—you know—"

He did know, for he had read the report. He knew exactly the water ration for each person in the boat—a cupful twice a day which had been reduced after twenty-one days to half a cupful. That had been maintained until within twenty-four hours of the rescue mainly because the deaths had left a small surplus. Behind the school buildings of Seaport, the totem pole of the netball game, he was aware of the intolerable surge, lifting the boat and dropping it again, lifting it and dropping it. "I was miserable when I left—it was the end of July. I cried in the taxi all the way to the station." Scobie counted the months—July to April: nine months: the period of gestation, and what had been born was a husband's death and the Atlantic pushing them like wreckage towards the long flat African beach and the sailor throwing himself over the side. He said, "This is more interesting. I can guess the other."

"What a lot I've talked. Do you know, I think I shall sleep tonight."

"Haven't you been sleeping?"

"It was the breathing all round me at the hospital. People turning and breathing and muttering. When the light was out, it was just like—you know."

"You'll sleep quietly here. No need to be afraid of anything. There's a watchman always on duty. I'll have a word with him."

"You've been so kind," she said. "Mrs. Carter and the others—they've all been kind." She lifted her worn frank childish face and said, "I like you so much."

"I like you too," he said gravely. They both had an immense sense of security: they were friends who could never

120

be anything else than friends—they were safely divided by a dead husband, a living wife, a father who was a clergyman, a games mistress called Helen, and years and years of experience. They hadn't got to worry about what they should say to each other.

He said, "Good night. Tomorrow I'm going to bring you some stamps for your album."

"How did you know about my album?"

"That's my job. I'm a policeman."

"Good night."

He walked away, feeling an extraordinary happiness, but this he would not remember as happiness, as he would remember setting out in the darkness, in the rain, alone.

2

From eight-thirty in the morning until eleven he dealt with a case of petty larceny: there were six witnesses to examine, and he didn't believe a word that any of them said. In European cases there are words one believes and words one distrusts: it is possible to draw a speculative line between the truth and the lies: at least the *cui bono* principle to some extent operates, and it is usually safe to assume, if the accusation is theft and there is no question of insurance, that something has at least been stolen. But here one could make no such assumption: one could draw no lines. He had known police officers whose nerves broke down in the effort to separate a single grain of incontestable truth: they ended, some of them, by striking a witness, they were pilloried in the local Creole papers and were invalided home or transferred. It woke in some men a virulent hatred of a black skin, but Scobie had long ago, during his fifteen years, passed through the dangerous stages: now lost in the tangle of lies he felt an extraordinary affection for these people who paralyzed an alien form of justice by so simple a method.

At last the office was clear again: there was nothing further on the charge sheet, and taking out a pad and placing some blotting paper under his wrist to catch the sweat, he prepared to write to Louise. Letter-writing never came easily to him. Perhaps because of his police training, he could never put even a comfortable lie upon paper over

121

his signature. He had to be accurate: he could comfort only by omission. So now, writing the two words *My dear* upon the paper, he prepared to omit. He wouldn't write that he missed her, but he would leave out any phrase that told unmistakably that he was content. *My dear, you must forgive a short letter again. You know I'm not much hand at letter-writing. I got your third letter yesterday, the one telling me that you were staying with Mrs. Halifax's friend for a week outside Durban. Here everything is quiet. We had an alarm last night, but it turned out that an American pilot had mistaken a school of porpoises for submarines. The rains have started, of course. The Mrs. Rolt I told you about in my last letter is out of hospital and they've put her to wait for a boat in one of the Nissen huts behind the transport park. I'll do what I can to make her comfortable. The boy is still in hospital but all right. I really think that's about all the news. The Tallit affair drags on —I don't think anything will come of it in the end. Ali had to go and have a couple of teeth out the other day. What a fuss he made! I had to drive him to the hospital or he'd never have gone.* He paused: he hated the idea of the censors—who happened to be Mrs. Carter and Calloway —reading these last phrases of affection. *Look after yourself, my dear, and don't worry about me. As long as you are happy, I'm happy. In another nine months I can take my leave and we'll be together.* He was going to write, "You are in my mind always," but that was not a statement he could sign. He wrote instead, *You are in my mind so often during the day,* and then pondered the signature. Reluctantly, because he believed it would please her, he wrote *Your Ticki.* Ticki—for a moment he was reminded of that other letter signed "Dicky" which had come back to him two or three times in dreams.

The sergeant entered, marched to the middle of the floor, turned smartly to face him, saluted. He had time to address the envelope while all this was going on. "Yes, sergeant?"

"The Commissioner, sah, he ask you to see him."

"Right."

The Commissioner was not alone. The Colonial Secretary's face shone gently with sweat in the dusky room, and beside him sat a tall bony man Scobie had not seen before —he must have arrived by air, for there had been no ship in during the last ten days. He wore a colonel's badges as though they didn't belong to him on his loose untidy uniform.

"This is Major Scobie. Colonel Wright." He could tell the Commissioner was worried and irritated. He said, "Sit down, Scobie. It's about this Tallit business." The rain darkened the room and kept out the air. "Colonel Wright has come up from Cape Town to hear about it."

"From Cape Town, sir?" The Commissioner moved his legs, playing with a penknife. He said, "Colonel Wright is the M.I.5. representative."

The Colonial Secretary said softly, so that everybody had to bend their heads to hear him, "The whole thing's been unfortunate." The Commissioner began to whittle the corner of his desk, ostentatiously not listening. "I don't think the police should have acted—quite in the way they did—not without consultation."

Scobie said, "I've always understood it was our duty to stop diamond-smuggling."

In his soft obscure voice the Colonial Secretary said, "There weren't a hundred pounds' worth of diamonds found."

"They are the only diamonds that have ever been found."

"The evidence against Tallit, Scobie, was too slender for an arrest."

"He wasn't arrested. He was interrogated."

"His lawyers say he was brought forcibly to the police station."

"His lawyers are lying. You surely realize that much."

The Colonial Secretary said to Colonel Wright, "You see the kind of difficulty we are up against. The Roman Catholic Syrians are claiming they are a persecuted minority and that the police are in the pay of the Moslem Syrians."

Scobie said, "The same thing would have happened the other way round—only it would have been worse. Parliament has more affection for Moslems than Catholics." He had a sense that no one had mentioned the real purpose of this meeting. The Commissioner flaked chip after chip off his desk, disowning everything, and Colonel Wright sat back on his shoulder-blades saying nothing at all.

"Personally," the Colonial Secretary said, "I would always . . ." and the soft voice faded off into inscrutable murmurs which Wright, stuffing his fingers into one ear and leaning his head sideways as though he were trying to hear something through a defective telephone, might possibly have caught.

Scobie said, "I couldn't hear what you said."

"I said personally I'd always take Tallit's word against Yusef's."

"That," Scobie said, "is because you have only been in this colony five years."

Colonel Wright suddenly interjected, "How many years have you been here, Major Scobie?"

"Fifteen."

Colonial Wright grunted non-committally.

The Commissioner stopped whittling the corner of his desk and drove his knife viciously into the top. He said, "Colonel Wright wants to know the source of your information, Scobie."

"You know that, sir. Yusef." Wright and the Colonial Secretary sat side by side watching him: he stood back with lowered head, waiting for the next move. But no move came: he knew they were waiting for him to amplify his bald reply, and he knew too that they would take it for a confession of weakness if he did. The silence became more and more intolerable: it was like an accusation. Weeks ago he had told Yusef that he intended to let the Commissioner know the details of his loan: perhaps he had really had that intention: perhaps he had been bluffing: he couldn't remember now. He only knew that now it was too late. That information should have been given before taking action against Tallit: it could not be an afterthought. In the corridor behind the office Fraser passed whistling his favourite tune: he opened the door of the office, said, "Sorry, sir," and retreated again, leaving a whiff of warm zoo smell behind him. The murmur of the rain went on and on. The Commissioner took the knife out of the table and began to whittle again: it was as if, for a second time, he were deliberately disowning the whole business. The Colonial Secretary cleared his throat. "Yusef," he repeated.

Scobie nodded.

Colonel Wright said, "Do you consider Yusef trustworthy?"

"Of course not, sir. But one has to act on what informa-

124

tion is available—and this information proved correct up to a point."

"Up to what point?"

"The diamonds were there."

The Colonial Secretary said, "Do you get much information from Yusef?"

"This is the first time I've had any at all."

He couldn't catch what the Colonial Secretary said, beyond the word "Yusef."

"I can't hear what you say, sir."

"I said are you in touch with Yusef?"

"I don't know what you mean by that."

"Do you see him often?"

"I think in the last three months I have seen him three—no, four times."

"On business?"

"Not necessarily. Once I gave him a lift home when his car had broken down. Once he came to see me when I had fever at Bamba. Once . . ."

"We are not cross-examining you, Scobie," the Commissioner said.

"I had an idea, sir, that these gentlemen were."

Colonel Wright uncrossed his long legs and said, "Let's boil it down to one question. Tallit, Major Scobie, has made counter-accusations—against the police, against you. He says in effect that Yusef has given you money. Has he?"

"No, sir. Yusef has given me nothing." He felt an odd relief that he had not yet been called upon to lie.

The Colonial Secretary said, "Naturally, sending your wife to South Africa was well within your private means." Scobie sat back in his chair, saying nothing. Again he was aware of the hungry silence waiting for his words.

"You don't answer?" the Colonial Secretary said impatiently.

"I didn't know you had asked a question. I repeat—Yusef has given me nothing."

"He's a man to beware of, Scobie."

"Perhaps when you have been here as long as I have you'll realize the police are meant to deal with people who are not received at the Secretariat."

"We don't want our tempers to get warm, do we?"

Scobie stood up. "Can I go, sir? If these gentlemen have finished with me . . . I have an appointment." The sweat

125

stood on his forehead: his heart jumped with fury. This should be the moment of caution, when the blood runs down the flanks and the red cloth waves.

"That's all right, Scobie," the Commissioner said.

Colonel Wright said, "You must forgive me for bothering you. I received a report. I had to take the matter up officially. I'm quite satisfied."

"Thank you, sir." But the soothing words came too late: the damp face of the Colonial Secretary filled his field of vision. The Colonial Secretary said softly, "It's just a matter of discretion, that's all."

"If I'm wanted for the next half an hour, sir," Scobie said to the Commissioner, "I shall be at Yusef's."

3

After all they had forced him to tell a lie: he had no appointment with Yusef. All the same he wanted a few words with Yusef: it was just possible that he might yet clear up, for his own satisfaction, if not legally, the Tallit affair. Driving slowly through the rain—his windscreen-wiper had long ceased to function—he saw Harris struggling with his umbrella outside the Bedford Hotel.

"Can I give you a lift? I'm going your way."

"The most exciting things have been happening," Harris said. His hollow face shone with rain and enthusiasm. "I've got a house at last."

"Congratulations."

"At least it's not a house: it's one of the huts up your way. But it's a home," Harris said. "I'll have to share it, but it's a home."

"Who's sharing it with you?"

"I'm asking Wilson, but he's gone away—to Lagos for a week or two. The damned elusive Pimpernel. Just when I wanted him. And that brings me to the second exciting thing. Do you know I've discovered we were both at Downham?"

"Downham?"

"The school, of course. I went into his room to borrow his ink while he was away, and there on his table I saw a copy of the *Old Downhamian*."

"What a coincidence," Scobie said.

126

"And do you know—it's really been a day of extraordinary happenings—I was looking through the magazine and there at the end there was a page which said, 'The Secretary of the Old Downhamian Association would like to get into touch with the following old boys with whom we have lost touch'—and there halfway down was my own name, in print, large as life. What do you think of that?"

"What did you do?"

"Directly I got to the office I sat down and wrote—before I touched a cable, except of course the 'Most Immediates,' but then I found I'd forgotten to put down the Secretary's address, so back I had to go for the paper. You wouldn't care to come in, would you, and see what I've written?"

"I can't stay long." Harris had been given an office in a small unwanted room in the Elder Dempster Company's premises. It was the size of an old-fashioned servant's bedroom and this appearance was enhanced by a primitive wash-basin with one cold tap and a gas ring. A table littered with cable forms was squashed between the wash-basin and a window no larger than a porthole which looked straight out onto the water-front and the grey creased bay. An abridged version of *Ivanhoe* for the use of schools, and half a loaf of bread, stood in an out-tray. "Excuse the muddle," Harris said. "Take a chair," but there was no spare chair.

"Where've I put it?" Harris wondered aloud, turning over the cables on his desk. "Ah, I remember." He opened *Ivanhoe* and fished out a folded sheet. "It's only a rough draft," he said with anxiety. "Of course I've got to pull it together. I think I'd better keep it back till Wilson comes. You see, I've mentioned him."

Scobie read, *Dear Secretary, It was just by chance I came on a copy of the Old Downhamian which another Old Downhamian, E. Wilson (1923-1928), had in his room. I'm afraid I've been out of touch with the old place for a great many years and I was very pleased and a bit guilty to see that you have been trying to get into touch with me. Perhaps you'd like to know a bit about what I'm doing in 'the white man's grave,' but as I'm a cable censor you will understand that I can't tell you much about my work. That will have to wait till we've won the war. We are in the middle of the rains now—and how it does rain. There's a* lot of fever about, but I've only had one dose, and E. Wilson has so far escaped altogether. We are sharing a little house together, so that you can feel that Old Downhamians even in this wild and distant part stick together. We've even got an Old Downhamian team of two and go out hunting together, but only cockroaches (Ha! Ha!). Well, I must stop now and get on with winning the war. Cheerio to all Old Downhamians from quite an old Coaster.

Scobie looking up met Harris's anxious and embarrassed gaze. "Do you think it's on the right lines?" he asked. "I was a bit doubtful about 'Dear Secretary.'"

"I think you've caught the tone admirably."

"Of course you know it wasn't a very good school, and I wasn't very happy there. In fact I ran away once."

"And now they've caught up with you."

"It makes you think, doesn't it?" said Harris. He stared out over the grey water with tears in his bloodshot worried eyes. "I've always envied people who were happy there," he said.

Scobie said consolingly, "I didn't much care for school myself."

"To start off happy," Harris said. "It must make an awful difference afterwards. Why, it might become a habit, mightn't it?" He took the piece of bread out of the out-tray and dropped it into the wastepaper basket. "I always mean to get this place tidied up," he said.

"Well, I must be going, Harris. I'm glad about the house —and the Old Downhamian."

"I wonder if Wilson was happy there," Harris brooded. He took Ivanhoe out of the out-tray and looked around for somewhere to put it, but there wasn't any place. He put it back again. "I don't suppose he was," he said, "or why should he have turned up here?"

4

Scobie left his car immediately outside Yusef's door: it was like a gesture of contempt in the face of the Colonial Secretary. He said to the steward, "I want to see your master. I know the way."

"Massa out."

"Then I'll wait for him." He pushed the steward to one

128

side and walked in. The bungalow was divided into a succession of small rooms identically furnished with sofas and cushions and low tables for drinks like the rooms in a brothel. He passed from one to another, pulling the curtains aside, till he reached the little room where nearly two months ago now he had lost his integrity. On the sofa Yusef lay asleep.

He lay on his back in his white duck trousers with his mouth open, breathing heavily. A glass was on a table at his side, and Scobie noticed the small white grains at the bottom. Yusef had taken a bromide. Scobie sat down at his side and waited. The window was open, but the rain shut out the air as effectively as a curtain. Perhaps it was merely the want of air that caused the depression which now fell on his spirits: perhaps it was because he had returned to the scene of a crime. Useless to tell himself that he had committed no offence. Like a woman who has made a loveless marriage he recognized in the room as anonymous as a hotel bedroom the memory of an adultery.

Just over the window there was a defective gutter which emptied itself like a tap, so that all the time you could hear the two sounds of the rain—the murmur and the gush. Scobie lit a cigarette, watching Yusef. He couldn't feel any hatred of the man. He had trapped Yusef as consciously and as effectively as Yusef had trapped him. The marriage had been made by both of them. Perhaps the intensity of the watch he kept broke through the fog of bromide: the fat thighs shifted on the sofa: Yusef grunted, murmured, "dear chap" in his deep sleep, and turned on his side, facing Scobie. Scobie stared again round the room, but he had examined it already thoroughly enough when he came here to arrange his loan: there was no change—the same hideous mauve silk cushions, the threads showing where the damp was rotting the covers: the tangerine curtains: even the blue siphon of soda was in the same place: they had an eternal air like the furnishings of hell. There were no bookshelves, for Yusef couldn't read: no desk, because he couldn't write. It would have been useless to search for papers—papers were useless to Yusef. Everything was inside that large Roman head.

"Why . . . Major Scobie . . ." The eyes were open and sought his: blurred with bromide, they found it difficult to focus.

"Good morning, Yusef." For once Scobie had him at a disadvantage: for a moment Yusef seemed about to sink again into drugged sleep: then with an effort he got on an elbow.

"I wanted to have a word about Tallit, Yusef."

"Tallit . . . forgive me, Major Scobie . . ."

"And the diamonds."

"Crazy about diamonds," Yusef brought out with difficulty in a voice halfway to sleep. He shook his head, so that the white lick of hair flapped: then putting out a vague hand he stretched for the siphon.

"Did you frame Tallit, Yusef?"

Yusef dragged the siphon towards him across the table, knocking over the bromide glass: he turned the nozzle towards his face and pulled the trigger: the soda water broke on his face and splashed all round him on the mauve silk. He gave a sigh of relief and satisfaction, like a man under a shower on a hot day. "What is it, Major Scobie, is anything wrong?"

"Tallit is not going to be prosecuted."

He was like a tired man dragging himself out of the sea: the tide followed him. He said, "You must forgive me, Major Scobie. I have not been sleeping." He shook his head up and down thoughtfully as a man might shake a box to see whether anything rattles. "You were saying something about Tallit, Major Scobie," and he explained again, "It is the stock-taking. All the figures. Three four stores. They try to cheat me because it's all in my head."

"Tallit," Scobie repeated, "won't be prosecuted."

"Never mind. One day he will go too far."

"Were they your diamonds, Yusef?"

"My diamonds? They have made you suspicious of me, Major Scobie."

"Was the small boy in your pay?"

Yusef mopped the soda-water off his face with the back of his hand. "Of course he was, Major Scobie. That was where I got my information."

The moment of inferiority had passed: the great head had shaken itself free of the bromide even though the limbs still lay sluggishly spread over the sofa. "Yusef, I'm not your enemy. I have a liking for you."

"When you say that, Major Scobie, how my heart beats." He pulled his shirt wider as though to show the actual

130

movement of the heart, and little streams of soda-water irrigated the black bush on his chest. "I am too fat," he said.

"I would like to trust you, Yusef. Tell me the truth. Were the diamonds yours or Tallit's?"

"I always want to speak the truth to you, Major Scobie. I never told you the diamonds were Tallit's."

"They were yours?"

"Yes, Major Scobie."

"What a fool you have made of me, Yusef. If only I had a witness here, I'd run you in."

"I didn't mean to make a fool of you, Major Scobie. I wanted Tallit sent away. It would be for the good of everybody if he was sent away. It is no good the Syrians being in two parties. If they were in one party you would be able to come to me and say, 'Yusef, the Government wants the Syrians to do this or that,' and I should be able to answer, 'It shall be so.'"

"And the diamond-smuggling would be in one pair of hands."

"Oh, the diamonds, diamonds, diamonds," Yusef wearily complained. "I tell you, Major Scobie, that I make more money in one year from my smallest store than I would make in three years from diamonds. You cannot understand how many bribes are necessary."

"Well, Yusef, I'm taking no more information from you. This ends our relationship. Every month, of course, I shall send you the interest." He felt a strange unreality in his own words: the tangerine curtains hung there immovably. There are certain places one never leaves behind: the curtains and cushions of this room joined an attic bedroom, an ink-stained desk, a lacy altar in Ealing—they would be there so long as consciousness lasted.

Yusef put his feet on the floor and sat bolt upright. He said, "Major Scobie, you have taken my little joke too much to heart."

"Good-bye, Yusef, you aren't a bad chap, but good-bye."

"You are wrong, Major Scobie. I am a bad chap." He said earnestly, "My friendship with you is the only good thing in this black heart. I cannot give it up. We must stay friends always."

"I'm afraid not, Yusef."

"Listen, Major Scobie. I am not asking you to do anything for me except sometimes—after dark perhaps when nobody can see—to visit me and talk to me. Nothing else. Just that. I will tell you no more tales about Tallit. I will tell you nothing. We will sit here with the siphon and the whisky bottle . . ."

"I'm not a fool, Yusef. I know it would be of great use to you if people believed we were friends. I'm not giving you that help."

Yusef put a finger in his ear and cleared it of soda water. He looked bleakly and brazenly across at Scobie. This must be how he looks, Scobie thought, at the store-manager who has tried to deceive him about the figures he carries in his head. "Major Scobie, did you ever tell the Commissioner about our little business arrangement or was that all bluff?"

"Ask him yourself."

"I think I will. My heart feels rejected and bitter. It urges me to go to the Commissioner and tell him everything."

"Always obey your heart, Yusef."

"I will tell him you took my money and together we planned the arrest of Tallit. But you did not fulfil your bargain, so I have come to him in revenge. In revenge," Yusef repeated gloomily, his Roman head sunk on his fat chest.

"Go ahead. Do what you like, Yusef. We are through." But he couldn't believe in any of this scene, however hard he played it: it was like a lovers' quarrel. He couldn't believe in Yusef's threats and he had no belief in his own calmness: he did not even believe in this good-bye. What had happened in the mauve-and-orange room had been too important to become part of the enormous equal past. He was not surprised when Yusef, lifting his head, said, "Of course I shall not go. One day you will come back and want my friendship. And I shall welcome you."

Shall I be really so desperate? Scobie wondered, as though in the Syrian's voice he had heard the genuine accent of prophecy.

5

On his way home Scobie stopped his car outside the Catholic church and went in. It was the first Saturday of the month and he always went to Confession on that day.

Half a dozen old women, their hair bound like char-women's in dusters, waited their turn: a nursing sister: a private soldier with a Royal Ordnance insignia. Father Rank's voice whispered monotonously from the box.

Scobie with his eyes fixed on the Cross prayed—the Our Father, the Hail Mary, the Act of Contrition. The awful languor of routine fell on his spirits. He felt like a specta-tor—one of those many people round the Cross over whom the gaze of Christ must have passed, seeking the face of a friend or an enemy. It sometimes seemed to him that his profession and his uniform classed him inexorably with all those anonymous Romans keeping order in the streets a long way off. One by one the old Kru women passed into the box and out again, and Scobie prayed—vaguely and ramblingly—for Louise, that she might be happy now at this moment and so remain, that no evil should ever come to her through him. The soldier came out of the box and he rose.

"In the name of the Father, the Son and the Holy Ghost." He said, "Since my last Confession a month ago I have missed one Sunday Mass and one holy day of obliga-tion."

"Were you prevented from going?"

"Yes, but with a little effort I could have arranged my duties better."

"Yes?"

"All through this month I have done the minimum. I've been unnecessarily harsh to one of my men . . ." He paused a long time.

"Is that everything?"

"I don't know how to put it, Father, but I feel—tired of my religion. It seems to mean nothing to me. I've tried to love God, but—" he made a gesture which the priest could not see, turned sideways through the grille. "I'm not sure that I even believe."

"It's easy," the priest said, "to worry too much about that. Especially here. The penance I would give to a lot of people if I could is six months' leave. The climate gets you down. It's easy to mistake tiredness for—well, dis-belief."

"I don't want to keep you, Father. There are other people waiting. I know these are just fancies. But I feel—empty. Empty."

133

"That's sometimes the moment God chooses," the priest said. "Now go along with you and say a decade of your rosary."

"I haven't a rosary. At least . . ."

"Well, five Our Fathers and five Hail Marys then." He began to speak the words of Absolution, but the trouble is, Scobie thought, there's nothing to absolve. The words brought no sense of relief because there was nothing to relieve. They were a formula: the Latin words hustled together—a hocus-pocus. He went out of the box and knelt down again, and this too was part of a routine. It seemed to him for a moment that God was too accessible. There was no difficulty in approaching Him. Like a popular demagogue He was open to the least of His followers at any hour. Looking up at the Cross he thought: He even suffers in public.

III. "I'VE BROUGHT YOU SOME STAMPS," SCOBIE said. "I've been collecting them for a week—from everybody. Even Mrs. Carter has contributed a magnificent parakeet—look at it—from somewhere in South America. And here's a complete set of Liberians surcharged for the American occupation. I got those from the Naval Observer."

They were completely at ease: it seemed to both of them for that very reason they were safe.

"Why do you collect stamps?" he asked. "It's an odd thing to do—after sixteen."

"I don't know," Helen Rolt said. "I don't really collect. I carry them round. I suppose it's habit." She opened the album and said, "No, it's not just habit. I do love the things. Do you see this green George V halfpenny stamp? It's the first I ever collected. I was eight. I steamed it off an envelope and stuck it in a notebook. That's why my father gave me an album. My mother had died, so he gave me a stamp-album."

She tried to explain more exactly. "They are like snapshots. They are so portable. People who collect china—they

134

can't carry it around with them. Or books. But you don't have to tear the pages out like you do with snapshots."

"You've never told me about your husband," Scobie said.

"No."

"It's not really much good tearing out a page, because you can see the place where it's been torn."

"Yes."

"It's easier to get over a thing," Scobie said, "if you talk about it."

"That's not the trouble," she said. "The trouble is—it's so terribly easy to get over." She took him by surprise: he hadn't believed she was old enough to have reached that stage in her lessons, that particular turn of the screw. She said, "He's been dead—how long—is it eight weeks yet? and he's so dead. So completely dead. What a little bitch I must be."

Scobie said, "You needn't feel that. It's the same with everybody, I think. When we say to someone, 'I can't live without you,' what we really mean is, 'I can't live feeling you may be in pain, unhappy, in want.' That's all it is. When they are dead our responsibility ends. There's nothing more we can do about it. We can rest in peace."

"I didn't know I was so tough," Helen said. "Horribly tough."

"I had a child," Scobie said, "who died. I was out here. My wife sent me two cables from Bexhill, one at five in the evening and one at six, but they mixed up the order. You see, she meant to break the thing gently. I got one cable just after breakfast. It was eight o'clock in the morning—a dead time of day for any news." He had never mentioned this before to anyone, not even to Louise. Now he brought out the exact words of each cable, carefully. "The cable said, *Catherine died this afternoon no pain God bless you.* The second cable came at lunch time. It said, *Catherine seriously ill. Doctor has hope my diving.* That was the one sent off at five. 'Diving' was a mutilation—I suppose for 'darling.' You see there was nothing more hopeless she could have put to break the news than 'doctor has hope.'"

"How terrible for you," Helen said.

"No, the terrible thing was that when I got the second telegram, I was so muddled in my head, I thought: There's been a mistake. She must be still alive. For a moment, un-
135

til I realized what had happened, I was—disappointed. That was the terrible thing. I thought: Now the anxiety begins, and the pain, but when I realized what had happened, then it was all right, she was dead, I could begin to forget her."

"Have you forgotten her?"

"I don't remember her often. You see, I escaped seeing her die. My wife had that."

It was astonishing to him how easily and quickly they had become friends. They came together over two deaths without reserve. She said, "I don't know what I'd have done without you."

"Everybody would have looked after you."

"I think they are scared of me," she said.

He laughed.

"They are. Flight-Lieutenant Bagster took me to the beach this afternoon, but he was scared. Because I'm not happy and because of my husband. Everybody on the beach was pretending to be happy about something, and I sat there grinning and it didn't work. Do you remember when you went to your first party and coming up the stairs you heard all the voices and you didn't know how to talk to people? That's how I felt, so I sat and grinned in Mrs. Carter's bathing dress, and Bagster stroked my leg, and I wanted to go home."

"You'll be going home soon."

"I don't mean that home. I mean here, where I can shut the door and not answer when they knock. I don't want to go away yet."

"But surely you aren't happy here?"

"I'm so afraid of the sea," she said.

"Do you dream about it?"

"No. I dream of John sometimes—that's worse. Because I've always had bad dreams of him, and I still have bad dreams of him. I mean we were always quarrelling in the dreams and we still go on quarrelling."

"Did you quarrel?"

"No. He was sweet to me. We were only married a month, you know. It would be easy being sweet as long as that, wouldn't it? When this happened I hadn't really had time to know my way around." It seemed to Scobie that she had never known her way around—at least not since she had left her netball team, was it a year ago? Sometimes he saw her lying back in the boat on that oily featureless sea, day after day, with the other child near death and the sailor going mad, and Miss Malcott, and the chief engineer who felt his responsibility to the owners: and sometimes he saw her carried past him on a stretcher grasping her stamp-album, and now he saw her in the borrowed unbecoming bathing dress grinning at Bagster as he stroked her legs, listening to the laughter and the splashes, not knowing the adult etiquette. . . . Sadly, like an evening tide, he felt responsibility bearing him up the shore.

"You've written to your father?"

"Oh, yes, of course. He's cabled that he's pulling strings about the passage. I don't know what strings he can pull from Bury, poor dear. He doesn't know anybody at all. He cabled too about John, of course." She lifted a cushion off the chair and pulled the cable out. "Read it. He's very sweet, but of course he doesn't know a thing about me."

Scobie read: *Terribly grieved for you dear child but remember his happiness Your loving father.* The date stamp with the Bury mark made him aware of the enormous distance between father and child. He said, "How do you mean, he doesn't know a thing?"

"You see, he believes in God and heaven, all that sort of thing."

"You don't?"

"I gave up all that when I left school. John used to pull his leg about it, quite gently, you know. Father didn't mind. But he never knew I felt the way John did. If you are a clergyman's daughter there are a lot of things you have to pretend about. He would have hated knowing that John and I—went together, oh, a fortnight before we were married."

Again he had that vision of someone who didn't know her way around: no wonder Bagster was scared of her. Bagster was not a man to accept responsibility, and how could anyone lay the responsibility for any action, he thought, on this stupid bewildered child? He turned over the little pile of stamps he had accumulated for her and said, "I wonder what you'll do when you get home?"

"I suppose," she said, "they'll conscript me."

He thought: If my child had lived, she too would have

been conscriptable, flung into some grim dormitory, to find her own way. After the Atlantic, the A.T.S. or the W.A.A.F., the blustering sergeant with the big bust, the cook-house and the potato peelings, the Lesbian officer with the thin lips and the tidy gold hair, and the men waiting on the Common outside the camp, among the gorse bushes . . . compared to that, surely even the Atlantic was more a home. He said, "Haven't you got any shorthand? Any languages?" Only the clever and the astute and the influential escaped in war.

"No," she said, "I'm not really any good at anything."

It was impossible to think of her being saved from the sea and then flung back like a fish that wasn't worth catching.

He said, "Can you type?"

"I can get along quite fast with one finger."

"You could get a job here, I think. We are very short of secretaries. All the wives, you know, are working in the Secretariat, and we still haven't enough. But it's a bad climate for a woman."

"I'd like to stay. Let's have a drink on it." She called, "Boy, boy."

"You are learning," Scobie said. "A week ago you were so frightened of him . . ." The boy came in with a tray set out with glasses, limes, water, a new gin bottle.

"This isn't the boy I talked to," Scobie said.

"No, that one went. You talked to him too fiercely."

"And this one came?"

"Yes."

"What's your name, boy?"

"Vande, sah."

"I've seen you before, haven't I?"

"No, sah."

"Who am I?"

"You big policeman, sah."

"Don't frighten this one away," Helen said.

"Who were you with?"

"I was with D.C. Pemberton up bush, sah. I was small boy."

"Is that where I saw you?" Scobie said. "I suppose I did. You look after this missus well now, and when she goes home, I get you big job. Remember that."

138

"Yes, sah."

"You haven't looked at the stamps," Scobie said.

"No, I haven't, have I?" A spot of gin fell upon one of the stamps and stained it. He watched her pick it out of the pile, taking in the straight hair falling in rats' tails over the nape as though the Atlantic had taken the strength out of it forever, the hollowed face. It seemed to him that he had not felt so much at ease with another human being for years—not since Louise was young. But this case was different, he told himself: they were safe with each other. He was more than thirty years the older: his body in this climate had lost the sense of lust: he watched her with sadness and affection and enormous pity because a time would come when he couldn't show her around in a world where she was at sea. When she turned and the light fell on her face she looked ugly, with the temporary ugliness of a child. The ugliness was like handcuffs on his wrists.

He said, "That stamp's spoilt. I'll get you another."

"Oh, no," she said, "it goes in as it is. I'm not a real collector."

He had no sense of responsibility towards the beautiful and the graceful and the intelligent. They could find their own way. It was the face for which nobody would go out of his way, the face that would never catch the covert look, the face which would soon be used to rebuffs and indifference, that demanded his allegiance. The word "pity" is used as loosely as the word "love": the terrible promiscuous passion which so few experience.

She said, "You see, whenever I see that stain I'll see this room. . . ."

"Then it's like a snapshot."

"You can pull a stamp out," she said with a terrible youthful clarity, "and you don't know that it's ever been there." She turned suddenly to him and said, "It's so good to talk to you. I can say anything I like. I'm not afraid of hurting you. You don't want anything out of me. I'm safe."

"We're both safe." The rain surrounded them, falling regularly on the iron roof. She said suddenly, passionately, "My God, how good you are."

"No."

She said, "I have a feeling that you'd never let me down." The words came to him like a command he would

139

have to obey, however difficult. Her hands were full of the absurd scraps of paper he had brought her. She said, "I'll keep these always. I'll never have to pull these out."

Somebody knocked on the door and a voice said, "Freddie Bagster. It's only me. Freddie Bagster," cheerily.

"Don't answer," she whispered, "don't answer." She put her arm in his and watched the door with her mouth a little open as though she were out of breath. He had the sense of an animal which had been chased to its hole.

"Let Freddie in," the voice wheedled. "Be a sport, Helen. Only Freddie Bagster." The man was a little drunk.

She stood pressed against him with her hand on his side. When the sound of Bagster's feet receded, she raised her mouth and they kissed. What they had both thought was safety proved to have been the camouflage of an enemy who works in terms of friendship, trust, and pity.

2

The rain poured steadily down, turning the little patch of reclaimed ground on which his house stood back into swamp again. The window of his room blew to and fro: at some time during the night the catch had been broken by a squall of wind. Now the rain had blown in, his dressing-table was soaking wet, and there was a pool of water on the floor. His alarm clock pointed to four-twenty-five. He felt as though he had returned to a house that had been abandoned years ago. It would not have surprised him to find cobwebs over the mirror, the mosquito net hanging in shreds, and the dirt of mice upon the floor.

He sat down on a chair and the water drained off his trousers and made a second pool around his mosquito boots. He had left his umbrella behind, setting out on his walk home with an odd jubilation, as though he had rediscovered something he had lost, something which belonged to his youth. In the wet and noisy darkness he had even lifted his voice and tried out a line from Fraser's song, but his voice was tuneless. Now somewhere between the Nissen hut and home he had mislaid his joy.

At four in the morning he had woken. Her head lay in his side and he could feel her hair against his breast. Putting his hand outside the net he found the light. She lay in the odd cramped attitude of someone who has been shot in escaping. It seemed to him for a moment even then, before his tenderness and pleasure awoke, that he was looking at a bundle of cannon fodder. The first words she said when the light had roused her were, "Bagster can go to hell."

"Were you dreaming?"

She said, "I dreamed I was lost in a marsh and Bagster found me."

He said, "I've got to go. If we sleep now, we shan't wake again till it's light." He began to think for both of them, carefully. Like a criminal he began to fashion in his own mind the undetectable crime: he planned the moves ahead: he embarked for the first time in his life on the long legalistic arguments of deceit. If so-and-so . . . then what follows. He said, "What time does your boy turn up?"

"About six, I think. I don't know. He calls me at seven."

"Ali starts boiling my water about a quarter to six. I'd better go, my dear." He looked carefully everywhere for signs of his presence; he straightened a mat and hesitated over an ash-tray. Then at the end of it all he had left his umbrella standing against the wall. It seemed to him the typical action of a criminal. When the rain reminded him of it, it was too late to go back. He would have to hammer on her door, and already in one hut a light had gone on. Standing in his own room with a mosquito boot in his hand he thought wearily and drearily. "In the future I must do better than that."

In the future—that was where the sadness lay. Was it the butterfly that died in the act of love? But human beings were condemned to consequences. The responsibility as well as the guilt was his—he was not a Bagster; he knew what he was about. He had sworn to preserve Louise's happiness, and now he had accepted another and contradictory responsibility. He felt tired by all the lies he would sometime have to tell: he felt the wounds of those victims who had not yet bled. Lying back on the pillow he stared sleeplessly out towards the grey early morning tide. Somewhere on the face of those obscure waters moved the sense of yet another wrong and another victim, not Louise, not Helen. Away in the town the cocks began to crow for the false dawn.

Part Two

"THERE. WHAT DO YOU THINK OF IT?" HARRIS asked with ill-concealed pride. He stood in the doorway of the hut while Wilson preceded him in, moving cautiously forward between the brown sticks of Government furniture like a setter through stubble.

"Better than the hotel," Wilson said cautiously, pointing his muzzle towards a Government easy chair.

"I thought I'd give you a surprise when you got back from Lagos." Harris had curtained the Nissen hut into three: a bedroom for each of them and a common sitting room. "There's only one point that worries me. I'm not sure whether there are any cockroaches."

"Well, we only played the game to get rid of them."

"I know, but it seems almost a pity, doesn't it?"

"Who are our neighbours?"

"There's the Mrs. Rolt who was submarined, and there are two chaps in the Department of Works, and somebody called Clive from the Agricultural Department, Boling who's in charge of Sewage—they all seem a nice friendly lot. And Scobie, of course, is just down the road."

"Yes."

Wilson moved restlessly around the hut and came to a stop in front of a photograph which Harris had propped against a Government inkstand. It showed three long rows of boys on a lawn: the first row sitting cross-legged on the grass: the second on chairs, wearing high stiff collars, with an elderly man and two women (one had a squint) in the centre: the third row standing. Wilson said, "That woman with the squint—I could swear I'd seen her somewhere before."

"Does the name Snakey convey anything to you?"

"Why, yes, of course." He looked closer. "So you were at that hole too?"

"I saw the *Downhamian* in your room and I fished this out to surprise you. I was in Jagger's house. Where were you?"

"I was a Prog," Wilson said.

"Oh, well," Harris admitted in a tone of disappointment, "there were some good chaps among the Prog bugs." He laid the photograph flat down again as though it were something that hadn't quite come off. "I was thinking we might have an Old Downhamian dinner."

"Whatever for?" Wilson asked. "There are only two of us."

"We could invite a guest each."

"I don't see the point."

Harris said bitterly, "Well, you are the real Downhamian, not me. I never joined the association. You get the magazine. I thought perhaps you had an interest in the place."

"My father made me a life member and he always forwards the bloody paper," Wilson said abruptly.

"It was lying beside your bed. I thought you'd been reading it."

"I may have glanced at it."

"There was a bit about me in it. They wanted my address."

"Oh, but you know why that is," Wilson said. "They are sending out appeals to any Old Downhamian they can rake up. The panelling in the Founders' Hall is in need of repair. I'd keep your address quiet if I were you." He was one of those, it seemed to Harris, who always knew what was on: who gave advance information on extra halves: who knew why old So-and-so had not turned up to school, and what the row brewing at the Masters' special meeting was about. A few weeks ago he had been a new boy whom Harris had been delighted to befriend, to show around: he remembered the evening when Wilson would have put on evening dress for a Syrian's dinner party if he hadn't been warned. But Harris from his first year at school had been fated to see how quickly new boys grew up: one term he was their kindly mentor—the next he was discarded. He could never progress as quickly as the newest unlicked boy. He remembered how even in the cockroach game—that he

143

had invented—his rules had been challenged on the first evening. He said sadly, "I expect you are right. Perhaps I won't send a letter after all." He added humbly, "I took the bed on this side, but I don't a bit mind which I have. . ."

"Oh, that's all right," Wilson said.

"I've only engaged one steward. I thought we could save a bit by sharing."

"The less boys we have knocking about here the better," Wilson said.

That night was the first night of their new comradeship. They sat reading on their twin Government chairs behind the black-out curtains. On the table was a bottle of whisky for Wilson and a bottle of barley water flavoured with lime for Harris. A sense of extraordinary peace came to Harris while the rain tingled steadily on the roof and Wilson read a Wallace. Occasionally a few drunks from the R.A.F. mess passed by, shouting or revving their cars, but this only enhanced the sense of peace inside the hut. Sometimes his eyes strayed to the walls seeking a cockroach, but you couldn't have everything.

"Have you got the *Downhamian* handy, old man? I wouldn't mind another glance at it. This book's so dull."

"There's a new one unopened on the dressing-table."

"You don't mind my opening it?"

"Why the hell should I?"

Harris turned first to the Old Downhamian notes and read again how the whereabouts of H.R. Harris (1917-1921) was still wanted. He wondered whether it was possible that Wilson was wrong: there was no word here about the panelling in Hall. Perhaps after all he would send that letter, and he pictured the reply he might receive from the secretary. *My dear Harris, it would go something like that, We were all delighted to receive your letter from those romantic parts. Why not send us a full-length contribution to the mag. and while I'm writing to you, what about membership of the Old Downhamian Association? I notice you've never joined. I'm speaking for all Old Downhamians when I say that we'll be glad to welcome you.* He tried out "proud to welcome you" on his tongue, but rejected that. He was a realist.

The Old Downhamian had had a fairly successful Christmas term. They had beaten Harpenden by one goal, Merchant Taylors by two, and had drawn with Lancing. Ducker and Tierney were coming on well as forwards, but the scrum was still slow in getting the ball out. He turned a page and read how the Opera Society had given an excellent rendering of *Patience* in the Founders' Hall. F.J.K., who was obviously the English master, wrote: *Lane as Bunthorne displayed a degree of æstheticism which surprised all his companions of Vb. We would not hitherto have described his hand as mediæval or associated him with lilies, but he persuaded us that we had misjudged him. A great performance, Lane.*

Harris skimmed through the accounts of Fives Matches, a fantasy called "The Tick of the Clock" beginning *There was once a little old lady whose most beloved possession . . .* The walls of Downham—the red brick laced with yellow, the extraordinary crockets, the mid-Victorian gargoyles—rose around him: boots beat on stone stairs and a cracked dinner bell rang to rouse him to another miserable day. He felt the loyalty we all feel to unhappiness—the sense that that is where we really belong. His eyes filled with tears, he took a sip of his barley water and thought, "I'll post that letter, whatever Wilson says." Somebody outside shouted, "Bagster. Where are you, Bagster, you sod?" and stumbled in a ditch. He might have been back at Downham, except of course that they wouldn't have used *that* word.

Harris turned a page or two and the title of a poem caught his eye. It was called "West Coast" and it was dedicated to "L.S." He wasn't very keen on poetry, but it struck him as interesting that somewhere on this enormous coast line of sand and smells there existed a third Old Downhamian. He read,

> Another Tristram on this distant coast
> Raises the poisoned chalice to his lips,
> Another Mark upon the palm-fringed shore
> Watches his love's eclipse.

It seemed to Harris obscure: his eye passed rapidly over the intervening verses to the initials at the foot: E.W. He nearly exclaimed aloud, but he restrained himself in time. In such close quarters as they now shared it was necessary to be circumspect. There wasn't space to quarrel in. Who

is L.S., he wondered, and thought: Surely it can't be . . .
the very idea crinkled his lips in a cruel smile. He said,
"There's not much in the mag. We beat Harpenden.
There's a poem called 'West Coast.' Another poor devil
out here, I suppose."

"Oh."

"Lovelorn," Harris said. "But I don't read poetry."

"Nor do I," Wilson lied behind the barrier of the
Wallace.

2

It had been a very narrow squeak. Wilson lay on his
back in bed and listened to the rain on the roof and the
heavy breathing of the Old Downhamian beyond the curtain. It was as if the hideous years had extended through
the intervening mist to surround him again. What madness had induced him to send that poem to the Downhamian? But it wasn't madness: he had long since become in-
capable of anything so honest as madness: he was one of
those condemned in childhood to complexity. He knew
what he had intended to do: to cut the poem out with no
indication of its source and to send it to Louise. It wasn't
quite her sort of poem, he knew, but surely, he had argued,
she would be impressed to some extent by the mere fact
that the poem was in print. If she asked him where it had
appeared, it would be easy to invent some convincing co-
terie name. The Downhamian luckily was well printed and
on good paper. It was true, of course, that he would have to
paste the cutting on opaque paper to disguise what was
printed on the other side, but it would be easy to think up
an explanation of that. It was as if his profession were
slowly absorbing his whole life, just as school had done. His
profession was to lie, to have the quick story ready, never to
give himself away, and his private life was taking the same
pattern. He lay on his back in a nausea of self-disgust.

The rain had momentarily stopped. It was one of those
cool intervals that were the consolation of the sleepless. In
Harris's heavy dreams the rain went on. Wilson got softly
out and mixed himself a bromide: the grains fizzed in the
bottom of the glass and Harris spoke hoarsely and turned
over behind the curtain. Wilson flashed his torch on his

146

watch and read two-twenty-five. Tiptoeing to the door so as not to waken Harris, he felt the little sting of a jigger under his toe-nail. In the morning he must get his boy to scoop it out. He stood on the small cement pavement above the marshy ground and let the cool air play on him with his pyjama jacket flapping open. All the huts were in darkness, and the moon was patched with the rainclouds coming up. He was going to turn away when he heard someone stumble a few yards away and he flashed his torch. It lit on a man's bowed back moving between the huts towards the road. "Scobie," Wilson exclaimed, and the man turned.

"Hullo, Wilson," Scobie said. "I didn't know you lived up here."

"I'm sharing with Harris," Wilson said, watching the man who had watched his tears.

"I've been taking a walk," Scobie said unconvincingly. "I couldn't sleep." It seemed to Wilson that Scobie was still a novice in the world of deceit: he hadn't lived in it since childhood, and he felt an odd elderly envy for Scobie, much as an old lag might envy the young crook serving his first sentence to whom all this was new.

3

Wilson sat in his little stuffy room in the U.A.C. office. Several of the firm's journals and daybooks bound in quarter pigskin formed a barrier between him and the door. Surreptitiously, like a schoolboy using a crib, Wilson behind the barrier worked at his code books, translating a cable. A commercial calendar showed a week-old date— June 20—and a motto: *The best investments are honesty and enterprise. William P. Cornforth.* A clerk knocked and said, "There's a nigger for you, Wilson, with a note."

"Who from?"

"He says Brown."

"Keep him a couple of minutes, there's a good chap, and then boot him in." However diligently Wilson practised, the slang phrase sounded unnatural on his lips. He folded up the cable and stuck it in the code book to keep his place: then he put the cable and the code book in the safe and pulled the door to. Pouring himself out a glass of water he looked out on the street; the mammies, their heads tied up in bright cotton clothes, passed, under their coloured umbrellas. Their shapeless cotton gowns fell to the ankle: one with a design of match-boxes: another with kerosene lamps: the third—the latest from Manchester—covered with mauve cigarette lighters on a yellow ground. Naked to the waist a young girl passed gleaming through the rain and Wilson watched her out of sight with melancholy lust. He swallowed and turned as the door opened.

"Shut the door."

The boy obeyed. He had apparently put on his best clothes for this morning call: a white cotton shirt fell outside his white shorts. His gym shoes were immaculate in spite of the rain except that his toes protruded.

"You small boy at Yusef's?"

"Yes, sah."

"You got a message," Wilson said, "from my boy. He tell you what I want, eh? He's your young brother, isn't he?"

"Yes, sah."

"Same father?"

"Yes, sah."

"He says you good boy, honest. You want to be a steward, eh?"

"Yes, sah."

"Can you read?"

"No, sah."

"Write?"

"No, sah."

"You got eyes in your head? Good ears? You see everything? You hear everything?"

The boy grinned—a gash of white in the smooth grey elephant-hide of his face: he had a look of sleek intelligence. Intelligence, to Wilson, was more valuable than honesty. Honesty was a double-edged weapon, but intelligence looked after number one. Intelligence realized that a Syrian might one day go home to his own land, but the English stayed. Intelligence knew that it was a good thing to work for government, whatever the government. "How much you get as small boy?"

"Ten shillings."

"I pay you five shillings more. If Yusef sack you I pay you ten shillings. If you stay with Yusef one year and give

148

me good information—true information, no lies—I give you job as steward with white man. Understand?"

"Yes, sah."

"If you give me lies, then you go to prison. Maybe they shoot you. I don't know. I don't care. Understand?"

"Yes, sah."

"Every day you see your brother at meat market. You tell him who comes to Yusef's house. Tell him where Yusef goes. You tell him any strange boys who come to Yusef's house. You no tell lies, you tell truth. No humbug. If no one comes to Yusef's house you say no one. You no make big lie. If you tell lie, I know it and you go to prison straightaway." The wearisome recital went on. He was never quite sure how much was understood. The sweat ran off Wilson's forehead and the cool contained grey face of the boy irritated him like an accusation he couldn't answer. "You go to prison and you stay in prison plenty long time." He could hear his own voice cracking with the desire to impress: he could hear himself, like the parody of a white man on the halls. He said, "Scobie? Do you know Major Scobie?"

"Yes, sah. He very good man, sah." They were the first words apart from yes and no the boy had uttered.

"You see him at your master's?"

"Yes, sah."

"How often?"

"Once, twice, sah."

"He and your master—they are friends?"

"My master he think Major Scobie very good man, sah."

The reiteration of the phrase angered Wilson. He broke furiously out, "I don't want to hear whether he's good or not. I want to know where he meets Yusef, see? What do they talk about? You bring them in drinks sometime when steward's busy? What do you hear?"

"Last time they have big palaver," the boy brought ingratiatingly out as if he were showing a corner of his wares.

"I bet they did. I want to know all about their palaver."

"When Major Scobie go away one time, my master he put pillow right on his face."

"What on earth do you mean by that?"

The boy folded his arms over his eyes in a gesture of great dignity and said, "His eyes make pillow wet."

"Good God," Wilson said, "what an extraordinary thing."

"Then he drink plenty whisky and go to sleep—ten, twelve hours. Then he go to his store in Bond Street and make plenty hell."

"Why?"

"He say they humbug him."

"What's that got to do with Major Scobie?"

The boy shrugged. As so many times before, Wilson had the sense of a door closed in his face: he was always on the outside of the door.

When the boy had gone he opened his safe again, moving the knob of the combination first left to 32—his age, secondly right to 10—the year of his birth, left again to 65—the number of his home in Western Avenue, Pinner, and took out the code books. 32946 78523 97042. Row after row of groups swam before his eyes. The telegram was headed "Important," or he would have postponed the decoding till the evening. He knew how little important it really was—the usual ship had left Lobito carrying the usual suspects—diamonds, diamonds, diamonds. When he had decoded the telegram he would hand it to the long-suffering Commissioner, who had already received the same information or contradictory information from M.I.5. or one of the other secret organizations which took root on the coast like mangroves. *Leave alone but do not repeat not pinpoint P. Ferreira passenger 1st class Repeat P. Ferreira passenger 1st class.* Ferreira was presumably an agent his organization had recruited on board. It was quite possible that the Commissioner would receive simultaneously a message from Colonel Wright that P. Ferreira was suspected of carrying diamonds and should be rigorously searched. 72391 87052 63847 92034. How did one simultaneously leave alone, not repeat not pinpoint, and rigorously search Mr. Ferreira? That, luckily, was not his worry. Perhaps it was Scobie who would suffer any headache there was.

Again he went to the window for a glass of water and again he saw the same girl pass. Or maybe it was not the same girl. He watched the water trickling down between the two thin winglike shoulder-blades. He remembered there was a time when he had not noticed a black skin. He felt as though he had passed years and not months on this coast, all the years between puberty and manhood.

4

"Going out?" Harris asked with surprise. "Where to?"

"Just into town," Wilson said, loosening the knot around his mosquito boots.

"What on earth can you find to do in town at this hour?"

"Business," Wilson said.

Well, he thought, it was business of a kind, the kind of joyless business one did alone, without friends. He had bought a second-hand car a few weeks ago, the first he had ever owned, and he was not yet a very reliable driver. No gadget survived the climate long and every few hundred yards he had to wipe the windscreen with his handkerchief. In Kru Town the hut doors were open and families sat around the kerosene lamps waiting till it was cool enough to sleep. A dead pye-dog lay in the gutter with the rain running over its white swollen belly. He drove in second gear at little more than a walking pace, for civilian head-lamps had to be blacked out to the size of a visiting card and he couldn't see more than fifteen paces ahead. It took him ten minutes to reach the great cotton tree near the police station. There were no lights on in any of the officers' rooms, and he left his car outside the main entrance. If anyone saw it there they would assume he was inside. For a moment he sat with the door open, hesitating. The image of the girl passing in the rain conflicted with the sight of Harris on his shoulder-blades reading a book with a glass of squash at his elbow. He thought sadly, as lust won the day, what a lot of trouble it was; the sadness of the after-taste fell upon his spirits beforehand.

He had forgotten to bring his umbrella and he was wet through before he had walked a dozen yards down the hill. It was the passion of curiosity more than of lust that impelled him now. Sometime or another, if one lived in a place, one must try the local product. It was like having a bar of chocolate shut in a bedroom drawer. Until the box was empty it occupied the mind too much. He thought: When this is over I shall be able to write another poem to Louise.

151

The brothel was a tin-roofed bungalow halfway down the hill on the right-hand side. In the dry season the girls sat outside in the gutter like sparrows: they chatted with the policeman on duty at the top of the hill. The road was never made up, so that nobody drove by the brothel on the way to the wharf or the Cathedral: it could be ignored. Now it turned a shuttered silent front to the muddy street, except where a door, propped open with a rock out of the roadway, opened on a passage. Wilson looked quickly this way and that and stepped inside.

Years ago the passage had been whitewashed and plastered, but rats had torn holes in the plaster and human beings had mutilated the whitewash with scrawls and pencilled names. The walls were tattooed like a sailor's arm: with initials, dates—there were even a pair of hearts interlocked. At first it seemed to Wilson that the place was entirely deserted: on either side of the passage there were little cells nine feet by four with curtains instead of doorways and beds made out of old packing cases spread with a native cloth. He walked rapidly to the end of the passage: then, he told himself, he would turn and go back to the quiet and somnolent security of the room where the Old Downhamian dozed over his book.

He felt an awful disappointment as though he had not found what he was looking for when he reached the end and discovered that the left-hand cell was occupied: in the light of an oil lamp burning on the floor he saw a girl in a dirty shift spread out on the packing cases like a fish on a counter: her bare pink soles dangled over the words "Tate's Sugar." She lay there on duty, waiting for a customer. She grinned at Wilson, not bothering to sit up, and said, "Want jig jig, darling? Ten bob." He had a vision of a girl with a rain-wet back moving for ever out of his sight.

"No," he said, "no," shaking his head and thinking: What a fool I was, what a fool, to drive all the way for only this. The girl giggled as if she understood his stupidity and he heard the slop slop of bare feet coming up the passage from the road: the way was blocked by an old mammy carrying a striped umbrella. She said something to the girl in her native tongue and received a grinning explanation. He had the sense that all this was strange only to him, that it was one of the stock situations the old woman was accustomed to meet in the dark region that she ruled. He said weakly, "I'll just go and get a drink first."

"She get drink," the mammy said. She commanded the girl sharply in the language he couldn't understand and the girl swung her legs off the sugar cases. "You stay here," the mammy said to Wilson, and mechanically, like a hostess whose mind is elsewhere but who must make conversation with however uninteresting a guest, she said, "Pretty girl, jig jig, one pound." Market values here were reversed: the price rose steadily with his reluctance.

"I'm sorry. I can't wait," Wilson said. "Here's ten bob," and he made the preliminary motions of departure, but the old woman paid him no attention at all, blocking the way, smiling steadily like a dentist who knows what's good for you. Here a man's colour had no value: he couldn't bluster as a white man could elsewhere: by entering this narrow plaster passage he had shed every racial, social, and individual trait, he had reduced himself to human nature. If he had wanted to hide, here was the perfect hiding place: if he had wanted to be anonymous, here he was simply a man. Even his reluctance, disgust, and fear were not personal characteristics: they were so common to those who came here for the first time that the old woman knew exactly what each move would be. First the suggestion of a drink, then the offer of money, after that . . .

Wilson said weakly, "Let me by," but he knew that she wouldn't move: she stood watching him, as though he were a tethered animal on whom she was keeping an eye for its owner. She wasn't interested in him, but occasionally she repeated calmingly, "Pretty girl jig jig by an' by." He held out a pound to her and she pocketed it and went on blocking the way. When he tried to push by, she thrust him backwards with a casual pink palm, saying, "By an' by. Jig jig." It had all happened so many hundreds of times before.

Down the passage the girl came carrying a vinegar bottle filled with palm wine, and with a sigh of reluctance Wilson surrendered. The heat between the walls of rain, the musty smell of his companion, the dim and wayward light of the kerosene lamp, reminded him of a vault newly opened for another body to be let down upon its floor. A grievance stirred in him, a hatred of those who had brought him here. In their presence he felt as though his dead veins would bleed again.

Part Three

I. HELEN SAID, "I SAW YOU AT THE BEACH THIS afternoon." Scobie looked apprehensively up from the glass of whisky he was measuring. Something in her voice reminded him oddly of Louise. He said, "I had to find Rees —the Naval Intelligence man."

"You didn't even speak to me."

"I was in a hurry."

"You are so careful, always," she said, and now he realized what was happening and why he had thought of Louise. He wondered sadly whether love always inevitably took the same road. It was not only the act of love itself that was the same. . . . How often in the last two years he had tried to turn away at the critical moment from just such a scene—to save himself but also to save the other victim. He laughed with half a heart and said, "For once I wasn't thinking of you. I had other things in mind."

"What other things?"

"Oh, diamonds . . ."

"Your work is much more important to you than I am," Helen said, and the banality of the phrase, read in how many books, wrung his heart like the too mature remark of a child.

"Yes," he said gravely, "but I'd sacrifice it for you."

"Why?"

"I suppose because you are a human being. One may love a dog more than any other possession, but one wouldn't run down even a strange child to save it."

"Oh," she said impatiently, "why do you always tell me the truth? I don't want the truth all the time."

He put the whisky glass in her hand and said, "My dear,
154

you are unlucky. You are tied up with a middle-aged man. We can't be bothered to lie all the time like the young."

"If you knew," she said, "how tired I get of all your caution. You come here after dark and you go after dark. It's so—so ignoble."

"Yes."

"We always make love—here. Among the junior official's furniture. I don't believe we'd know how to do it anywhere else."

"Poor dear," he said.

She said furiously, "I don't want your pity." But it was not a question of whether she wanted it—she had it. Pity smouldered like decay at his heart. He would never rid himself of it. He knew from experience how passion died away and how love went, but pity always stayed. Nothing ever diminished pity. The conditions of life nurtured it. There was only one person in the world who was unpitiable—himself.

"Can't you ever risk anything? she asked. "You never even write a line to me. You go away on trek for days, but you won't leave anything behind. I can't even have a photograph to make this place human."

"But I haven't got a photograph."

"I suppose you think I'd use your letters against you." He thought wearily: If I shut my eyes it might almost be Louise speaking—the voice was younger, that was all, and perhaps less capable of giving pain. Standing with the whisky glass in his hand he remembered another night—a hundred yards away—the glass had then contained gin. He said gently, "You talk such nonsense, dear."

"You think I'm a child. You tiptoe in—bringing me stamps."

"I'm trying to protect you."

"I don't care a bloody damn if people talk." He recognized the hard swearing of the netball team.

He said, "If they talked enough, my dear, this would come to an end."

"You are not protecting me. You are protecting your wife."

"It comes to the same thing."

"Oh," she said, "to couple me with—that woman." He couldn't prevent the wince that betrayed him. He had underrated her power of giving pain. He could see how she

155

had spotted her success: he had delivered himself into her hands. Now she would always know how to inflict the sharpest stab. She was like a child with a pair of dividers who knows her power to injure. You could never trust a child not to use her advantage.

"My dear," he said, "it's too soon to quarrel."

"That woman," she repeated, watching his eyes. "You'd never leave her, would you?"

"We are married," he said.

"If she knew of this, you'd go back like a whipped dog." No, he thought with tenderness, she hasn't read the best books, unlike Louise.

"I don't know."

"You'll never marry me."

"I can't. You know that. I'm a Catholic. I can't have two wives."

"It's a wonderful excuse," she said. "It doesn't stop you sleeping with me—it only stops you marrying me."

"Yes," he said heavily as though he were accepting a penance. He thought: How much older she is than she was a month ago. She hadn't been capable of a scene then, but she had been educated by love and secrecy: he was beginning to form her. He wondered whether, if this went on long enough, she would be indistinguishable from Louise. In my school, he thought wearily, they learn bitterness and frustration and how to grow old.

"Go on," Helen said, "justify yourself."

"It would take too long," he said. "One would have to begin with the arguments for a God."

"What a twister you are."

He felt appallingly tired—and disappointed. He had looked forward to the evening. All day in the office dealing with a rent case and a case of juvenile delinquency he had looked forward to the Nissen hut, the bare room, the junior official's furniture like his own youth, everything that she had abused. He said, "I meant well."

"What do you mean?"

"I meant to be your friend. To look after you. To make you happier than you were."

"Wasn't I happy?" she asked, as though she were speaking of years ago.

He said, "You were shocked, lonely . . ."

"I couldn't have been as lonely as I am now," she said.

"I go out to the beach with Mrs. Carter when the rain stops. Bagster makes a pass, they think I'm frigid. I come back here before the rain starts and wait for you . . . we drink a glass of whisky . . . you give me some stamps as though I were your small girl . . ."

"I'm sorry," Scobie said, "I've been such a failure. . . ." He put out his hand and covered hers: the knuckles lay under his palm like a small backbone that had been broken. He went slowly and cautiously on, choosing his words carefully, as though he were pursuing a path through evacuated country sown with booby traps: every step he took he expected the explosion. "I'm sorry about everything. I'd do anything—almost anything—to make you happy. I'd stop coming here. I'd go right away—retire . . ."

"You'd be so glad to be rid of me," she said.

"It would be like the end of life."

"Go away if you want to."

"I don't want to go. I want to do what you want."

"You can go if you want to—or you can stay," she said with contempt. "I can't move, can I?"

"If you wanted it, I'd get you on the next boat somehow."

"Oh, how glad you'd be if this were over," she said, and began to weep. He envied her the tears. When he put out a hand to touch her she screamed at him, "Go to hell. Go to hell. Clear out."

"I'll go," he said.

"Yes, go and don't come back."

Outside the door, with the rain cooling his face, running down his hands, it occurred to him how much easier life might be if he took her at her word. He would go into his house and close the door and be alone again: he would write a letter to Louise without a sense of deceit: sleep as he hadn't slept for weeks, dreamlessly. Next day the office, the quiet going home, the evening meal, the locked door. . . . But down the hill, past the transport park, where the lorries crouched under the dripping tarpaulins, the rain fell like tears. He thought of her alone in the hut, wondering whether the irrevocable words had been spoken: if all the tomorrows would consist of Mrs. Carter and Bagster until the boat came and she went home with nothing to remember but misery. He thought: I would never go back there, to the Nissen hut, if it meant that she were happy

and I suffered. But if I were happy and she suffered . . .
That was what he could not face. Inexorably the other's
point of view rose on the path like a murdered innocent.
She's right, he thought, who could bear my caution?

As he opened his door a rat that had been nosing at his
food-safe retreated without haste up the stairs. This was
what Louise had hated and feared: he had at least made
her happy, and now ponderously, with planned and careful
recklessness, he set about trying to make things right for
Helen. He sat down at his table and taking a sheet of type-
writing paper—official paper stamped with the Government water-mark—he began to compose a letter.

He wrote: *My darling*—he wanted to put himself entirely in her hands, but to leave her anonymous. He looked
at his watch and added in the right-hand corner, as though
he were making a police report, *12:35 a.m. Burnside, September 5.* He went carefully on, *I love you more than myself, more than my wife, more than God I think. Please
keep this letter. Don't burn it. When you are angry with
me, read it. I am trying very hard to tell the truth. I want
more than anything in the world to make you happy. . . .*
The banality of the phrases saddened him: they seemed
to have no truth personal to herself: they had been used
too often. If I were young, he thought, I would be able to
find the right words, the new words, but all this has happened to me before. He wrote again, *I love you. Forgive
me*, signed and folded the paper.

He put on his mackintosh and went out again in the
rain. Wounds festered in the damp, they never healed.
Scratch your finger and in a few hours there would be a
little coating of green skin. He carried a sense of corruption
up the hill. A soldier shouted something in his sleep in the
transport park—a single word like a hieroglyphic on a wall
which Scobie could not interpret—the men were Nigerians.
The rain hammered on the Nissen roofs, and he thought:
Why did I write that? Why did I write "more than God"?
She would have been satisfied with "more than Louise."
Even if that's true, why did I write it? The sky wept end-
lessly around him: he had the sense of wounds that never
healed. He said softly aloud, "O God, I have deserted you.
Do not you desert me." When he came to her door he
thrust the letter under it: he heard the rustle of the paper
on the cement floor but nothing else. Remembering the
158

childish figure carried past him on the stretcher, he was saddened to think how much had happened, how uselessly, to make him now say to himself with resentment: She will never again be able to accuse me of caution.

2

"I was just passing by," Father Rank said, "so I thought I'd look in." The evening rain fell in grey ecclesiastical folds, and a lorry howled its way towards the hills.

"Come in," Scobie said. "I'm out of whisky. But there's beer—or gin."

"I saw you up at the Nissens, so I thought I'd follow you down. You are not busy?"

"I'm having dinner with the Commissioner, but not for another hour."

Father Rank moved restlessly around the room, while Scobie took the beer out of the ice-box. "Would you have heard from Louise lately?" he asked.

"Not for a fortnight," Scobie said, "but there've been some sinkings in the south."

Father Rank let himself down in the Government arm-chair with his glass between his knees. There was no sound but the rain scraping on the roof. Scobie cleared his throat and then the silence came back. He had the odd sense that Father Rank, like one of his own junior officers, was waiting there for orders.

"The rains will soon be over," Scobie said.

"It must be six months now since your wife went."

"Seven."

"Will you be taking your leave in South Africa?" Father Rank asked, looking away and taking a draught of his beer.

"I've postponed my leave. The young men need it more."

"Everybody needs leave."

"You've been here twelve years without it, Father."

"Ah, but that's different," Father Rank said. He got up again and moved restlessly down one wall and along another. He turned an expression of undefined appeal towards Scobie. "Sometimes," he said, "I feel as though I weren't a working man at all." He stopped and stared and half raised his hands, and Scobie remembered Father Clay dodging an unseen figure in his restless walk. He felt as though an appeal were being made to which he couldn't find an answer. He said weakly, "There's no one works harder than you, Father."

Father Rank returned draggingly to his chair. He said, "It'll be good when the rains are over."

"How's the mammy out by Congo Creek? I heard she was dying."

"She'll be gone this week. She's a good woman." He took another draught of beer and then doubled up in the chair with his hand on his stomach. "The wind," he said. "I get the wind badly."

"You shouldn't drink bottled beer, Father."

"The dying," Father Rank said, "that's what I'm here for. They send for me when they are dying." He raised eyes bleary with too much quinine and said harshly and hopelessly, "I've never been any good to the living, Scobie."

"You are talking nonsense, Father."

"When I was a novice, I thought that people talked to their priests, and I thought God somehow gave the right words. Don't mind me, Scobie, don't listen to me. It's the rains—they always get me down about this time. God doesn't give the right words, Scobie. I had a parish once in Northampton. They make boots there. They used to ask me out to tea, and I'd sit and watch their hands pouring out, and we'd talk of the Children of Mary and repairs to the church roof. They were very generous in Northampton. I only had to ask and they'd give. I wasn't of any use to a single living soul, Scobie. I thought, in Africa things will be different. You see, I'm not a reading man, Scobie: I never had much talent for loving God as some people do. I wanted to be of use, that's all. Don't listen to me. It's the rains. I haven't talked like this for five years. Except to the mirror. If people are in trouble they'd go to you, Scobie, not to me. They ask me to dinner to hear the gossip. And if you were in trouble where would you go?" And Scobie was again aware of those bleary and appealing eyes, waiting, through the dry seasons and the rains, for something that never happened. Could I shift my burden there, he wondered: Could I tell him that I love two women: that I don't know what to do? What would be the use? I know the answers as well as he does. One should look after one's own soul at whatever cost to another, and that's what I can't do, what I shall never be able to do. It wasn't he who required the magic word, it was the priest, and he couldn't give it.

"I'm not the kind of man to get into trouble, Father. I'm dull and middle-aged," and looking away, unwilling to see distress, he heard Father Rank's clapper miserably sounding, "Ho! ho! ho!"

3

On his way to the Commissioner's bungalow, Scobie looked in at his office. A message was written in pencil on his pad: *I looked in to see you. Nothing important. Wilson.* It struck him as odd: he had not seen Wilson for some weeks, and if his visit had no importance why had he so carefully recorded it? He opened the drawer of his desk to find a packet of cigarettes and noticed at once that something was out of order: he considered the contents carefully: his indelible pencil was missing. Obviously Wilson had looked for a pencil with which to write his message and had forgotten to put it back. But why the message?

In the charge room the sergeant said, "Mr. Wilson come to see you, sah."

"Yes, he left a message."

So that was it, he thought: I would have known anyway, so he considered it best to let me know himself. He returned to his office and looked again at his desk. It seemed to him that a file had been shifted, but he couldn't be sure. He opened his drawer, but there was nothing there which would interest a soul. Only the broken rosary caught his eye—something which should have been mended a long while ago. He took it out and put it in his pocket.

"Whisky?" the Commissioner asked.

"Thank you," Scobie said, holding the glass up between himself and the Commissioner. "Do you trust me?"

"Yes."

"Am I the only one who doesn't know about Wilson?"

The Commissioner smiled, lying back at ease, unembarrassed. "Nobody knows officially—except myself and the manager of the U.A.C.—that was essential, of course. The Governor too and whoever deals with the cables marked 'Most Secret.' I'm glad you've tumbled to it."

"I wanted you to know that—up to date of course—I've been trustworthy."

"You don't need to tell me, Scobie."

"In the case of Tallit's cousin, we couldn't have done anything different."

"Of course not."

Scobie said, "There is one thing you don't know, though. I borrowed two hundred pounds from Yusef so that I could send Louise to South Africa. I pay him four per cent interest. The arrangement is purely commercial, but if you want my head for it . . ."

"I'm glad you told me," the Commissioner said. "You see, Wilson got the idea that you were being black-mailed. He must have dug up those payments somehow."

"Yusef wouldn't black-mail for money."

"I told him that."

"Do you want my head . . . ?"

"I need your head, Scobie, here. You're the only officer I really trust."

Scobie stretched out a hand with an empty glass in it: it was like a handclasp.

"Say when."

"When."

Men can become twins with age: the past was their common womb: the six months of rain and the six months of sun was the period of their common gestation. They needed only a few words and a few gestures to convey their meaning. They had graduated through the same fevers: they were moved by the same love and contempt.

"Derry reports there've been some big thefts from the mines."

"Commercial?"

"Gem stones. Is it Yusef—or Tallit?"

"It might be Yusef," Scobie said. "I don't think he deals in industrial diamonds. He calls them gravel. But of course one can't be sure."

"The *Esperança* will be in in a few days. We've got to be careful."

"What does Wilson say?"

"He swears by Tallit. Yusef is the villain of his piece—and you, Scobie."

"I haven't seen Yusef for a long while."

"I know."

"I begin to know what these Syrians feel—watched and reported on."

"He reports on all of us, Scobie. Fraser, Tod, Thimble-rigg, myself. He thinks I'm too easygoing. It doesn't really matter, though. Wright tears up his reports, and of course Wilson reports on him."

"Does anybody report on Wilson?"

"I suppose so."

He walked up, at midnight, to the Nissen huts: in the black-out he felt momentarily safe, unwatched, unreported on: in the soggy ground his footsteps made the smallest sounds, but as he passed Wilson's hut he was aware again of the deep necessity for caution. An awful weariness touched him, and he thought: I will go home: I won't creep by to her tonight. Her last words had been "Don't come back": couldn't one, for once, take somebody at their word? He stood twenty yards from Wilson's hut, watching the crack of light between the curtains. A drunken voice shouted somewhere up the hill and the first spatter of the returning rain licked his face. He thought: I'd go back and go to bed, in the morning I'd write to Louise and in the evening go to Confession: the day after that God would return to me in a priest's hands: life would be simple again. He would be at peace sitting under the handcuffs in the office. Virtue, the good life, tempted him in the dark like a sin. The rain blurred his eyes: the ground sucked at his feet as they trod reluctantly towards the Nissen hut.

He knocked twice and the door immediately opened. He had prayed between the two knocks that anger might still be there behind the door, that he wouldn't be wanted. He couldn't shut his eyes or his ears to any human need of him: he was not the centurion, but a man in the ranks who had to do the bidding of a hundred centurions, and when the door opened, he could tell the command was going to be given again—the command to stay, to love, to accept responsibility, to lie.

"Oh, my dear," she said, "I thought you were never coming. I bitched you so."

"I'll always come if you want me."

"Will you?"

"Always. If I'm alive." God can wait, he thought: how can one love God at the expense of one of his creatures? Would a woman accept a love for which a child had to be sacrificed?

Carefully they drew the curtains close before turning up the lamps: they lifted discretion between them like a cradle.

She said, "I've been afraid all day that you wouldn't come."

"Of course I came."

"I told you to go away. Never pay any attention to me when I tell you to go away. Promise."

"I promise," he said, with a sense of despair, as though he were signing away the whole future.

"If you hadn't come back . . ." she said, and became lost in thought between the lamps. He could see her searching for herself, frowning in the effort to see where she would have been. . . . "I don't know. Perhaps I'd have slutted with Bagster, or killed myself, or both. I think both."

He said anxiously, "You mustn't think like that. I'll always be here if you need me, as long as I'm alive."

"Why do you keep on saying as long as I'm alive?"

"There are thirty years between us."

For the first time that night they kissed. She said, "I can't feel the years."

"Why did you think I wouldn't come?" Scobie said. "You got my letter."

"Your letter?"

"The one I pushed under your door last night."

She said, with fear, "I never saw a letter. What did you say?"

He touched her face and smiled to hide the danger. "Everything. I didn't want to be cautious any longer. I put down everything."

"Even your name?"

"I think so. Anyway, it's signed with my handwriting."

"There's a mat by the door. It must be under the mat."

But they both knew it wouldn't be there. It was as if all along they had foreseen how disaster would come in by that particular door.

"Who would have taken it?"

He tried to soothe her nerves. "Probably your boy threw it away, thought it was waste-paper. It wasn't in an envelope. Nobody could know whom I was writing to."

"As if that mattered. Darling," she said, "I feel sick. Really sick. Somebody's getting something on you. I wish I'd died in that boat."

"You're imagining things. Probably I didn't push the note far enough. When your boy opened the door in the morning it blew away or got trampled in the mud." He spoke with all the conviction he could summon: it was just possible.

"Don't let me ever do you any harm," she implored, and every phrase she used fastened the fetters more firmly round his wrists. He put out his hands to her and lied firmly, "You'll never do me harm. Don't worry about a lost letter. I exaggerated. It said nothing really—nothing that a stranger would understand. My dear, don't worry."

"Listen, dear. Don't stay tonight. I'm nervous. I feel—watched. Say good night now and go away. But come back. Oh, my dear, come back."

The light was still on in Wilson's hut as he passed. Opening the door of his own dark house he saw a piece of paper on the floor. It gave him an odd shock as though the missing letter had returned, like a cat, to its old home. But when he picked it up, it wasn't his letter, though this too was a message of love. It was a telegram addressed to him at police headquarters, and the signature, written in full for the sake of censorship, Louise Scobie, was like a blow struck by a boxer with a longer reach than he possessed. *Have written am on my way home have been a fool stop love*—and then that name as formal as a seal.

He sat down and said aloud, "I've got to think": his head swam with nausea. He thought: If I had never written that other letter, if I had taken Helen at her word and gone away, how easily then life could have been arranged again. But he remembered his words in the last ten minutes: "I'll always be here if you need me as long as I'm alive." That constituted an oath as ineffaceable as the vow by the Ealing altar. The wind was coming up from the sea—the rains ended, as they began, with typhoons: the curtains blew in and he ran to the windows and pulled them to. Upstairs the bedroom windows clattered to and fro, tearing at hinges.

Turning from closing them he looked at the bare dressing-table where soon the photographs and the pots would be back again—one photograph in particular. The happy Scobie, he thought, my one success. A child in hospital said "Father" as the shadow of a rabbit shifted on the pillow: a girl went by on a stretcher clutching a stamp-album —Why me, he thought, why do they need me—a dull, middle-aged police officer who had failed for promotion? I've got nothing to give them that they can't get elsewhere: why can't they leave me in peace? Elsewhere there was younger and better love, more security. It sometimes seemed to him now that all he could share with them was his despair.

Leaning back against the dressing-table, he tried to pray. The Lord's Prayer lay as dead on his tongue as a legal document: it wasn't his daily bread that he wanted, but so much more. He wanted happiness for others and solitude and peace for himself. "I don't want to plan any more," he said suddenly aloud. "They wouldn't need me if I were dead. No one needs the dead. The dead can be forgotten. O God, give me death before I give them unhappiness." But the words sounded melodramatically in his own ears. He told himself that he mustn't get hysterical: there was far too much planning to do for an hysterical man, and going downstairs again he thought three aspirins or perhaps four were what he required in this situation—this banal situation. He took a bottle of filtered water out of the ice-box and dissolved the aspirins. He wondered how it would feel to drain death as simply as these aspirins which now stuck sourly in his throat. The priests told you it was the unforgivable sin, the final expression of an unrepentant despair, and of course one accepted the Church's teaching. But they taught also that God had sometimes broken his own laws, and was it more impossible for him to put out a hand of forgiveness into the suicidal darkness and chaos than to have woken himself in the tomb, behind the stone? Christ had not been murdered: you couldn't murder God: Christ had killed himself: he had hanged himself on the Cross as surely as Pemberton from the picture rail.

He put his glass down and thought again: I must not get hysterical. Two people's happiness were in his hands, and he must learn to juggle with strong nerves. Calmness was everything. He took out his diary and began to write against the date Wednesday, September 6: *Dinner with the Commissioner. Satisfactory talk about W. Called on Helen for a few minutes. Telegram from Louise that she is on the way home.*

He hesitated for a moment and then wrote: *Father Rank called in for drink before dinner. A little overwrought. He needs leave.* He read this over and scored out the last two sentences. It was seldom in the record that he allowed himself an expression of opinion.

II. THE TELEGRAM LAY ON HIS MIND ALL DAY: ordinary life—the two hours in court on a perjury case—had the unreality of a country one is leaving for ever. One says, At this hour, in that village, these people I once knew are sitting down at table just as they did a year ago when I was there, but one is not convinced that any life goes on the same as ever outside the consciousness. All Scobie's consciousness was on the telegram, on that nameless boat edging its way now up the African coast line from the south. God forgive me, he thought, when his mind lit for a moment on the possibility that it might never arrive. In our hearts there is a ruthless dictator, ready to contemplate the misery of a thousand strangers if it will ensure the happiness of the few we love.

At the end of the perjury case Fellowes, the Sanitary Inspector, caught him at the door. "Come to chop tonight, Scobie. We've got a bit of real Argentine beef." It was too much of an effort in this dream world to refuse an invitation. "Wilson's coming," Fellowes said. "To tell you the truth, he helped us with the beef. You like him, don't you?"

"Yes. I thought it was you who didn't."

"Oh, the Club's got to move with the times, and all sorts of people go into trade nowadays. I admit I was hasty.

Bit boozed up, I wouldn't be surprised. He was at Downham: we used to play them when I was at Lancing."

Driving out to the familiar house he had once occupied himself on the hills Scobie thought listlessly, I must speak to Helen soon. She mustn't learn this from someone else. Life always repeated the same pattern: there was always, sooner or later, bad news that had to be broken, comforting lies to be uttered, pink gins to be consumed to keep misery away.

He came to the long bungalow living-room and there at the end of it was Helen. With a sense of shock he realized that never before had he seen her like a stranger in another man's house: never before had he seen her dressed for an evening's party. "You know Mrs. Rolt, don't you?" Fellowes said. There was no irony in his voice. Scobie thought, with a tremor of self-disgust: How clever we've been: how successfully we've deceived the gossipers of a small colony. It oughtn't to be possible for lovers to deceive so well. Wasn't love supposed to be spontaneous, reckless . . . ?

"Yes," he said, "I'm an old friend of Mrs. Rolt. I was at Pende when she was brought across." He stood by the table a dozen feet away while Fellowes mixed the drinks, and watched her while she talked to Mrs. Fellowes, talked easily, naturally, as if there had been no moment in that dark Nissen hut below the hill when she had cried out in his arms. Would I, he wondered, if I had come in tonight and seen her for the first time, ever have felt any love at all?

"Now which was yours, Mrs. Rolt?"

"A pink gin."

"I wish I could get my wife to drink them. I can't bear her gin and orange."

Scobie said, "If I'd known you were going to be here, I'd have called for you."

"I wish you had," Helen said. "You never come and see me." She turned to Fellowes and said with an ease that horrified him, "He was so kind to me in hospital at Pende, but I think he only likes the sick."

Fellowes stroked his little ginger moustache, poured himself out some more gin, and said, "He's scared of you, Mrs. Rolt. All we married men are." At the phrase "married men" Scobie could see that tired exhausted figure on the stretcher turn away from them both as from strong sunlight. She said with false blandness, "Do you think I could have one more without getting tight?"

"Ah, here's Wilson," Fellowes said, and there he was with his pink innocent self-distrustful face and his badly tied cummerbund. "You know everybody, don't you? You and Mrs. Rolt are neighbours."

"We haven't met, though," Wilson said, and began automatically to blush.

"I don't know what's come over the men in this place," said Fellowes. "You and Scobie both neighbours and neither of you see anything of Mrs. Rolt," and Scobie was immediately aware of Wilson's gaze speculatively turned upon him. "*I* wouldn't be so bashful," Fellowes said, pouring out the pink gins.

"Dr. Sykes late as usual," Mrs. Fellowes commented from the end of the room, but at that moment, treading heavily up the outside stairs, sensible in a dark dress and mosquito boots, came Dr. Sykes. "Just in time for a drink, Jessie," Fellowes said. "What's it to be?"

"Double Scotch," Dr. Sykes said. She glared around through her thick glasses and added, "Evening all."

As they went in to dinner Scobie said, "I've got to see you," but catching Wilson's eye he added, "about your furniture."

"My furniture?"

"I think I could get you some extra chairs." As conspirators they were much too young: they had not yet absorbed a whole code book into their memory: he was uncertain whether she had understood the mutilated phrase. All through dinner he sat silent, dreading the time when he would be alone with her, afraid to lose the least opportunity; when he put his hand in his pocket for a handkerchief the telegram crumpled in his fingers . . . *have been a fool stop love.*

"Of course you know more about it than we do, Major Scobie," Dr. Sykes said.

"I'm sorry. I missed . . ."

"We were talking about the Pemberton case." So already in a few months it had become a case. When something became a case it no longer seemed to concern a human being: there was no shame or suffering in a case: the boy on the bed was cleaned and tidied, laid out for the text-book of psychology.

169

"I was saying," Wilson said, "that Pemberton chose an odd way to kill himself. I would have chosen a sleeping draught."

"It wouldn't be easy to get a sleeping draught in Bamba," Dr. Sykes said. "It was probably a sudden decision."

"I wouldn't have caused all that fuss," said Fellowes. "A chap's got the right to take his own life, of course, but there's no need for fuss. An overdose of sleeping draught— I agree with Wilson—that's the way."

"You still have to get your prescription," Dr. Sykes said.

Scobie with his fingers on the telegram remembered the letter signed "Dicky": the immature handwriting: the marks of cigarettes on the chairs: the novels of Wallace: the stigmata of loneliness. Through two thousand years, he thought, we have discussed Christ's agony in just this disinterested way.

"Pemberton was always a bit of a fool," Fellowes said.

"A sleeping draught is invariably tricky," Dr. Sykes said. Her big lenses reflected the electric globe as she turned them like a lighthouse in Scobie's direction. "Your experience will tell you how tricky. Insurance companies never like sleeping draughts, and no coroner could lend himself to a deliberate fraud."

"How can they tell?" Wilson asked.

"Take luminal, for instance. Nobody could really take enough luminal by accident . . ."

Scobie looked across the table at Helen: she ate slowly, without appetite, her eyes on her plate. Their silences seemed to isolate them: this was a subject the unhappy could never discuss impersonally. Again he was aware of Wilson looking from one to another of them, and Scobie drew desperately at his mind for any phrase that would end their dangerous solitude. They could not even be silent together with safety.

He said, "What's the way out you'd recommend, Dr. Sykes?"

"Well, there are bathing accidents—but even they need a good deal of explanation. If a man's brave enough to step in front of a car, but it's too uncertain . . ."

"And involves somebody else," Scobie said.

"Personally," Dr. Sykes said, grinning under her glasses, "I should have no difficulties. In my position, I should

170

classify myself as a false angina case and then get one of my colleagues to prescribe . . ."

Helen said with sudden violence, "What a beastly talk this is. You've got no business to tell . . ."

"My dear," Dr. Sykes said, revolving her malevolent beams, "when you've been a doctor as long as I have been you know your company. I don't think any of us are likely . . ."

Mrs. Fellowes said, "Have another helping of fruit salad, Mrs. Rolt."

"Are you a Catholic, Mrs. Rolt?" Fellowes asked. "Of course they take very strong views."

"No, I'm not a Catholic."

"But they do, don't they, Scobie?"

"We are taught," Scobie said, "that it's the unforgivable sin."

"That you'll go to hell?"

"To hell."

"But do you really, seriously, Major Scobie," Dr. Sykes asked, "believe in hell?"

"Oh, yes, I do."

"In flames and torment?"

"Perhaps not quite that. They tell us it may be a permanent sense of loss."

"That sort of hell wouldn't worry me," Fellowes said.

"Perhaps you've never lost anything of any importance," Scobie said.

The real object of the dinner party had been the Argentine beef. With that consumed there was nothing to keep them together (Mrs. Fellowes didn't play cards). Fellowes busied himself about the beer, and Wilson was wedged between the sour silence of Mrs. Fellowes and Dr. Sykes's garrulity.

"Let's get a breath of air," Scobie suggested.

"Wise?"

"It would look odd if we didn't," Scobie said.

"Going to look at the stars?" Fellowes called, pouring out the beer. "Making up for lost time, Scobie? Take your glasses with you."

They balanced their glasses on the rail of the verandah. Helen said, "I haven't found your letter."

"Forget it, dear."

171

"Wasn't that what you wanted to see me about?"

"No."

He could see the outline of her face against the sky, doomed to go out as the rain clouds advanced. He said, "My dear, I've got bad news."

"Somebody knows?"

"Oh, no, nobody knows." He said, "Last night I had a telegram from my wife. She's on the way home." One of the glasses fell from the rail and smashed in the yard.

The lips repeated bitterly the word "home" as if that were the only word she had grasped. He said quickly, moving his hand along the rail and failing to reach her, "Her home. It will never be my home again."

"Oh, yes, it will. Now it will be."

He swore carefully, "I shall never again want any home without you." The rain clouds had reached the moon and her face went out like a candle in a sudden draught of wind. He had the sense that he was embarking now on a longer journey than he had ever intended: if he looked back he knew that he would see only a ravaged countryside. A light suddenly shone on both of them as a door opened. He said sharply, "Mind the black-out," and thought: at least we were not standing together, but how, how did our faces look? Wilson's voice said, "We thought a fight was going on. We heard a glass break."

"Mrs. Rolt lost all her beer."

"For God's sake call me Helen," she said drearily, "everybody else does, Major Scobie."

"Am I interrupting something?"

"A scene of unbridled passion," Helen said. "It's left me shaken. I want to go home."

"I'll drive you down," Scobie said. "It's getting late."

"I wouldn't trust you, and anyway Dr. Sykes is dying to talk to you about suicide. I won't break up the party. Haven't you got a car, Mr. Wilson?"

"Of course. I'd be delighted."

"You could always drive down and come straight back."

"I'm an early bird myself," Wilson said.

"I'll just go in then and say good night."

When he saw her face again in the light he thought: Do I worry too much? Couldn't this for her be just the end of an episode? He heard her saying to Mrs. Fellowes, "The Argentine beef certainly was lovely."

172

"We've got Mr. Wilson to thank for it."

The phrases went to and fro like shuttlecocks. Somebody laughed (it was Fellowes or Wilson) and said, "You're right there," and Dr. Sykes's spectacles made a dot dash dot on the ceiling. He couldn't watch the car move off without disturbing the black-out: he listened to the starter retching and retching, the racing of the engine, and then the slow decline to silence.

Dr. Sykes said, "They should have kept Mrs. Rolt in hospital a while longer."

"Why?"

"Nerves. I could feel it when she shook hands."

He waited another half an hour and then he drove home. As usual Ali was waiting for him, dozing uneasily on the kitchen step. He lit Scobie to the door with his torch. "Missus leave letter," he said, and took an envelope out of his shirt.

"Why didn't you leave it on my table?"

"Massa in there."

"What massa?" But by that time the door was open and he saw Yusef stretched in a chair, asleep, breathing so gently that the hair lay motionless on his chest.

"I tell him go away," Ali said with contempt, "but he stay."

"That's all right. Go to bed."

He had a sense that life was closing in on him. Yusef had never been here since the night he came to enquire after Louise and to lay his trap for Tallit. Quietly, so as not to disturb the sleeping man and bring *that* problem on his heels, he opened the note from Helen. She must have written it immediately she got home. He read, *My darling, this is serius. I can't say this to you, so I'm putting it on paper. Only I'll give it to Ali. You trust Ali. When I heard your wife was coming back . . .*

Yusef opened his eyes and said, "Excuse me, Major Scobie, for intruding."

"Do you want a drink? Beer. Gin. My whisky's finished."

"May I send you a case?" Yusef began automatically, and then laughed. "I always forget. I must not send you things."

Scobie sat down at the table and laid the note open in front of him. Nothing could be so important as those next sentences. He said, "What do you want, Yusef?" and read

173

on. When I heard your wife was coming back, I was angry and bitter. It was stupid of me. Nothing is your fault. You are a Catholic. I wish you weren't, but even if you weren't you hate not keeping your word.

"Finish your reading, Major Scobie, I can wait."

"It isn't really important," Scobie said, dragging his eyes from the large immature letters, the mistake in spelling which was like a pain in his heart. "Tell me what you want, Yusef," and back his eyes went to the letter. *That's why I'm writing. Because last night you made promises about not leaving me and I don't want you ever to be bound to me with promises. My dear, all your promises . . .*

"Major Scobie, when I lent you money, I swear it was for friendship, just friendship. I never wanted to ask anything of you, anything at all, not even the four per cent. I wouldn't even have asked for your friendship . . . I was your friend . . . this is very confusing, words are very complicated, Major Scobie."

"You've kept the bargain, Yusef. I don't complain about Tallit's cousin." He read on: *. . . belong to your wife. Nothing you say to me is a promise. Please please remember that. If you never want to see me again, don't write, don't speak. And, dear, if you just want to see me sometimes, see me sometimes. I'll tell any lies you like.*

"Do finish what you are reading, Major Scobie. Because what I have to speak about is very very important."

My dear my dear leave me if you want to or have me as your hore if you want to. He thought: She's only heard the word, never seen it spelt: they cut it out of the school Shakespeares. *Good night. Don't worry, my darling.* He said savagely, "All right, Yusef. What is it that's so important?"

"Major Scobie, I have got after all to ask you a favour. It has nothing to do with the money I lent you. If you can do this for me it will be friendship, just friendship."

"It's late, Yusef, tell me what it is."

"The Esperança will be in the day after tomorrow. I want a small packet taken on board for me and left with the captain."

"What's in the packet?"

"Major Scobie, don't ask. I am your friend. I would rather have this a secret. It will harm no one at all."

174

"Of course, Yusef, I can't do it. You know that."

"I assure you, Major Scobie, on my word"—he leant forward in the chair and laid his hand on the black fur of his chest—"on my word as a friend, the package contains nothing, nothing for the Germans. No industrial diamonds, Major Scobie."

"Gem stones?"

"Nothing for the Germans. Nothing that will hurt your country."

"Yusef, you can't really believe that I'd agree?"

The tight drill trousers squeezed to the edge of the chair: for one moment Scobie thought that Yusef was going on his knees to him. He said, "Major Scobie, I implore you . . . It is important for you as well as for me." His voice broke with genuine emotion: "I want to be a friend. I want to be a friend."

Scobie said, "I'd better warn you before you say any more, Yusef, that the Commissioner *does* know about our arrangement."

"I daresay. I daresay, but this is so much worse. Major Scobie, on my word of honour, this will do no harm to anyone. Just do this one act of friendship, and I'll never ask another. Do it of your own free will, Major Scobie. There is no bribe. I offer no bribe."

His eye went back to the letter: *My darling, this is serius.* Serius—his eye this time read it as *servus*—a slave: a servant of the servants of God. It was like an unwise command which he had none the less to obey. He felt as though he were turning his back on peace for ever. With his eyes open, knowing the consequences, he entered the territory of lies without a passport for return.

"What were you saying, Yusef? I didn't catch . . ."

"Just once more I ask you . . ."

"No, Yusef."

"Major Scobie," Yusef said, sitting bolt upright in his chair, speaking with a sudden odd formality, as though a stranger had joined them and they were no longer alone, "you remember Pemberton?"

"Of course."

"His boy came into my employ."

"Pemberton's boy?" (*Nothing you say to me is a promise.*)

"Pemberton's boy is Mrs. Rolt's boy."

Scobie's eyes remained on the letter, but he no longer read what he saw.

"Her boy brought me a letter. You see I asked him to keep his eyes—skinned—is that the right word?"

"You have a very good knowledge of English, Yusef. Who read it to you?"

"That doesn't matter."

The formal voice suddenly stopped and the old Yusef implored again: "Oh, Major Scobie, what made you write such a letter? It was asking for trouble."

"One can't be wise all the time, Yusef. One would die of disgust."

"You see, it has put you in my hands."

"I wouldn't mind that so much. But to put three people in your hands . . ."

"If only you would have done an act of friendship . . ."

"Go on, Yusef. You must complete your blackmail. You can't get away with half a threat."

"I wish I could dig a hole and put the package in it. But the war's going badly, Major Scobie. I am doing this not for myself, but for my father and mother, my half-brother, my three sisters—and there are cousins too."

"Quite a family."

"You see, if the English are beaten all my stores have no value at all."

"What do you propose to do with the letter, Yusef?"

"I hear from a clerk in the cable company that your wife is on her way back. I will have the letter handed to her as soon as she lands."

He remembered the telegram signed Louise Scobie: . . . *have been a fool stop love.* It would be a cold welcome, he thought.

"And if I give your package to the captain of the *Esperança?*"

"My boy will be waiting on the wharf. In return for the captain's receipt he will give you an envelope with your letter inside."

"You trust your boy?"

"Just as you trust Ali."

"Suppose I demand the letter first and give you my word . . ."

176

"It is the penalty of the black-mailer, Major Scobie, that he has no debts of honour. You would be quite right to cheat me."

"Suppose you cheat me?"

"That wouldn't be right. And formerly I was your friend."

"You very nearly were," Scobie reluctantly admitted.

"I am the base Indian."

"The base Indian?"

"Who threw away a pearl," Yusef sadly said. "That was in the play by Shakespeare the Ordnance Corps gave in the Memorial Hall. I have always remembered it."

2

"Well," Druce said, "I'm afraid we'll have to get to work now."

"One more glass," the captain of the *Esperança* said.

"Not if we are going to release you before the boom closes. See you later, Scobie."

When the door of the cabin closed the captain said breathlessly, "I am still here."

"So I see. I told you there are often mistakes—minutes go to the wrong place, files are lost."

"I believe none of that," the captain said. "I believe you helped me." He dripped gently with sweat in the stuffy cabin. He added, "I pray for you at Mass, and I have brought you this. It was all that I could find for you in Lobito. She is a very obscure Saint"—and he slid across the table between them a holy medal the size of a nickel piece. "Santa . . . I don't remember her name. She had something to do with Angola, I think," the captain explained.

"Thank you," Scobie said. The package in his pocket seemed to him to weigh as heavily as a gun against his thigh. He let the last drops of port settle in the well of his glass and then drained them. He said, "This time I have something for you." A terrible reluctance cramped his fingers.

"For me?"

"Yes."

How light the little package actually was now that it

was on the table between them. What had weighed like a gun in the pocket might now have contained little more than fifty cigarettes. He said, "Someone who comes on board with the pilot at Lisbon will ask you if you have any American cigarettes. You will give him this package."

"Is this Government business?"

"No. The Government would never pay as well as this." He laid a packet of notes upon the table.

"This surprises me," the captain said, with an odd note of disappointment. "You have put yourself in my hands."

"You were in mine," Scobie said.

"I don't forget. Nor will my daughter. She is married outside the Church, but she has faith. She prays for you too."

"The prayers we pray then don't count, surely?"

"No, but when the moment of Grace comes they rise"— the captain raised his fat arms in an absurd and touching gesture—"all at once together like a flock of birds."

"I shall be glad of them," Scobie said.

"You can trust me, of course."

"Of course. Now I must search your cabin."

"You do not trust me very far."

"That package," Scobie said, "has nothing to do with the war."

"Are you sure?"

"I am nearly sure."

He began his search. Once, pausing by a mirror, he saw poised over his own shoulder a stranger's face, a fat sweating unreliable face. Momentarily he wondered: Who can that be? before he realized that it was only this new unfamiliar look of pity that made it strange to him. He thought: Am I really one of those whom people pity?

Book 3

Part One

Part One

I. THE RAINS WERE OVER AND THE EARTH STEAMED. Flies everywhere settled in clouds, and the hospital was full of malaria patients. Further up the coast they were dying of blackwater, and yet for a while there was a sense of relief. It was as if the world had become quiet again, now that the drumming on the iron roofs was over. In the town the deep scent of flowers modified the zoo smell in the corridors of the police station. An hour after the boom was opened the liner moved in from the south unescorted.

Scobie went out in the police boat as soon as the liner anchored. His mouth felt stiff with welcome: he practised on his tongue phrases which would seem warm and unaffected, and he thought: what a long way I have travelled to make me rehearse a welcome. He hoped he would find Louise in one of the public rooms: it would be easier to greet her in front of strangers, but there was no sign of her anywhere. He had to ask at the purser's office for her cabin number.

Even then, of course, there was the hope that it would be shared. No cabin nowadays held less than six passengers.

But when he knocked and the door was opened, nobody was there but Louise. He felt like a caller at a strange house with something to sell. There was a question-mark at the end of his voice when he said, "Louise?"

"Henry." She added, "Come inside." When once he was within the cabin there was nothing to do but kiss. He avoided her mouth—the mouth reveals so much, but she wouldn't be content until she had pulled his face round and left the seal of her return on his lips. "Oh, my dear, here I am."

"Here you are," he said, seeking desperately for the phrases he had rehearsed.

"They've all been so sweet," she explained. "They are keeping away so that I can see you alone."

"You've had a good trip?"

"I think we were chased once."

"I was very anxious," he said, and thought: That is the first lie. I may as well take the plunge now. He said, "I've missed you so much."

"I was a fool to go away, darling." Through the port-hole the houses sparkled like mica in the haze of heat. The cabin smelt closely of women, of powder, nail varnish, and night-dresses. He said, "Let's get ashore."

But she detained him a little while yet. "Darling," she said, "I've made a lot of resolutions while I've been away. Everything now is going to be different. I'm not going to rattle you any more." She repeated, "Everything will be different," and he thought sadly that that at any rate was the truth, the bleak truth.

Standing at the window of his house while Ali and the small boy carried in the trunks he looked up the hill towards the Nissen huts: it was as if a landslide had suddenly put an immeasurable distance between him and them. They were so distant that at first there was no pain, any more than for an episode of youth remembered with the faintest melancholy. Did my lies really start, he wondered, when I wrote that letter? Can I really love her more than Louise? Do I, in my heart of hearts, love either of them, or is it only that this automatic terrible pity goes out to any human need—and makes it worse? Any victim demands allegiance. Upstairs silence and solitude were being hammered away: tin-tacks were being driven in: weights fell on the floor and shook the ceiling. Louise's voice was raised in cheerful peremptory commands. There was a rattle of objects on the dressing-table. He went upstairs and from the doorway saw the face in the white communion veil staring back at him again: the dead too had returned. Life was not the same without the dead. The mosquito net hung, a grey ectoplasm, over the double bed.

"Well, Ali," he said, with the phantom of a smile which was all he could raise at this séance, "Missus back. We're all together again." Her rosary lay in a small pool on the dressing-table, and he thought of the broken one in his pocket. He had always meant to get it mended: now it hardly seemed worth the trouble.

"Darling," Louise said, "I've finished up here. Ali can do the rest. There are so many things I want to speak to you about . . ." She followed him downstairs and said at once, "I must get the curtains washed."

"They don't show the dirt."

"Poor dear, you wouldn't notice, but I've been away." She said, "I really want a bigger bookcase now. I've brought a lot of books back with me."

"You haven't told me yet what made you . . ."

"Darling, you'd laugh at me. It was so silly. But suddenly I saw what a fool I'd been to worry like that about the commissionership. I'll tell you one day when I don't mind your laughing." She put her hand out and tentatively touched his arm. "You're really glad . . .?"

"So glad," he said.

"Do you know one of the things that worried me? I was afraid you wouldn't be much of a Catholic without me around, keeping you up to things, poor dear."

"I don't suppose I have been."

"Have you missed Mass often?"

He said with rather forced jocularity, "I've hardly been at all."

"Oh, Ticki." She pulled herself quickly up and said, "Henry, darling, you'll think I'm very sentimental, but tomorrow's Sunday and I want us to go to Communion together. A sign that we've started again—in the right way." It was extraordinary the points in a situation one missed—this he had not considered. He said, "Of course," but his brain momentarily refused to work.

"You'll have to go to Confession this afternoon."

"I haven't done anything very terrible."

"Missing Mass on Sunday's a mortal sin, just as much as adultery."

"Adultery's more fun," he said with attempted lightness.

"It's time I came back."

"I'll go along this afternoon—after lunch. I can't confess on an empty stomach," he said.

"Darling, you *have* changed, you know."

"I was only joking."

"I don't mind your joking. I like it. You didn't do it much, though, before."

"You don't come back every day, darling." The strained good humour, the jest with dry lips, went on and on: at lunch he laid down his fork for yet another "crack." "Dear Henry," she said, "I've never known you so cheerful." The ground had given way beneath his feet, and all through the meal he had the sensation of falling, the relaxed stomach, the breathlessness, the despair—because you couldn't fall so far as this and survive. His hilarity was like a scream from a crevasse.

When lunch was over (he couldn't have told what it was he'd eaten) he said, "I must be off."

"Father Rank?"

"First I've got to look in on Wilson. He's living in one of the Nissens now. A neighbour."

"Won't he be in town?"

"I think he comes back for lunch."

He thought as he went up the hill: What a lot of times in future I shall have to call on Wilson. But no—that wasn't a safe alibi. It would only do this once, because he knew that Wilson lunched in town. None the less, to make sure, he knocked and was taken aback momentarily when Harris opened to him. "I didn't expect to see you."

"I had a touch of fever," Harris said.

"I wondered whether Wilson was in."

"He always lunches in town," Harris said.

"I just wanted to tell him he'd be welcome to look in. My wife's back, you know."

"I thought I saw the activity through the window."

"You must call on us too."

"I'm not much of a calling man," Harris said, drooping in the doorway. "To tell you the truth, women scare me."

"You don't see enough of them, Harris."

"I'm not a squire of dames," Harris said with a poor attempt at pride, and Scobie was aware of how Harris watched him as he picked his way reluctantly towards a woman's hut, watched with the ugly asceticism of the unwanted man. He knocked and felt that disapproving gaze boring into his back. He thought: There goes my alibi: he will tell Wilson and Wilson . . . He thought: I will say that as I was up here, I called . . . and he felt his whole personality crumble with the slow disintegration of lies.

"Why did you knock?" Helen said. She lay on her bed in the dusk of drawn curtains.

"Harris was watching me."

"I didn't think you'd come today."

"How did you know?"

"Everybody here knows everything—except one thing. How clever you are about that. I suppose it's because you are a police officer."

"Yes." He sat down on the bed and put his hand on her arm: immediately the sweat began to run between them. He said, "What are you doing here? You are not ill?"

"Just a headache."

He said mechanically, without even hearing his own words, "Take care of yourself."

"Something's worrying you, dear," she said. "Have things gone—wrong?"

"Nothing of that kind."

"Poor dear, do you remember the first night you stayed here? We didn't worry about anything. You even left your umbrella behind. We were happy. Doesn't it seem odd?— we were happy."

"Yes."

"Why do we go on like this—being unhappy?"

"It's a mistake to mix up the ideas of happiness and love," Scobie said with desperate pedantry as though if he could turn the whole situation into a text-book case—as they had turned Pemberton—peace might return to both of them, a kind of resignation.

"Sometimes you are so damnably old," Helen said, but immediately she expressed with a motion of her hand towards him that she wasn't serious. Today, he thought with pity, she can't afford to quarrel—or so she believes. "My dear," she added, "a penny for your thoughts."

One ought not to lie to two people if it could be avoided: that way lay complete chaos, but he was tempted terribly to lie as he watched her face on the pillow. She seemed to him like one of those plants in nature films which you watch age under your eye. Already she had the look of the coast about her. She shared it with Louise. He said: "It's just a worry I have to think out for myself. Something I hadn't considered."

"Tell me, dear. Two brains . . ." She closed her eyes and he could see her mouth steady for a blow.

He said, "Louise wants me to go to Mass with her, to Communion. I'm supposed to be on the way to Confession now."

"Oh, is that all?" she asked with immense relief, and irritation at her ignorance moved like hatred unfairly in his brain. "All?" he said. "All?" Then justice reclaimed him. He said gently, "If I don't go to Communion, you see, she'll know there's something wrong—seriously wrong."

"But can't you simply go?"

He said, "To me that means—well, damnation. To take my God in mortal sin."

"You don't really believe in hell?"

"That was what Fellowes asked me."

"But I simply don't understand. If you believe in hell, why are you with me now?"

How often, he thought, lack of faith helps one to see more clearly than faith. He said, "You are right, of course: it ought to prevent all this. But the villagers on the slopes of Vesuvius go on. . . . And then, against all the teaching of the Church, one has the conviction that love—any kind of love—does deserve a bit of mercy. One will pay, of course, pay terribly, but I don't believe one will pay for ever. Perhaps one will be given time before one dies. . . ."

"A death-bed repentance," she said with contempt.

"It wouldn't be easy," he said, "to repent of this." He kissed the sweat off her hand. "I can regret the lies, the mess, the unhappiness, but if I were dying now I wouldn't know how to repent the love."

"Well," she said with the same undertone of contempt that seemed to pull her apart from him, in to the safety of the shore, "can't you go and confess everything now? After all, it doesn't mean you won't do it again."

"It's no good confessing if I don't intend to try. . . ."

"Well, then," she said triumphantly, "be hung for a sheep. You are in mortal sin—so you think—now. What difference does it make if you add just one more?"

He thought: Pious people, I suppose, would call this the Devil speaking, but he knew that evil never spoke in these crude answerable terms: this was innocence. He said, "There is a difference—a big difference. It's not easy to explain. Now I'm just putting our love above—well, my safety. But the other—the other's really evil. It's like the

186

Black Mass, the man who steals the sacrament to desecrate it. It's striking God when he's down—in my power."

She turned her head wearily away and said, "I don't understand a thing you are saying. It's all hooey to me."

"I wish it were to me. But I believe it."

She said sharply, "I suppose you do. Or is it just a trick? I didn't hear so much about God when we began, did I? You aren't turning pious on me to give you an excuse . . .?"

"My dear," Scobie said, "I'm not leaving you ever. I've got to think, that's all."

2

At a quarter past six next morning Ali called them. Scobie woke at once, but Louise remained sleeping—she had had a long day. Scobie, turning his head on the pillow, watched her—this was the face he had loved: this was the face he loved. She was terrified of death by sea and yet she had come back, to make him comfortable. She had borne a child by him in one agony, and in another agony had watched the child die. It seemed to him that he had escaped everything. If only, he thought, I could so manage that she never suffers again, but he knew that he had set himself an impossible task. He could delay the suffering, that was all, but he carried it about with him, an infection which sooner or later she must contract. Perhaps she was contracting it now, for she turned and whimpered in her sleep. He put his hand against her cheek to soothe her. He thought: If only she will go on sleeping, then I will sleep on too, I will oversleep, we shall miss Mass, another problem will be postponed. But as if his thoughts had been an alarm clock she awoke.

"What time is it, darling?"

"Nearly half past six."

"We'll have to hurry." He felt as though he were being urged by a kindly and remorseless gaoler to dress for execution. Yet he still put off the saving lie: there was always the possibility of a miracle. Louise gave a final dab of powder (but the powder caked as it touched the skin) and said, "We'll be off now." Was there the faintest note of triumph in her voice? Years and years ago, in the other life of childhood, someone with his name, Henry Scobie, had

187

acted in the school play, had acted Hotspur. He had been chosen for his seniority and his physique, but everyone said that it had been a good performance. Now he had to act again—surely it was as easy as the simpler verbal lie?

Scobie suddenly leant back against the wall and put his hand on his chest. He couldn't make his muscles imitate pain, so he simply closed his eyes. Louise, looking in her mirror, said, "Remind me to tell you about Father Davis in Durban. He was a very good type of priest, much more intellectual than Father Rank." It seemed to Scobie that she was never going to look round and notice him. She said, "Well, we really must be off," and dallied by the mirror. Some sweat-lank hairs were out of place. Through the curtain of his lashes at last he saw her turn and look at him. "Come along, dear," she said, "you look sleepy."

He kept his eyes shut and stayed where he was. She said sharply, "Ticki, what's the matter?"

"A little brandy."

"Are you ill?"

"A little brandy," he repeated sharply and when she had fetched it for him and he felt the taste on his tongue he had an immeasurable sense of reprieve. He sighed and relaxed, "That's better."

"What was it, Ticki?"

"Just a pain in my chest. It's gone now."

"Have you had it before?"

"Once or twice while you've been away."

"You must see a doctor."

"Oh, it's not worth a fuss. They'll just say overwork."

"I oughtn't to have dragged you up, but I wanted us to have Communion together."

"I'm afraid I've ruined that—with the brandy."

"Never mind, Ticki." Carelessly she sentenced him to eternal death. "We can go any day."

He knelt in his seat and watched Louise kneel with the other communicants at the altar rail: he had insisted on coming to the service with her. Father Rank turning from the altar came to them with God in his hands. Scobie thought: God has just escaped me, but will He always escape? *Domine, non sum dignus . . . domine, non sum dignus . . . domine, non sum dignus . . .* His hand formally, as though he were at drill, beat on a particular button of his uniform. It seemed to him for a moment cruelly

188

unfair to God to have exposed himself in this way, a man, a wafer of bread, first in the Palestinian villages and now here in the hot port, there, everywhere, allowing man to have his will of Him. Christ had told the rich young man to sell all and follow him, but that was an easy rational step compared with this that God had taken, to put Himself at the mercy of men who hardly knew the meaning of the word. How desperately God must love, he thought with shame. The priest had reached Louise in his slow interrupted patrol, and suddenly Scobie was aware of the sense of exile. Over there, where all these people knelt, was a country to which he would never return. The sense of love stirred in him, the love one always feels for what one has lost, whether a child, a woman, or even pain.

II. WILSON TORE THE PAGE CAREFULLY OUT OF the *Downhamian* and pasted a thick sheet of Colonial Office notepaper on the back of the poem. He held it up to the light: it was impossible to read the sports results on the other side of his verses. Then he folded the page carefully and put it in his pocket: there it would probably stay, but one never knew.

He had seen Scobie drive away towards the town, and with beating heart and a sense of breathlessness, much the same as he had felt when stepping into the brothel, even with the same reluctance—for who wanted at any given moment to change the routine of his life?—he made his way downhill towards Scobie's house.

He began to rehearse what he considered another man in his place would do: pick up the threads at once: kiss her quite naturally, upon the mouth if possible, say "I've missed you," no uncertainty. But his beating heart sent out its message of fear which drowned thought.

"It's Wilson at last," Louise said. "I thought you'd forgotten me," and held out her hand. He took it like a defeat.

"Have a drink."

"I was wondering whether you'd like a walk."

"It's too hot, Wilson."

"I haven't been up there, you know, since . . ."

"Up where?" He realized that for those who do not love, time never stands still.

"Up at the old station."

She said vaguely with a remorseless lack of interest, "Oh, yes . . . yes, I haven't been up there myself yet."

"That night when I got back"—he could feel the awful immature flush expanding—"I tried to write some verse."

"What, you, Wilson?"

He said furiously, "Yes, me, Wilson. Why not? And it's been published."

"I wasn't laughing. I was just surprised. Who published it?"

"A new paper called *The Circle*. Of course they don't pay much."

"Can I see it?"

Wilson said breathlessly, "I've got it here." He explained, "There was something on the other side I couldn't stand. It was just too modern for me." He watched her with hungry embarrassment.

"It's quite pretty," she said weakly.

"You see the initials?"

"I never had a poem dedicated to me before."

Wilson felt sick: he wanted to sit down. Why, he wondered, does one ever begin this humiliating process: why does one imagine that one is in love? He had read somewhere that love had been invented in the eleventh century by the troubadours. Why had they not left us with lust? He said with hopeless venom, "I love you." He thought: It's a lie: the word means nothing off the printed page. He waited for her laughter.

"Oh, no, Wilson," she said, "no. You don't. It's just Coast fever."

He plunged blindly: "More than anything in the world."

She said gently, "No one loves like that, Wilson.

He walked restlessly up and down, his shorts flapping, waving the bit of paper from the *Downhamian*. "You ought to believe in love. You're a Catholic. Didn't God love the world?"

"Oh, yes," she said. "He's capable of it. But not many of us are."

"You love your husband. You told me so. And it's brought you back."

Louise said sadly, "I suppose I do. All I can. It's not the kind of love though you want to imagine you feel. No poisoned chalices, eternal doom, black sails. We don't die for love, Wilson—except, of course, in books. And sometimes a boy play-acting. Don't let's play-act, Wilson—it's no fun at our age."

"I'm not play-acting," he said with a fury in which he could hear too easily the histrionic accent. He confronted her bookcase as though it were a witness she had forgotten. "Do they play-act?"

"Not much," she said. "That's why I like them better than your poets."

"All the same you came back." His face lit up with wicked inspiration. "Or was that just jealousy?"

She said, "Jealousy? What on earth have I got to be jealous about?"

"They've been careful," Wilson said, "but not as careful as all that."

"I don't know what you are talking about."

"Your Ticki and Helen Rolt."

Louise struck at his cheek and, missing, got his nose, which began to bleed copiously. She said, "That's for calling him Ticki. Nobody's going to do that except me. You know he hates it. Here, take my handkerchief if you haven't got one of your own."

Wilson said, "I bleed awfully easily. Do you mind if I lie on my back?" He stretched himself on the floor between the table and the meat-safe, among the ants. First there had been Scobie watching his tears at Pende, and now—this.

"You wouldn't like me to put a key down your back?" Louise asked.

"No. No thank you." The blood had stained the Down-hamian page.

"I really am sorry. I've got a vile temper. This will cure you, Wilson." But if romance is what one lives by, one must never be cured of it. The world has too many spoilt priests of this faith or that: better surely to pretend a belief than wander in that vicious vacuum of cruelty and despair. He said obstinately, "Nothing will cure me, Louise. I love you. Nothing," bleeding into her handkerchief.

"How strange," she said, "it would be if it were true."

He grunted a query from the ground.

"I mean," she explained, "if you were one of those people who really love. I thought Henry was. It would be strange if really it was you all the time." He felt an odd fear that after all he was going to be accepted at his own valuation, rather as a minor staff officer might feel during a rout when he finds that his claim to know the handling of the tanks will be accepted. It is too late to admit that he knows nothing but what he has read in the technical journals—O lyric love, half angel and half bird . . . Bleeding into the handkerchief, he formed his lips carefully round a generous phrase "I expect he loves—in his way."

"Who?' Louise said. "Me? This Helen Rolt you are talking about? Or just himself?"

"I shouldn't have said that."

"Isn't it true? Let's have a bit of truth, Wilson. You don't know how tired I am of comforting lies. Is she beautiful?"

"Oh, no, no. Nothing of that sort."

"She's young, of course, and I'm middle-aged. But surely she's a bit worn after what she's been through."

"She's very worn."

"But she's not a Catholic. She's lucky. She's free, Wilson."

Wilson sat up against the leg of the table. He said with genuine passion, "I wish to God you wouldn't call me Wilson."

"Edward. Eddie. Ted. Teddy."

"I'm bleeding again," he said dismally, and lay back on the floor.

"What do you know about it all, Teddy?"

"I think I'd rather be Edward. Louise, I've seen him come away from her hut at two in the morning. He was up there yesterday afternoon."

"He was at Confession."

"Harris saw him."

"You're certainly watching him."

"It's my belief Yusef is using him."

"That's fantastic. You're going too far."

She stood over him as though he were a corpse: the blood-stained handkerchief lay in his palm. They neither of them heard the car stop or the footsteps up to the threshold. It was strange to both of them, hearing a third voice

192

from an outside world speaking into this room which had become as close and intimate and airless as a vault. "Is anything wrong?" Scobie's voice asked.

"It's just . . ." Louise said, and made a gesture of bewilderment—as though she were saying: where does one start explaining? Wilson scrambled to his feet and at once his nose began again to bleed.

"Here," Scobie said, and taking out his bundle of keys dropped them inside Wilson's shirt-collar. "You'll see," he said, "the old-fashioned remedies are always best," and sure enough the bleeding did stop within a few seconds. "You should never lie on your back," Scobie went reasonably on. "Seconds use a sponge of cold water, and you certainly look as though you'd been in a fight, Wilson."

"I always lie on my back," Wilson said. "Blood makes me ill."

"Have a drink?"

"No," Wilson said, "no. I must be off." He retrieved the keys with some difficulty and left the tail of his shirt dangling. He discovered it only when Harris pointed it out to him on his return to the Nissen, and he thought: That is how I looked while I walked away and they watched side by side. He looked out over the landscape of baking earth and bleak iron huts towards the Scobies' house as though he were examining the scene of a battle after the defeat. He wondered how all that dreary scene would have appeared if he had been victorious, but in human love there is never such a thing as victory: only a few minor tactical successes before the final defeat of death or indifference.

2

"What did he want?" Scobie said.

"He wanted to make love to me."

"Does he love you?"

"He thinks he does. You can't ask much more than that, can you?"

"You seem to have hit him rather hard," Scobie said, "on the nose?"

"He made me angry. He called you Ticki. Darling, he's spying on you."

"I know that."

"Is he dangerous?"

"He might be—under some circumstances. But then it would be my fault."

"Henry, do you never get furious at anyone? Don't you mind him making love to me?"

He said, "I'd be a hypocrite if I were angry at that. It's the kind of thing that happens to people. You know, quite pleasant normal people do fall in love."

"Have you ever fallen in love?"

"Oh, yes, yes." He watched her closely while he excavated his smile. "You know I have."

"Henry, did you really feel ill this morning?"

"Yes."

"It wasn't just an excuse?"

"No."

"Then, darling, let's go to Communion together tomorrow morning."

"If you want to," he said. It was the moment he had known would come. With bravado, to show that his hand was not shaking, he took down a glass. "Drink?"

"It's too early, dear," Louise said: he knew she was watching him closely—like all the others. He put the glass down and said, "I've just got to run back to the station for some papers. When I get back it will be time for drinks."

He drove unsteadily down the road, his eyes blurred with nausea. O God, he thought, the decisions you force on people, suddenly, with no time to consider. I am too tired to think: this ought to be worked out on paper like a problem in mathematics, and the answer arrived at without pain. But the pain made him physically sick so that he retched over the wheel. The trouble is, he thought, we know the answers—we Catholics are damned by our knowledge. There's no need for me to work anything out—there is only one answer: to kneel down in the Confessional and say, "Since my last confession I have committed adultery so many times et cetera and et cetera": to hear Father Rank telling me to avoid the occasion: never see the woman alone (speaking in those terrible abstract terms: Helen— the woman, the occasion, no longer the bewildered child clutching the stamp-album, listening to Bagster howling outside the door: that moment of peace and darkness and tenderness and pity, "adultery"). And I to make my Act of Contrition, the promise "never more to offend thee," and then tomorrow the Communion: taking God in my mouth in what they call the State of Grace. That's the right answer—there is no other answer: to save my own soul and abandon her to Bagster and despair. One must be reasonable, he told himself, and recognize that despair doesn't last (is that true?), that love doesn't last (but isn't that the very reason that despair does?), that in a few weeks or months she'll be all right again. She has survived forty days in an open boat and the death of her husband, and can't she survive the mere death of love? As I can, as I know I can.

He drew up outside the church and sat hopelessly at the wheel. Death never comes when one desires it most. He thought, Of course there's the ordinary honest wrong answer: to leave Louise, forget that private vow, resign my job. To abandon Helen to Bagster or Louise to what? I am trapped, he told himself, catching sight of an expressionless stranger's face in the driving mirror, trapped. Nevertheless he left the car and went into the church. While he was waiting for Father Rank to go into the confessional he knelt and prayed: the only prayer he could rake up. Even the words of the Our Father and the Hail Mary deserted him. He prayed for a miracle, "O God, convince me, help me, convince me. Make me feel that I am more important than that child." It was not Helen's face he saw as he prayed but the dying child who called him "Father": a face in a photograph staring from the dressing-table: the face of a black girl of twelve a sailor had raped and killed glaring blindly up at him in a yellow paraffin light. "Make me put my own soul first. Give me trust in your mercy to the one I abandon." He could hear Father Rank close the door of his box, and nausea twisted him again on his knees. "O God," he said, "if, instead, I should abandon you, punish me, but let the others get some happiness." He went into the box. He thought: A miracle may still happen. Even Father Rank may for once find the word, the right word. . . . Kneeling in the space of an upturned coffin he said, "Since my last confession I have committed adultery."

"How many times?"

"I don't know, Father, many times."

"Are you married?"

"Yes." He remembered that evening when Father Rank had nearly broken down before him, admitting his failure to help. . . . Was he, even while he was struggling to retain the complete anonymity of the Confessional, remembering it too? He wanted to say, "Help me, Father. Convince me that I would do right to abandon her to Bagster. Make me believe in the mercy of God," but he knelt silently waiting: he was unaware of the slightest tremor of hope. Father Rank said, "Is it one woman?"

"Yes."

"You must avoid seeing her. Is that possible?"

He shook his head.

"If you must see her, you must never be alone with her. Do you promise to do that, promise God, not me?" He thought: How foolish it was of me to expect the magic word. This is the formula used so many times on so many people. Presumably people promised and went away and came back and confessed again. Did they really believe they were going to try? He thought: I am cheating human beings every day I live, I am not going to try to cheat myself or God. He replied, "It would be no good my promising that, Father."

"You must promise. You can't desire the end without desiring the means."

Ah, but one can, he thought, one can: one can desire the peace of victory without desiring the ravaged towns.

Father Rank said, "I don't need to tell you surely that there's nothing automatic in the Confessional or in Absolution. It depends on your state of mind whether you are forgiven. It's no good coming and kneeling here unprepared. Before you come here you must know the wrong you've done."

"I do know that."

"And you must have a real purpose of amendment. We are told to forgive our brother seventy times seven and we needn't fear that God will be any less forgiving than we are, but nobody can begin to forgive the uncontrite. It's better to sin seventy times and repent each time than sin once and never repent." He could see Father Rank's hand go up to wipe the sweat out of his eyes: it was like a gesture of weariness. He thought: What is the good of keeping him in this discomfort? He's right, of course, he's right. I was a fool to imagine that somehow in this airless box I would

196

find a conviction. . . . He said, "I think I was wrong to come, Father."

"I don't want to refuse you absolution, but I think if you would just go away and turn things over in your mind, you'd come back in a better frame of mind."

"Yes, Father."

"I will pray for you."

When he came out of the box it seemed to Scobie that for the first time his footsteps had taken him out of sight of hope. There was no hope anywhere he turned his eyes: the dead figure of the God upon the Cross, the plaster Virgin, the hideous Stations, representing a series of events that had happened a long time ago. It seemed to him that he had left for his exploration only the territory of despair.

He drove down to the station, collected a file, and returned home. "You've been a long time," Louise said. He didn't even know the lie he was going to tell before it was on his lips. "That pain came back," he said, "so I waited for a while."

"Do you think you ought to have a drink?"

"Yes, until anybody tells me not to."

"And you'll see a doctor?"

"Of course."

That night he dreamed that he was in a boat drifting down just such an underground river as his boyhood hero Allan Quatermain had taken towards the lost city of Milosis. But Quatermain had companions, while he was alone, for you couldn't count the dead body on the stretcher as a companion. He felt a sense of urgency, for he told himself that bodies in this climate kept for a very short time, and the smell of decay was already in his nostrils. Then, sitting there guiding the boat down the midstream, he realized that it was not the dead body that smelt but his own living one. He felt as though his blood had ceased to run: when he tried to lift his arm it dangled uselessly from his shoulder. He woke, and it was Louise who had lifted his arm. She said, "Darling, it's time to be off."

"Off?" he asked.

"We're going to Mass together," and again he was aware of how closely she was watching him. What was the good of yet another delaying lie? He wondered what Wilson had said to her. Could he go on lying week after week, finding some reason of work, of health, of forgetfulness, for

197

avoiding the issue at the altar rail? He thought hopelessly: I am damned already—I may as well go the whole length of my chain. "Yes," he said, "of course. I'll get up," and was suddenly surprised by her putting the excuse into his mouth, giving him his chance. "Darling," she said, "if you aren't well, stay where you are. I don't want to drag you to Mass."

But the excuse it seemed to him was also a trap. He could see where the turf had been replaced over the hidden stakes. If he took the excuse she offered he would have all but confessed his guilt. Once and for all now, at whatever eternal cost, he was determined that he would clear himself in her eyes and give her the reassurance she needed. He said, "No, no. I will come with you." When he walked beside her into the church it was as if he had entered this building for the first time—a stranger. An immeasurable distance already separated him from these people who knelt and prayed and would presently receive God in peace. He knelt and pretended to pray.

The words of the Mass were like an indictment. "I will go in unto the altar of God: to God who giveth joy to my youth." But there was no joy anywhere. He looked up from between his hands, and the plaster images of the Virgin and the Saints seemed to be holding out hands to everyone, on either side, beyond him. He was the unknown guest at a party who is introduced to no one. The gentle painted smiles were unbearably directed elsewhere. When the Kyrie Eleison was reached he again tried to pray. "Lord, have mercy . . . Christ, have mercy . . . Lord, have mercy . . ." but the fear and the shame of the act he was going to commit chilled his brain. Those ruined priests who presided at a Black Mass, consecrating the Host over the naked body of a woman, consuming God in an absurd and horrifying ritual, were at least performing the act of damnation with an emotion larger than human love: they were doing it from hate of God or some odd perverse devotion to God's enemy. But he had no love of evil or hate of God: how was he to hate this God who of His own accord was surrendering Himself into his power? He was desecrating God because he loved a woman—was it even love, or was it just a feeling of pity and responsibility? He tried again to excuse himself: "You can look after yourself. You survive the Cross every day. You can only suffer.

You can never be lost. Admit that you must come second to these others." And myself, he thought, watching the priest pour the wine and water into the chalice, his own damnation being prepared like a meal at the altar. I must come last: I am the Deputy Commissioner of Police: a hundred men serve under me: I am the responsible man. It is my job to look after the others. I am conditioned to serve.

Sanctus. Sanctus. Sanctus. The Canon of the Mass had started: Father Rank's whisper at the altar hurried remorselessly towards the consecration. "To order our days in thy peace . . . that we be preserved from eternal damnation . . ." *Pax, pacis, pacem:* all the declinations of the word "peace" drummed on his ears through the Mass. He thought: I have left even the hope of peace for ever. I am the responsible man. I shall soon have gone too far in my design of deception ever to go back. *Hoc est enim Corpus:* the bell rang, and Father Rank raised God in his fingers —this God as light now as a wafer whose coming lay on Scobie's heart as heavily as lead. *Hic est enim Calix Sanguinis* and the second bell.

Louise touched his hand. "Dear, are you well?" He thought: Here is the second chance. The return of my pain. I can go out. And who indeed is in pain if I am not in pain? But if he went out of church now, he knew that there would be only one thing left to do—to follow Father Rank's advice, to settle his affairs, to desert, to come back in a few days' time and take God with a clear conscience and a knowledge that he had pushed innocence back where it properly belonged—under the Atlantic surge. Innocence must die young if it isn't to kill the souls of men.

"Peace I leave with you, my peace I give unto you."

"I'm all right," he said, the old longing pricking at the eyeballs, and looking up towards the Cross on the altar he thought savagely: Take your sponge of gall. You made me what I am. Take the spear thrust. He didn't need to open his Missal to know how this prayer ended. "May the receiving of Thy Body, O Lord Jesus Christ, which I unworthy presume to take, turn not to my judgment and condemnation." He shut his eyes and let the darkness in. Mass rushed towards its end: *Domine, non sum dignus . . . Domine, non sum dignus . . . Domine, non sum dignus.* . . . At the foot of the scaffold he opened his eyes and saw

199

the old black women shuffling up towards the altar rail, a few soldiers, an aircraft mechanic, one of his own policemen, a clerk from the bank: they moved sedately towards peace, and Scobie felt an envy of their simplicity, their goodness. Yes, now at this moment of time they were good.

"Aren't you coming, dear?" Louise ased, and again the hand touched him: the kindly firm detective hand. He rose and followed her and knelt by her side like a spy in a foreign land who has been taught the customs and to speak the language like a native. Only a miracle can save me now, Scobie told himself, watching Father Rank at the altar opening the tabernacle, but God would never work a miracle to save Himself. I am the Cross, he thought: He will never speak the word to save Himself from the Cross, but if only wood were made so that it didn't feel, if only the nails were senseless as people believe.

Father Rank came down the steps from the altar bearing God. The saliva had dried in Scobie's mouth: it was as though his veins had dried. He couldn't look up: he saw only the priest's skirt like the skirt of the mediæval warhorse bearing down upon him: the flapping of feet: the charge of God. If only the archers would let fly from ambush: and for a moment he dreamed that the priest's steps had indeed faltered: perhaps after all something may yet happen before he reaches me: some incredible interposition. . . . But with open mouth (the time had come) he made one last attempt at prayer, "O God, I offer up my damnation to you. Take it. Use it for them," and was aware of the pale papery taste of his eternal sentence on the tongue.

III. THE BANK MANAGER TOOK A SIP OF ICED water and exclaimed with more than professional warmth, "How glad you must be to have Mrs. Scobie back well in time for Christmas."

"Christmas is a long way off still," Scobie said.

"Time flies when the rains are over," the bank manager

went on with his novel cheerfulness. Scobie had never before heard in his voice this note of optimism. He remembered the storklike figure pacing to and fro, pausing at the medical books, so many hundred times a day.

"I came along . . ." Scobie began.

"About your life insurance—or an overdraft, would it be?"

"Well, it wasn't either this time."

"You know I'll always be glad to help you, Scobie, whatever it is." How quietly Robinson sat at his desk. Scobie said with wonder, "Have you given up your daily exercise?"

"Ah, that was all stuff and nonsense," the manager said. "I had read too many books."

"I wanted to look in your medical encyclopædia," Scobie explained.

"You'd do much better to see a doctor," Robinson surprisingly advised him. "It's a doctor who's put me right, not the books. The time I would have wasted . . . I tell you, Scobie, the new young fellow they've got at the Argyll Hospital's the best man they've sent to this colony since they discovered it."

"And he's put you right?"

"Go and see him. His name's Travis. Tell him I sent you."

"All the same, if I could just have a look . . ."

"You'll find it on the shelf. I keep 'em there still because they look important. A bank manager has to be a reading man. People expect him to have solid books around."

"I'm glad your stomach's cured."

The manager took another sip of water. He said, "I'm not bothering about it any more. The truth of the matter is, Scobie, I'm . . ."

Scobie looked up from the encyclopædia. "Yes?"

"Oh, I was just thinking aloud."

Scobie had opened the encyclopædia at the word *Angina* and now he read on: *Character of the Pain. This is usually described as being "gripping," "as though the chest were in a vice." The pain is situated in the middle of the chest and under the sternum. It may run down either arm, perhaps more commonly the left, or up into the neck or down into the abdomen. It lasts a few seconds, or at the most a minute or so. The Behaviour of the Patient. This is characteristic. He holds himself absolutely still in whatever cir-*

201

cumstances he may find himself . . . Scobie's eye passed rapidly down the cross-headings: *Cause of the Pain. Treatment. Termination of the Disease.* Then he put the book back on the shelf. "Well," he said, "perhaps I'll drop in on your Doctor Travis. I'd rather see him than Doctor Sykes. I hope he cheers me up as he's done you."

"Well, my case," the manager said evasively, "had peculiar features."

"Mine looks straightforward enough."

"You seem pretty well."

"Oh, I'm all right—bar a bit of pain now and then and sleeping badly."

"Your responsibilities do that for you."

"Perhaps."

It seemed to Scobie that he had sowed enough—against what harvest? He couldn't himself have told. He said goodbye and went out into the dazzling street. He carried his helmet and let the sun strike vertically down upon his thin greying hair. He offered himself for punishment all the way to the police station and was rejected. It had seemed to him these last three weeks that the damned must be in a special category: like the young men destined for some unhealthy foreign post in a trading company, they were reserved from their humdrum fellows, protected from the daily task, preserved carefully at special desks, so that the worst might happen later. Nothing now ever seemed to go wrong. The sun would not strike, the Colonial Secretary asked him to dinner . . . He felt rejected by misfortune.

The Commissioner said, "Come in, Scobie. I've got good news for you," and Scobie prepared himself for yet another rejection.

"Baker is not coming here. They need him in Palestine. They've decided after all to let the right man succeed me." Scobie sat down on the window ledge and watched his hand tremble on his knee. He thought: So all this need not have happened. If Louise had stayed I should never have loved Helen: I would never have been black-mailed by Yusef, never have committed that act of despair. I would have been myself still—the same self that lay stacked in fifteen years of diaries, not this broken cast. But, of course, he told himself, it's only because I have done these things that success comes. I am of the Devil's party. He looks after his own in this world. I shall go now from damned success to damned success, he thought with disgust.

"I think Colonel Wright's word was the deciding factor. You impressed him, Scobie."

"It's come too late, sir."

"Why too late?"

"I'm too old for the job. It needs a younger man."

"Nonsense. You're only just fifty."

"My health's not good."

"It's the first I've heard of it."

"I was telling Robinson at the bank today. I've been getting pains, and I'm sleeping badly." He talked rapidly, beating time on his knee. "Robinson swears by Travis. He seems to have worked wonders with him."

"Poor Robinson."

"Why?"

"He's been given two years to live. That's in confidence, Scobie."

Human beings never cease to surprise: so it was the death-sentence that had cured Robinson of his imaginary ailments, his medical books, his daily walk from wall to wall. I suppose, Scobie thought, that is what comes of knowing the worst—one is left alone with the worst, and it's like peace. He imagined Robinson talking across the desk to his solitary companion. "I hope we all die as calmly," he said. "Is he going home?"

"I don't think so. I suppose presently he'll have to go to the Argyll."

Scobie thought: I wish I had known what I had been looking at: Robinson was exhibiting the most enviable possession a man can own—a happy death. This tour would bear a high proportion of deaths—or perhaps not so high when you counted them and remembered Europe. First Pemberton, then the child at Pende, now Robinson . . . no, it wasn't many, but of course he hadn't counted the blackwater cases in the military hospital.

"So that's how matters stand," the Commissioner said. "Next tour you will be Commissioner. Your wife will be pleased."

I must endure her pleasure, Scobie thought, without anger. I am the guilty man, and I have no right to criticize, to show vexation ever again. He said, "I'll be getting home."

203

Ali stood by his car, talking to another boy who slipped quietly away when he saw Scobie approach. "Who was that, Ali?"

"My small brother, sah," Ali said.

"I don't know him, do I? Same mother?"

"No, sah, same father."

"What does he do?" Ali worked at the starting handle, his face dripping with sweat, saying nothing.

"Who does he work for, Ali?"

"Sah?"

"I said who does he work for?"

"For Mr. Wilson, sah."

The engine started and Ali climbed into the back seat. "Has he ever made you a proposition, Ali? I mean has he asked you to report on me—for money?" He could see Ali's face in the driving mirror, set, obstinate, closed and rocky like a cave mouth. "No, sah."

"Lots of people are interested in me and pay good money for reports. They think me bad man, Ali."

Ali said, "I'm your boy," staring back through the medium of the mirror. It seemed to Scobie one of the qualities of deceit that you lost the sense of trust. If I can lie and betray, so can others. Wouldn't many people gamble on my honesty and lose their stake? Why should I lose my stake on Ali? I have not been caught and he has not been caught, that's all. An awful depression weighed his head towards the wheel. He thought: I know that Ali is honest: I have known that for fifteen years: I am just trying to find a companion in this region of lies. Is the next stage the stage of corrupting others?

Louise was not in when they arrived: presumably someone had called and taken her out—perhaps to the beach. She hadn't expected him back before sundown. He wrote a note for her, *Taking some furniture up to Helen. Will be back early with good news for you*, and then he drove up alone to the Nissen huts through the bleak empty middle day. Only the vultures were about—gathering round a dead chicken at the edge of the road, stooping their old men's necks over the carrion, their wings like broken umbrellas sticking out this way and that.

"I've brought you another table and a couple of chairs. Is your boy about?"

"No, he's at market."

They kissed as formally now when they met as a brother and sister. When the damage was done adultery became as unimportant as friendship. The flame had licked them and gone on across the clearing: it had left nothing standing except a sense of responsibility and a sense of loneliness. Only if you trod barefooted did you notice the heat in the grass. Scobie said, "I'm interrupting your lunch."

"Oh no. I've about finished. Have some fruit salad."

"It's time you had a new table. This one wobbles." He said, "They are making me Commissioner after all."

"It will please your wife," Helen said.

"It doesn't mean a thing to me."

"Oh, of course it does," she said briskly. This was another convention of hers—that only she suffered. He would for a long time resist, like Coriolanus, the exhibition of *his* wounds, but sooner or later he would give way: he would dramatize his pain in words until even to himself it seemed unreal. Perhaps, he would think, she is right after all: perhaps I don't suffer. She said, "Of course the Commissioner must be above suspicion, mustn't he, like Cæsar." (Her sayings, as well as her spelling, lacked accuracy.) "This is the end of us, I suppose."

"You know there is no end to us."

"Oh, but the Commissioner can't have a mistress hidden away in a Nissen hut." The sting, of course, was in the "hidden away," but how could he allow himself to feel the least irritation, remembering the letter she had written to him, offering herself as a sacrifice any way he liked, to keep or to throw away? Human beings couldn't be heroic all the time: those who surrendered everything—for God or love—must be allowed sometimes in thought to take back their surrender. So many had never committed the heroic act however rashly. It was the act that counted. He said, "If the Commissioner can't keep you, then I shan't be the Commissioner."

"Don't be silly. After all," she said with fake reasonableness, and he recognized this as one of her bad days, "what do we get out of it?"

"I get a lot," he said, and wondered: Is that a lie for the sake of comfort? There were so many lies nowadays he couldn't keep track of the small, the unimportant ones.

"An hour or two every other day perhaps when you can slip away. Never so much as a night."

205

He said hopelessly, "Oh, I have plans."

"What plans?"

He said, "They are too vague still."

She said with all the acid she could squeeze out, "Well, let me know in time. To fall in with your wishes, I mean."

"My dear, I haven't come here to quarrel."

"I sometimes wonder what you do come here for."

"Well, today I brought some furniture."

"Oh, yes, the furniture."

"I've got the car here. Let me take you to the beach."

"Oh, we can't be seen there together."

"That's nonsense. Louise is there now, I think."

"For God's sake," Helen said, "keep that smug woman out of my sight."

"All right, then. I'll take you for a run in the car."

"That would be safer, wouldn't it?"

Scobie took her by the shoulders and said, "I'm not always thinking of safety."

"I thought you were."

Suddenly he felt his resistance give away and he shouted at her, "The sacrifice isn't all on your side." With despair he could see from a distance the scene coming up on both of them: like the tornado before the rains, that wheeling column of blackness which would soon cover the whole sky.

"Of course work must suffer," she said with childish sarcasm. "All these snatched half-hours."

"I've given up hope," he said.

"What do you mean?"

"I've given up the future. I've damned myself."

"Don't be so melodramatic," she said. "I don't know what you are talking about. Anyway, you've just told me about the future—the commissionership."

"I mean the real future—the future that goes on."

She said, "If there's one thing I hate it's your Catholicism. I suppose it comes of having a pious wife. It's so bogus. If you really believed you wouldn't be here."

"But I do believe and I am here." He said with bewilderment, "I can't explain it, but there it is. My eyes are open. I know what I'm doing. When Father Rank came down to the rail carrying the sacrament . . ."

Helen exclaimed with scorn and impatience, "You've

told me all that before. You are trying to impress me. You don't believe in hell any more than I do."

He took her wrists and held them furiously. He said, "You can't get out of it that way. I believe, I tell you. I believe that I'm damned for all eternity—unless a miracle happens. I'm a policeman. I know what I'm saying. What I've done is far worse than murder—that's an act, a blow, a stab, a shot: it's over and done, but I'm carrying my corruption around with me. It's the coating of my stomach. I can never void it." He threw her wrists aside like seeds towards the stony floor. "Never pretend I haven't shown my love."

"Love for your wife, you mean. You were afraid she'd find out."

Anger drained out of him. He said, "Love for both of you. If it were just for her there'd be an easy straight way." He put his hands over his eyes, feeling hysteria beginning to mount again. He said, "I can't bear to see suffering, and I cause it all the time. I want to get out, get out."

"Where to?"

Hysteria and honesty receded: cunning came back across the threshold like a mongrel dog. He said, "Oh, I just mean take a holiday." He added, "I'm not sleeping well. And I've been getting an odd pain."

"Darling, are you ill?" The pillar had wheeled on its course: the storm was involving others now: it had passed beyond them. Helen said, "Darling, I'm a bitch. I get tired and fed up with things—but it doesn't mean anything. Have you seen a doctor?"

"I'll see Travis at the Argyll some time soon."

"Everybody says Dr. Sykes is better."

"No, I don't want to see Dr. Sykes." Now that the anger and hysteria had passed he could see her exactly as she was that first evening when the sirens blew. He thought, O God, I can't leave her. Or Louise. You don't need me as they need me. You have your good people, your Saints, all the company of the blessed. You can do without me. He said, "I'll take you for a spin now in the car. It will do us both good."

In the dusk of the garage he took her hands again and kissed her. He said, "There are no eyes here . . . Wilson can't see us. Harris isn't watching. Yusef's boys . . ."

207

"My dear, I'd leave you tomorrow if it would help."

"It wouldn't help." He said, "You remember when I wrote you a letter—which got lost. I tried to put down everything there, plainly, in black and white. So as not to be cautious any more. I wrote that I loved you more than my wife . . ." He hesitated. "More than God," and as he spoke, he heard another's breath behind his shoulder, beside the car. He said, sharply, "Who's that?"

"What, dear?"

"Somebody's here." He came round to the other side of the car and said sharply, "Who's there? Come out."

"It's Ali," Helen said.

"What are you doing here, Ali?"

"Missus sent me," Ali said. "I wait here for Massa tell him Missus back." He was hardly visible in the shadow.

"Why were you waiting here?"

"My head humbug me," Ali said. "I go for sleep, small small sleep."

"Don't frighten him," Helen said. "He's telling the truth."

"Go along home, Ali," Scobie told him, "and tell Missus I come straight down." He watched him pad out into the hard sunlight between the Nissen huts. He never looked back.

"Don't worry about him," Helen said. "He didn't understand a thing."

"I've had Ali for fifteen years," Scobie said. It was the first time he had been ashamed before him in all those years. He remembered Ali the night after Pemberton's death, cup of tea in hand, holding him up against the shaking lorry, and then he remembered Wilson's boy slinking off along the wall by the police station.

"You can trust him anyway."

"I don't know how," Scobie said. "I've lost the trick of trust."

2

Louise was asleep upstairs, and Scobie sat at the table with his diary open. He had written down against the date October 31: *Commissioner told me this morning I am to succeed him. Took some furniture to H.R. Told Louise news, which pleased her.* The other life—bare and undisturbed and built of facts—lay like Roman foundations under his hand. This was the life he was supposed to lead: no one reading this record would visualize the obscure shameful scene in the garage, the interview with the Portuguese captain, Louise striking out blindly with the painful truth, Helen accusing him of hypocrisy . . . He thought: This is how it ought to be: I am too old for emotion. I am too old to be a cheat. Lies are for the young. They have a lifetime of truth to recover in. He looked at his watch—eleven-forty-five—and wrote: *Temperature at 2 p.m. 92°.* The lizard pounced upon the wall, the tiny jaws clamping on a moth. Something scratched outside the door—a pye-dog? He laid his pen down again and loneliness sat across the table opposite him. No man surely was less alone, with his wife upstairs and his mistress little more than five hundred yards away up the hill, and yet it was loneliness that seated itself like a companion who doesn't need to speak. It seemed to him that he had never been so alone before.

There was nobody now to whom he could speak the truth. There were things the Commissioner must not know, Louise must not know, there were even limits to what he could tell Helen, for what was the use, when he had sacrificed so much in order to avoid pain, of inflicting it needlessly? As for God, he could speak to Him only as one speaks to an enemy—there was bitterness between them. He moved his hand on the table, and it was as though his loneliness moved too and touched the tips of his fingers. "You and I," his loneliness said, "you and I." It occurred to him that the outside world, if they knew the facts, might envy him: Bagster would envy him Helen, and Wilson, Louise. What a hell of a quiet dog, Fraser would exclaim with a lick of the lips. They would imagine, he thought with amazement, that I get something out of it, but it seemed to him that no man had ever got less. Even self-pity was denied him because he knew so exactly the extent of his guilt. He felt as though he had exiled himself so deeply in the desert that his skin had taken on the colour of the sand.

The door creaked gently open behind him. Scobie did not move. The spies, he thought, are creeping in. Is this Wilson, Harris, Pemberton's boy, Ali . . . ? "Massa," a voice whispered, and a bare foot slapped the concrete floor.

"Who are you?" Scobie asked, not turning round. A pink palm dropped a small ball of paper on the table and went out of sight again. The voice said, "Yusef say come very quiet nobody see."

"What does Yusef want now?"

"He send you dash—small small dash." Then the door closed again and silence was back. Loneliness said, "Let us open this together, you and I."

Scobie picked up the ball of paper: it was light, but it had a small hard centre. At first he didn't realize what it was: he thought it was a pebble put in to keep the paper steady and he looked for writing, which, of course, was not there, for whom would Yusef trust to write for him? Then he realized what it was—a diamond, a gem stone. He knew nothing about diamonds, but it seemed to him that it was probably worth at least as much as his debt to Yusef. Presumably Yusef had information that the stones he had sent by the *Esperança* had reached their destination safely. This was a mark of gratitude—not a bribe, Yusef would explain, the fat hand upon his sincere and shallow heart.

The door burst open and there was Ali. He had a boy by the arm who whimpered. Ali said, "This stinking Mende boy he go all round the house. He try doors."

"Who are you?" Scobie said.

The boy broke out in a mixture of fear and rage, "I Yusef's boy. I bring Massa letter," and he pointed at the table where the pebble lay in the screw of paper. Ali's eyes followed the gesture. Scobie said to his loneliness, "You and I have to think quickly." He turned on the boy and said, "Why you not come here properly and knock on the door? Why you come like a thief?"

He had the thin body and the melancholy soft eyes of all Mendes. He said, "I not a thief," with so slight an emphasis on the first word that it was just possible he was not impertinent. He went on, "Massa tell me to come very quiet."

Scobie said, "Take this back to Yusef and tell him I want to know where he gets a stone like that. I think he steals stones and I find out by an' by. Go on. Take it. Now, Ali, throw him out." Ali pushed the boy ahead of him through the door, and Scobie could hear the rustle of their feet on the path. Were they whispering together? He went to the door and called out after them, "Tell Yusef I call on
210

him one night soon and make hell of a palaver." He slammed the door again and thought, what a lot Ali knows, and he felt distrust of his boy moving again like fever with the bloodstream. He could ruin me, he thought: he could ruin *them*.

He poured himself out a glass of whisky and took a bottle of soda out of his ice-box. Louise called from upstairs, "Henry."

"Yes, dear?"

"Is it twelve yet?"

"Close on, I think."

"You won't drink anything after twelve, will you? You remember tomorrow?" and of course he did remember, draining his glass: it was November the first—All Saints' Day, and this Allhallows Eve. What ghost would pass over the whisky's surface? "You are coming to Communion, aren't you, dear?" and he thought wearily: There is no end to this: why should I draw the line now? one may as well go on damning oneself until the end. His loneliness was the only ghost his whisky could invoke, nodding across the table at him, taking a drink out of his glass. "The next occasion," loneliness told him, "will be Christmas—the Midnight Mass—you won't be able to avoid that, you know, and no excuse will serve you on that night, and after that" . . . the long chain of feast days, of early Masses in spring and summer, unrolled themselves like a perpetual calendar. He had a sudden picture before his eyes of a bleeding face, of eyes closed by the continuous shower of blows: the punch-drunk head of God reeling sideways.

"You are coming, Ticki?" Louise called with what seemed to him a sudden anxiety, as though perhaps suspicion had momentarily breathed on her again—and he thought again: Can Ali really be trusted? and all the stale Coast wisdom of the traders and the remittance-men told him, "Never trust a black. They'll let you down in the end. Had my boy fifteen years . . ." The ghosts of distrust came out on All Souls' Night and gathered around his glass.

"Oh, yes, my dear, I'm coming."

"You have only to say the word," he addressed God, "and legions of angels . . ." and he struck with his ringed hand under the eye and saw the bruised skin break. He

211

thought: And again at Christmas, thrusting the Child's face into the filth of the stable. He cried up the stairs, "What's that you said, dear?"

"Oh, only that we've got so much to celebrate tomorrow. Being together and the commissionership. Life is so happy, Ticki."

And that, he told his loneliness with defiance, is my reward, splashing the whisky across the table, defying the ghosts to do their worst, watching God bleed.

IV.

HE COULD TELL THAT YUSEF WAS WORKING late in his office on the quay. The little white two-storied building stood beside the wooden jetty on the edge of Africa, just beyond the army dumps of petrol, and a line of light showed under the curtains in the landward window. A policeman saluted Scobie as he picked his way between the crates. "All quiet, corporal?"

"All quiet, sah."

"Have you patrolled at the Kru Town end?"

"Oh, yes, sah. All quiet, sah." He could tell from the promptitude of the reply how untrue it was.

"The wharf rats out, eh?"

"Oh, no, sah. All very quiet like the grave." The stale literary phrase showed that the man had been educated at a mission school.

"Well, good night."

"Good night, sah."

Scobie went on. It was many weeks now since he had seen Yusef—not since the night of the black-mail, and now he felt an odd yearning towards his tormentor. The little white building magnetized him, as though concealed there was his only companionship, the only man he could trust. At least his black-mailer knew him as no one else did: he could sit opposite that fat absurd figure and tell the whole truth. In this new world of lies his black-mailer was at home: he knew the paths: he could advise: even help. . . .

Round the corner of a crate came Wilson. Scobie's torch lit his face like a map.

"Why, Wilson," Scobie said, "you are out late."

"Yes," Wilson said; and Scobie thought uneasily, how he hates me.

"You've got a pass for the quay?"

"Yes."

"Keep away from the Kru Town end. It's not safe there alone. No more nose-bleeding?"

"No," Wilson said. He made no attempt to move: it seemed always his way—to stand blocking a path: a man one had to walk round.

"Well, I'll be saying good night, Wilson. Look in any time. Louise . . ."

Wilson said, "I love her, Scobie."

"I thought you did," Scobie said. "She likes you, Wilson."

"I love her," Wilson repeated. He plucked at the tarpaulin over the crate and said, "You wouldn't know what that means."

"What means?"

"Love. You don't love anybody except yourself, your dirty self."

"You are overwrought, Wilson. It's the climate. Go and lie down."

"You wouldn't act as you do if you loved her." Over the black tide, from an invisible ship, came the sound of a gramophone playing some popular heart-rending tune. A sentry challenged, by the Field Security post, and somebody replied with a password. Scobie lowered his torch till it lit only Wilson's mosquito boots. He said, "Love isn't as simple as you think it is, Wilson. You read too much poetry."

"What would you do if I told her everything—about Mrs. Rolt?"

"But you have told her, Wilson. What you believe. But she prefers my story."

"One day I'll ruin you, Scobie."

"Would that help Louise?"

"I could make her happy," Wilson claimed ingenuously, with a breaking voice that took Scobie back over fifteen years—to a much younger man than this soiled specimen
213

who listened to Wilson at the sea's edge, hearing under the words the low sucking of water against wood. He said gently, "You'd try. I know you'd try. Perhaps . . ." but he had no idea himself how that sentence was supposed to finish, what vague comfort for Wilson had brushed his mind and gone again. Instead an irritation took him against the gangling romantic figure by the crate who was so ignorant and yet knew so much. He said, "I wish meanwhile you'd stop spying on me."

"It's my job," Wilson admitted, and his boots moved in the torch-light.

"The things you find out are so unimportant." He left Wilson beside the petrol dump and walked on. As he climbed the steps to Yusef's office he could see, looking back, an obscure thickening of the darkness where Wilson stood and watched and hated. He would go home and draft a report. "At 11:25 I observed Major Scobie going obviously by appointment . . ."

Scobie knocked and walked right in where Yusef half lay behind his desk, his legs upon it, dictating to a black clerk. Without breaking his sentence—"five hundred rolls match-box design, seven hundred and fifty bucket and sand, six hundred poker dot artificial silk"—he looked up at Scobie with hope and apprehension. Then he said sharply to the clerk, "Get out. But come back. Tell my boy that I see no one." He took his legs from the desk, rose and held out a flabby hand—"Welcome, Major Scobie"—then let it fall like an unwanted piece of material. "This is the first time you have ever honoured my office, Major Scobie."

"I don't know why I've come here now, Yusef."

"It is a long time since we have seen each other." Yusef sat down and rested his great head wearily on a palm like a dish. "Time goes so differently for two people—fast or slow. According to their friendship."

"There's probably a Syrian poem about that."

"There is, Major Scobie," he said eagerly.

"You should be friends with Wilson, not me, Yusef. He reads poetry. I have a prose mind."

"A whisky, Major Scobie?"

"I wouldn't say no." He sat down on the other side of the desk and the inevitable blue siphon stood between them.

"And how is Mrs. Scobie?"

214

"Why did you send me that diamond, Yusef?"

"I was in your debt, Major Scobie."

"Oh, no, you weren't. You paid me off in full with a bit of paper."

"I try so hard to forget that that was the way. I tell myself it was really friendship—at bottom it was friendship."

"It's never any good lying to oneself, Yusef. One sees through the lie too easily."

"Major Scobie, if I saw more of you, I should become a better man." The soda hissed in the glasses and Yusef drank greedily. He said, "I can feel in my heart, Major Scobie, that you are anxious, depressed . . . I have always wished that you would come to me in trouble."

Scobie said, "I used to laugh at the idea—that I should ever come to you."

"In Syria we have a story of a lion and a mouse . . ."

"We have the same story, Yusef. But I've never thought of you as a mouse, and I'm no lion. No lion."

"It is about Mrs. Rolt you are troubled. And your wife, Major Scobie?"

"Yes."

"You do not need to be ashamed with me, Major Scobie. I have had much woman trouble in my life. Now it is better because I have learned the way. The way is not to care a damn, Major Scobie. You say to each of them, 'I do not care a damn. I sleep with whom I please. You take me or leave me. I do not care a damn.' They always take you, Major Scobie." He sighed into his whisky. "Sometimes I have wished they would not take me."

"I've gone to great lengths, Yusef, to keep things from my wife."

"I know the lengths you have gone, Major Scobie."

"Not the whole length. The business with the diamonds was very small compared . . ."

"Yes?"

"You wouldn't understand. Anyway, somebody else knows now—Ali."

"But you trust Ali?"

"I think I trust him. But he knows about you too. He came in last night and saw the diamond there. Your boy was very indiscreet."

The big broad hand shifted on the table. "I will deal with my boy presently."

"Ali's half-brother is Wilson's boy. They see each other."

"That is certainly bad," Yusef said.

He had told all his worries now—all except the worst. He had the odd sense of having for the first time in his life shifted a burden elsewhere. And Yusef carried it—he obviously carried it. He raised himself from his chair now and moved his great haunches to the window, staring at the green black-out curtain as though it were a landscape. A hand went up to his mouth and he began to bite his nails—snip, snip, snip, his teeth closed on each nail in turn. Then he began on the other hand. "I don't suppose it's anything to worry about, really," Scobie said. He was touched by uneasiness as though he had accidentally set in motion a powerful machine he couldn't control.

"It is a bad thing not to trust," Yusef said. "One must always have boys one trusts. You must always know more about them than they do about you." That, apparently, was his conception of trust. Scobie said, "I used to trust him."

Yusef looked at his trimmed nails and took another bite. He said, "Do not worry. I will not have you worry. Leave everything to me, Major Scobie. I will find out for you whether you can trust him." He made the startling claim, "I will look after you."

"How can you do that?" I feel no resentment, he thought with weary surprise: I am being looked after—and a kind of nursery peace descended.

"You mustn't ask me questions, Major Scobie. You must leave everything to me just this once. I understand the way." Moving from the window Yusef turned on Scobie eyes like closed telescopes, blank and brassy. He said with a soothing nurse's gesture of the broad wet palm, "You will just write a little note to your boy, Major Scobie, asking him to come here. I will talk to him. My boy will take it to him."

"But Ali can't read."

"Better still then. You will send some token with my boy to show that he comes from you. Your signet ring."

"What are you going to do, Yusef?"

"I am going to help you, Major Scobie. That is all." Slowly, reluctantly, Scobie drew at his ring. He said, "He's been with me fifteen years. I always have trusted him until now."

"You will see," Yusef said. "Everything will be all right." He spread out his palm to receive the ring and their hands touched: it was like a pledge between conspirators. "Just a few words."

"The ring won't come off," Scobie said. He felt an odd unwillingness. "It's not necessary, anyway. He'll come if your boy tells him that I want him."

"I do not think so. They do not like to come to the wharf at night."

"He will be all right. He won't be alone. Your boy will be with him."

"Oh, yes, yes, of course. But I still think—if you would just send something to show—well, that it is not a trap. Yusef's boy is no more trusted, you see, than Yusef."

"Let him come tomorrow, then."

"Tonight is better," Yusef said.

Scobie felt in his pockets: the broken rosary grated on his nails. He said, "Let him take this, but it's not necessary . . ." and fell silent, staring back at those blank eyes.

"Thank you," Yusef said. "This is most suitable." At the door he said, "Make yourself at home, Major Scobie. Pour yourself another drink. I must give my boy instructions."

He was away a very long time. Scobie poured himself a third whisky and then, because the little office was so airless, he drew the seaward curtains after turning out the light and let what wind there was trickle in from the bay. The moon was rising and the naval depot ship glittered like grey ice. Restlessly he made his way to the other window that looked up the quay towards the sheds and lumber of the native town. He saw Yusef's clerk coming back from there, and he thought how Yusef must have the wharf rats well under control if his clerk could pass alone through their quarters. I came for help, he told himself, and I am being looked after—how, and at whose cost? This was the Day of All Saints, and he remembered how mechanically, almost without fear or shame, he had knelt at the rail this second time and watched the priest come. Even that act of damnation could become as unimportant as a habit. He thought: My heart has hardened, and he pictured the fossilized shells one picks up on a beach: the stony convolutions like arteries. One can strike God once too often. After that, does one care what happens? It seemed to him

217

that he had rotted so far that it was useless to make any effort. God was lodged in his body, and his body was corrupting outwards from that seed.

"It was too hot?" Yusef's voice said. "Let us leave the room dark. With a friend the darkness is kind."

"You have been a very long time."

Yusef said with what must have been deliberate vagueness, "There was much to see to." It seemed to Scobie that now or never he must ask what was Yusef's plan, but the weariness of his corruption halted his tongue. "Yes, it's hot," he said, "let's try and get a cross-draught," and he opened the side window onto the quay. "I wonder if Wilson has gone home."

"Wilson?"

"He watched me come here."

"You must not worry, Major Scobie. I think your boy can be made quite trustworthy."

He said with relief and hope, "You mean you have a hold on him?"

"Don't ask questions. You will see." The hope and the relief both wilted. He said, "Yusef, I must know . . ." but Yusef said, "I have always dreamed of an evening just like this with two glasses by our side and darkness and time to talk about important things, Major Scobie. God. The family. Poetry. I have great appreciation of Shakespeare. The Royal Ordnance Corps have very fine actors and they have made me appreciate the gems of English literature. I am crazy about Shakespeare. Sometimes because of Shakespeare I would like to be able to read, but I am too old to learn. And I think perhaps I would lose my memory. That would be bad for business, and though I do not live for business I must do business to live. There are so many subjects I would like to talk to you about. I should like to hear the philosophy of your life."

"I have none."

"The piece of cotton you hold in your hand in the forest."

"I've lost my way."

"Not a man like you, Major Scobie. I have such an admiration for your character. You are a just man."

"I never was, Yusef. I didn't know myself, that's all. There's a proverb, you know, about the end is the begin-
218

ning. When I was born I was sitting here with you drinking whisky, knowing . . ."

"Knowing what, Major Scobie?"

Scobie emptied his glass. He said, "Surely your boy must have got to my house now."

"He has a bicycle."

"Then they should be on their way back."

"We must not be impatient. We may have to sit a long time, Major Scobie. You know what boys are."

"I thought I did." He found his left hand was trembling on the desk and he put it between his knees to hold it still. He remembered the long trek beside the border: innumerable lunches in the forest shade, with Ali cooking in an old sardine tin, and again that last drive to Bamba came to mind—the long wait at the ferry, the fever coming down on him and Ali always at hand. He wiped the sweat off his forehead and he thought for a moment: This is just a sickness, a fever. I shall wake soon. The record of the last six months—the first night in the Nissen hut, the letter which said too much, the smuggled diamonds, the lies, the sacrament taken to put a woman's mind at ease—seemed as insubstantial as shadows over a bed cast by a hurricane lamp. He said to himself: I am waking up, and heard the sirens blowing the alert just as on that night, that night . . . He shook his head and came awake to Yusef sitting in the dark on the other side of the desk, to the taste of the whisky, and the knowledge that everything was the same. He said wearily, "They ought to be here by now."

Yusef said, "You know what boys are. They get scared by the siren and they take shelter. We must sit here and talk to each other, Major Scobie. It is a great opportunity for me. I do not want the morning ever to come."

"The morning? I am not going to wait till morning for Ali."

"Perhaps he will be frightened. He will know you have found him out and he will run away. Sometimes boys go back to bush . . ."

"You are talking nonsense, Yusef."

"Another whisky, Major Scobie?"

"All right. All right." He thought: Am I taking to drink too? It seemed to him that he had no shape left, nothing you could touch and say: This is Scobie.

219

"Major Scobie, there are rumours that after all justice is to be done and that you are to be Commissioner."

He said with care, "I don't think it will ever come to that."

"I just wanted to say, Major Scobie, that you need not worry about me. I want your good, nothing so much as that. I will slip out of your life, Major Scobie. I will not be a millstone. It is enough for me to have had tonight—this long talk in the dark on all sorts of subjects. I will remember tonight always. You will not have to worry. I will see to that." Through the window behind Yusef's head, from somewhere among the jumble of huts and warehouses, a cry came: pain and fear: it swam up like a drowning animal for air, and fell again into the darkness of the room, into the whisky, under the desk, into the basket of waste-paper, a discarded finished cry.

Yusef said too quickly, "A drunk man." He yelped apprehensively, "Where are you going, Major Scobie? It's not safe—alone." That was the last Scobie ever saw of Yusef, a silhouette stuck stiffly and crookedly on the wall, with the moonlight shining on the siphon and the two drained glasses. At the bottom of the stairs the clerk stood, staring down the wharf. The moonlight caught his eyes: like road studs they showed the way to turn.

There was no movement in the empty warehouses on either side or among the sacks and crates as he moved his torch: if the wharf rats had been out, that cry had driven them back to their holes. His footsteps echoed between the sheds, and somewhere a pye-dog wailed. It would have been quite possible to have searched in vain in this wilderness of litter until morning: what was it that brought him so quickly and unhesitatingly to the body, as though he had himself chosen the scene of the crime? Turning this way and that down the avenues of tarpaulin and wood, he was aware of a nerve in his forehead that beat out the where-abouts of Ali.

The body lay coiled and unimportant like a broken watchspring under a pile of empty petrol drums: it looked as though it had been shovelled there to wait for morning and the scavenger birds. Scobie had a moment of hope before he turned the shoulder over, for after all two boys had been together on the road. The seal-grey neck had been slashed and slashed again. Yes, he thought, I can trust him now. The yellow eyeballs stared up at him like a stranger's flecked with red. It was as if this body had cast him off, disowned him—"I know you not." He swore aloud, hysterically, "By God, I'll get the man who did this," but under that anonymous stare insincerity withered. He thought: I am the man. Didn't I know all the time in Yusef's room that something was planned? Couldn't I have pressed for an answer? A voice said, "Sah?"

"Who's that?"

"Corporal Laminah, sah."

"Can you see a broken rosary anywhere around? Look carefully."

"I can't see nothing, sah."

Scobie thought: If only I could weep, if only I could feel pain; have I really become so evil? Unwillingly he looked down at the body. The fumes of petrol lay all around in the heavy night and for a moment he saw the body as something very small and dark and a long way away—like a broken piece of the rosary he looked for: a couple of black beads and the image of God coiled at the end of it. O God, he thought, I've killed you: you've served me all these years and I've killed you at the end of them. God lay there under the petrol drums and Scobie felt the tears in his mouth, salt in the cracks of his lips. You served me and I did this to you. You were faithful to me, and I wouldn't trust you.

"What is it, sah?" the corporal whispered, kneeling by the body.

"I loved him," Scobie said.

Part Two

I. AS SOON AS HE HAD HANDED OVER HIS WORK TO Fraser and closed his office for the day, Scobie started out for the Nissen. He drove with his eyes half closed, looking straight ahead: he told himself, Now, today, I am going to clean up, whatever the cost. Life is going to start again: this nightmare of love is finished. It seemed to him that it had died for ever the previous night under the petrol drums. The sun blazed down on his hands which were sealed to the wheel by sweat.

His mind was so concentrated on what had to come—the opening of a door, a few words, and closing a door again for ever—that he nearly passed Helen on the road. She was walking down the hill towards him, hatless. She didn't even see the car. He had to run after her and catch her up. When she turned it was the face he had seen at Pende carried past him—defeated, broken, as ageless as a smashed glass.

"What are you doing here? In the sun, without a hat."

She said vaguely, "I was looking for you," standing there, dithering on the laterite.

"Come back to the car. You'll get sunstroke." A look of cunning came into her eyes. "Is it as easy as all that?" she asked, but she obeyed him.

They sat side by side in the car. There seemed to be no object in driving further: one could say good-bye here as easily as there. She said, "I heard this morning about Ali. Did you do it?"

"I didn't cut his throat myself," he said. "But he died because I existed."

"Do you know who did?"

"I don't know who held the knife. A wharf rat, I suppose.

222

Yusef's boy who was with him has disappeared. Perhaps he did it or perhaps he's dead too. We will never prove anything. I doubt if Yusef intended it."

"You know," she said, "this is the end for us. I can't go on ruining you any more. Don't speak. Let me speak. I never thought it would be like this. Other people seem to have love affairs which start and end and are happy, but with us it doesn't work. It seems to be all or nothing. So it's got to be nothing. Please don't speak. I've been thinking about this for weeks. I'm going to go away—right away."

"Where to?"

"I told you not to speak. Don't ask questions." He could see in the windscreen a pale reflexion of her desperation. It seemed to him as though he were being torn apart. "My dear," she said, "don't think it's easy. I've never done anything so hard. It would be so much easier to die. You come into everything. I can never again see a Nissen hut—or a Ford car. Or taste pink gin. See a black face. Even a bed . . . one has to sleep in a bed. I don't know where I'll get away from you. It's no use saying in a year it will be all right. It's a year I've got to get through. All the time knowing you are somewhere. I could send a telegram or a letter and you'd have to read it, even if you didn't reply." He thought: How much easier it would be for her if I were dead. "But I mustn't write," she said. She wasn't crying: her eyes when he took a quick glance were dry and red, as he remembered them in hospital, exhausted. "Waking up will be the worst. There's always a moment when one forgets that everything's different."

He said, "I came up here to say good-bye too. But there are things I can't do."

"Don't talk, darling. I'm being good. Can't you see I'm being good? You don't have to go away from me—I'm going away from you. You won't ever know where to. I hope I won't be too much of a slut."

"No," he said, "no."

"Be quiet, darling. You are going to be all right. You'll see. You'll be able to clean up. You'll be a Catholic again— that's what you really want, isn't it, not a pack of women?"

"I want to stop giving pain," he said.

"You want peace, dear. You'll have peace. You'll see. Everything will be all right." She put her hand on his knee and began at last to weep in this effort to comfort him. He thought: Where did she pick up this heart-breaking tenderness? Where do they learn to be so old so quickly?

"Look, dear. Don't come up to the hut. Open the car door for me. It's stiff. We'll say good-bye here, and you'll just drive home—or to the office if you'd rather. That's so much easier. Don't worry about me. I'll be all right." He thought: I missed that one death and now I'm having them all. He leant over her and wrenched at the car door: her tears touched his cheek. He could feel the mark like a burn. "There's no objection to a farewell kiss, dear. We haven't quarrelled. There hasn't been a scene. There's no bitterness." As they kissed he was aware of pain under his mouth like the beating of a bird's heart. They sat still, silent, and the door of the car lay open. A few black labourers passing down the hill looked curiously in.

She said, "I can't believe that this is the last time: that I'll get out and you'll drive away, and we won't see each other again ever. I won't go outside more than I can help till I get right away. I'll be up here and you'll be down there. Oh, God, I wish I hadn't got the furniture you brought me."

"It's just official furniture."

"The cane is broken in one of the chairs where you sat down too quickly."

"Darling, darling, this isn't the way."

"Don't speak, dear. I'm really being quite good, but I can't say these things to another living soul. In books there's always a confidant. But I haven't got a confidant. I must say them all once." He thought again: If I were dead, she would be free of me: one forgets the dead quite quickly; one doesn't wonder about the dead—what is he doing now, who is he with? This for her is the hard way.

"Now, dear, I'm going to do it. Shut your eyes. Count three hundred slowly, and I won't be in sight. Turn the car quickly, dear, and drive like hell. I don't want to see you go. And I'll stop my ears. I don't want to hear you change gear at the bottom of the hill. Cars do that a hundred times a day. I don't want to hear you change gear."

O God, he prayed, his hands dripping over the wheel, kill me now, now. My God, you'll never have more complete contrition. What a mess I am. I carry suffering with me like a body smell. Kill me. Put an end to me. Vermin

224

don't have to exterminate themselves. Kill me. Now. Now. Now. Before I hurt you again.

"Shut your eyes, dear. This is the end. Really the end." She said hopelessly, "It seems so silly, though."

He said, "I won't shut my eyes. I won't leave you. I promised that."

'You aren't leaving me. I'm leaving you."

"It won't work, darling. We love each other. It won't work. I'd be up this evening to see how you were. I couldn't sleep . . ."

"You can always sleep. I've never known such a sleeper. Oh, my dear, look. I'm beginning to laugh at you again just as though we weren't saying good-bye."

"We aren't. Not yet."

"But I'm only ruining you. I can't give you any happiness."

"Happiness isn't the point."

"I'd made up my mind."

"So had I."

"But, dear, what do we do?" She surrendered completely. "I don't mind going on as we are. I don't mind the lies. Anything."

"Just leave it to me. I've got to think." He leant over her and closed the door of the car. Before the lock had clicked he had made his decision.

2

Scobie watched the small boy as he cleared away the evening meal, watched him come in and go out, watched the bare feet flap the floor. Louise said, "I know it's a terrible thing, darling, but you've got to put it behind you. You can't help Ali now." A new parcel of books had come from England and he watched her cutting the leaves of a volume of verse. There was more grey in her hair than when she had left for South Africa, but she looked, it seemed to him, years younger because she was paying more attention to make-up: her dressing table was littered with the pots and bottles and tubes she had brought back from the south. Ali's death meant little to her: why should it? It was the sense of guilt that made it so important. Otherwise one didn't grieve for a death. When he was young, he had thought love had something to do with understanding, but with age he knew that no human being understood another. Love was the wish to understand, and presently with constant failure the wish died, and love died too perhaps or changed into this painful affection, loyalty, pity. . . . She sat there, reading poetry, and she was a thousand miles away from the torment that shook his hand and dried his mouth. She would understand, he thought, if I were in a book, but would I understand her if she were just a character?—I don't read that sort of book.

"Haven't you anything to read, darling?"

"I'm sorry. I don't feel much like reading."

She closed her book, and it occurred to him that after all she had her own effort to make: she tried to help. Sometimes he wondered with horror whether perhaps she knew everything, whether that complacent face she had worn since her return after all masked misery. She said, "Let's talk about Christmas."

"It's still a long way off," he said quickly.

"Before you know, it will be on us. I was wondering whether we couldn't give a party. We've always been out to dinner: it would be fun to have people here. Perhaps on Christmas Eve."

"Just what you like."

"We could all go on then to Midnight Mass. Of course you and I would have to remember to drink nothing after ten—but the others could do as they pleased."

He looked up at her with momentary hatred as she sat so cheerfully there, so smugly it seemed to him, arranging his further damnation. He was going to be Commissioner. She had what she wanted—her sort of success, everything was all right with her now. He thought: It was the hysterical woman who felt the world laughing behind her back that I loved. I love failure: I can't love success. And how successful she looks, sitting there: one of the saved—and he saw laid across that wide face like a news-screen the body of Ali under the black drums, the exhausted eyes of Helen, and all the faces of the lost, his companions in exile, the unrepentant thief, the soldier with the sponge. Thinking of what he had done and was going to do, he thought, with love, even God is a failure.

"What is it, Ticki? Are you still worrying . . . ?"

But he couldn't tell her the entreaty that was on his lips:
226

Let me pity you again, be disappointed, unattractive, be a failure so that I can love you once more without this bitter gap between us. Time is short. I want to love you too at the end. He said slowly, "It's the pain. It's over now. When it comes"—he remembered the phrase of the text-book—"it's like a vice."

"You must see the doctor, Ticki."

"I'll see him tomorrow. I was going to anyway because of my sleeplessness."

"Your sleeplessness? But, Ticki, you sleep like a log."

"Not the last week."

"You're imagining it."

"No. I wake up about two and can't sleep again—till just before we are called. Don't worry. I'll get some tablets."

"I hate drugs."

"I won't go on long enough to form a habit."

"We must get you right for Christmas, Ticki."

"I'll be all right by Christmas." He came stiffly across the room to her, imitating the bearing of a man who fears that pain may return again, and put his hand against her breast. "Don't worry." Hatred went out of him at the touch—she wasn't as successful as all that: she would never be married to the Commissioner of Police.

After she had gone to bed he took out his diary. In this record at least he had never lied. At the worst he had omitted. He had checked his temperatures as carefully as a sea captain making up his log. He had never exaggerated or minimized, and he had never indulged in speculation. All he had written here were facts. *November 1. Early Mass with Louise. Spent morning on larceny case at Mrs. Onoko's. Temperature 91° at 2. Saw Y. at his office. Ali found murdered.* The statement was as plain and simple as that other time when he had written: *C. died.*

November 2. He sat a long while with that date in front of him, so long that presently Louise called down to him. He replied carefully, "Go to sleep, dear. If I sit up late, I may be able to sleep properly." But already, exhausted by the day and by all the plans that had to be laid, he was near to nodding at the table. He went to his ice-box, and, wrapping a piece of ice in his handkerchief, rested it against his forehead until sleep receded. *November 2.* Again he picked up his pen: This was his death-warrant he was signing. He wrote: *Saw Helen for a few minutes.* (It

227

was always safer to leave no facts for anyone else to unearth.) *Temperature at 2, 92°. In the evening, return of pain. Fear angina.* He looked up the pages of the entries for a week back and added an occasional note. *Slept very badly. Bad night. Sleeplessness continues.* He read the entries over carefully: they would be read later by the coroner, by the insurance inspectors. They seemed to him to be in his usual manner. Then he put the ice back on his forehead to drive sleep away. It was still only half after midnight: it would be better not to go to bed before two.

II. "It grips me," Scobie said, "like a vice."

"And what do you do then?"

"Why, nothing. I stay as still as I can until the pain goes."

"How long does it last?"

"It's difficult to tell, but I don't think more than a minute."

The stethoscope followed like a ritual. Indeed there was something clerical in all that Dr. Travis did: an earnestness, almost a reverence. Perhaps because he was young he treated the body with great respect: when he rapped the chest he did it slowly, carefully, with his ear bowed close as though he really expected somebody or something to rap back. Latin words came softly onto his tongue as though in the Mass—*sternum* instead of *pacem*.

"And then," Scobie said, "there's the sleeplessness."

The young man sat back behind his desk and tapped with an indelible pencil: there was a mauve smear at the corner of his mouth which seemed to indicate that sometimes—off guard—he sucked it. "That's probably nerves," Dr. Travis said, "apprehension of pain. Unimportant."

"It's important to me. Can't you give me something to take? I'm all right when once I get to sleep, but I lie awake for hours, waiting . . . Sometimes I'm hardly fit for work. And a policeman, you know, needs his wits."

"Of course," Dr. Travis said. "I'll soon settle you. Evi-

228

pan's the stuff for you." It was as easy as all that. "Now as for the pain"—he began his tap, tap, tap, with the pencil. He said, "It's impossible to be certain, of course. I want you to note carefully the circumstances of every attack . . . what seems to bring it on. Then it will be quite possible to regulate it, avoid it almost entirely."

"But what's wrong?"

Dr. Travis said, "There are some words that always shock the layman. I wish we could call cancer by a symbol like H_2O. People wouldn't be nearly so disturbed. It's the same with the word angina?"

"You think it's angina?"

"It has all the characteristics. But men can live for years with angina—even work in reason. We have to see exactly how much you can do."

"Should I tell my wife?"

"There's no point in not telling her. I'm afraid this will mean—retirement."

"Is that all?"

"You may die of a lot of things before angina gets you—given care."

"On the other hand, I suppose it might happen any day?"

"I can't guarantee anything, Major Scobie. I'm not even absolutely satisfied that this is angina."

"I'll speak to the Commissioner then on the quiet. I don't want to alarm my wife until we are certain."

"If I were you, I'd tell her what I've said. It will prepare her. But tell her you may live for years with care."

"And the sleeplessness?"

"This will make you sleep."

Sitting in the car with the little package on the seat beside him, he thought, I have only now to choose the date. He didn't start his car for quite a while: he was touched by a feeling of awe as if he had in fact been given his death-sentence by the doctor. His eyes dwelt on the neat blob of sealing-wax like a dried wound. He thought, I have still got to be careful, so careful. If possible no one must even suspect. It was not only the question of his life insurance: the happiness of others had to be protected. It was not so easy to forget a suicide as a middle-aged man's death from angina.

He unsealed the package and studied the directions. He

had no knowledge of what a fatal dose might be, but surely if he took ten times the correct amount he would be safe. That meant every night for nine nights removing a dose and keeping it secretly for use on the tenth night. More evidence must be invented in his diary, which must be written right up to the end—November 12. He must make engagements for the following week. In his behaviour there must be no hint of farewells. This was the worst crime a Catholic could commit—it must be a perfect one.

First the Commissioner . . . He drove down towards the police station and stopped his car outside the church. The solemnity of the crime lay over his mind almost like happiness: it was action at last—he had fumbled and muddled too long. He put the package for safekeeping into his pocket and went in, carrying his death. An old mammy was lighting a candle before the Virgin's statue: another sat with her market basket beside her and her hands folded, staring up at the altar. Otherwise the church was empty. Scobie sat down at the back: he had no inclination to pray —what was the good? If one was a Catholic, one had all the answers: no prayer was effective in a state of mortal sin—but he watched the other two with sad envy. They were still inhabitants of the country he had left. This was what human love had done to him—it had robbed him of love for eternity. It was no use pretending as a young man might that the price was worth while.

If he couldn't pray he could at least talk, sitting there at the back, as far as he could get from Golgotha. He said, O God, I am the only guilty one because I've known the answers all the time. I've preferred to give you pain rather than give pain to Helen or my wife because I can't observe your suffering. I can only imagine it. But there are limits to what I can do to you—or them. I can't desert either of them while I'm alive, but I can die and remove myself from their blood-stream. They are ill with me and I can cure them. And you too, God—you are ill with me. I can't go on, month after month, insulting you. I can't face coming up to the altar at Christmas—your birthday feast—and taking your body and blood for the sake of a lie. I can't do that. You'll be better off if you lose me once and for all. I know what I'm doing. I'm not pleading for mercy. I am going to damn myself, whatever that means. I've longed for peace and I'm never going to know peace again. But you'll be at peace when I am out of your reach. It will be no use then sweeping the floor to find me or searching for me over the mountains. You'll be able to forget me, God, for eternity. One hand clasped the package in his pocket like a promise.

No one can speak a monologue for long alone: another voice will always make itself heard: every monologue sooner or later becomes a discussion. So now he couldn't keep the other voice silent: it spoke from the cave of his body: it was as if the sacrament which had lodged there for his damnation gave tongue: You say you love me, and yet you'll do this to me—rob me of you forever. I made you with love. I've wept your tears. I've saved you from more than you will ever know; I planted in you this longing for peace only so that one day I could satisfy your longing and watch your happiness. And now you push me away, you put me out of your reach. There are no capital letters to separate us when we talk together. I am not Thou but simply you, when you speak to me; I am humble as any other beggar. Can't you trust me as you'd trust a faithful dog? I have been faithful to you for two thousand years. All you have to do now is ring a bell, go into a box, confess . . . the repentance is already there, straining at your heart. It's not repentance you lack, just a few simple actions: to go up to the Nissen hut and say good-bye. Or if you must, continue rejecting me but without lies any more. Go to your house and say good-bye to your wife and live with your mistress. If you live you will come back to me sooner or later. One of them will suffer, but can't you trust me to see that the suffering isn't too great?

The voice was silent in the cave and his own voice replied hopelessly: No. I don't trust you. I love you, but I've never trusted you. If you made me, you made this feeling of responsibility that I've always carried about like a sack of bricks. I'm not a policeman for nothing—responsible for order, for seeing justice is done. There was no other profession for a man of my kind. I can't shift my responsibility to you. If I could, I would be someone else. I can't make one of them suffer so as to save myself. I'm responsible and I'll see it through the only way I can. A sick man's death means to them only a short suffering—everybody has to die. We are all of us resigned to death: it's life we aren't resigned to.

So long as you live, the voice said, I have hope. There's no human hopelessness like the hopelessness of God. Can't you just go on, as you are doing now? the voice pleaded, lowering the terms every time it spoke, like a dealer in a market. It explained: There are worse acts. But— No, he said, No. That's impossible. I love you and I won't go on insulting you at your own altar. You see, it's an *impasse*, God, an *impasse*, he said, clutching the package in his pocket. He got up and turned his back on the altar and went out. Only when he saw his face in the driving mirror did he realize that his eyes were bruised with suppressed tears. He drove on towards the police station and the Commissioner.

III. November 3. Yesterday I told the Commissioner that angina had been diagnosed and that I should have to retire as soon as a successor could be found. Temperature at 2 p.m. 91°. Much better night as the result of evipan.

November 4. Went with Louise to 7:30 Mass, but pain threatening to return did not wait for Communion. In the evening told Louise that I should have to retire before end of tour. Did not mention angina but spoke of strained heart. Another good night as result of evipan. Temperature at 2 p.m. 89°.

November 5. Lamp thefts in Wellington Street. Spent long morning at Azikawe's store checking story of fire in storeroom. Temperature at 2 p.m. 90°. Drove Louise to Club for library night.

November 6-10. First time I've failed to keep up daily entries. Pain has become more frequent and unwilling to take on any extra exertion. Like a vice. Lasts about one minute. Liable to come on if I walk more than half a mile. Last night or two have slept badly in spite of evipan, I think from the apprehension of pain.

November 11. Saw Travis again. There seems to be no doubt now that it is angina. Told Louise tonight, but also

that with care I may live for years. Discussed with Commis-
sioner an early passage home. In any case can't go for
another month as too many cases I want to see through the
courts in the next week or two. Agreed to dine with Fel-
lowes on 13th, Commissioner on 14th. Temperature at 2
p.m. 88°.

2

Scobie laid down his pen and wiped his wrist on the
blotting paper. It was just six o'clock on November 12,
and Louise was out at the beach. His brain was clear, but
the nerves tingled from his shoulder to his wrist. He
thought: I have come to the end. What years had passed
since he walked up through the rain to the Nissen hut,
while the sirens wailed: the moment of happiness. It was
time to die after so many years.

But there were still deceptions to be practised, just as
though he were going to live through the night, good-byes
to be said with only himself knowing that they were good-
byes. He walked very slowly up the hill in case he was observed—wasn't he a sick man?—and turned off by the Nissens. He couldn't just die without some word—what word?
O God, he prayed, let it be the right word, but when he
knocked there was no reply, no words at all. Perhaps she
was at the beach with Bagster.

The door was not locked and he went in. Years had
passed in his brain, but here time had stood still. It might
have been the same bottle of gin from which the boy had
stolen—how long ago? The junior official's chairs stood
stiffly around, as though on a film set: he couldn't believe
they had ever moved, any more than the pouf presented by
—was it Mrs. Carter? On the bed the pillow had not been
shaken after the siesta, and he laid his hand on the warm
mould of a skull. O God, he prayed, I'm going away from
all of you for ever: let her come back in time: let me see
her once more—but the hot day cooled around him and
nobody came. At six-thirty Louise would be back from the
beach. He couldn't wait any longer.

I must leave some kind of a message, he thought, and
perhaps before I have written it she will have come. He
felt a constriction in his breast worse than any pain he had
233

ever invented to Travis. I shall never touch her again. I shall leave her mouth to others for the next twenty years. Most lovers deceived themselves with the idea of an eternal union beyond the grave, but he knew all the answers: he went to an eternity of deprivation. He looked for paper and couldn't find so much as a torn envelope: he thought he saw a writing case, but it was the stamp-album that he unearthed, and opening it at random for no reason, he felt fate throw another shaft, for he remembered that particular stamp and how it came to be stained with gin. She will have to tear it out, he thought, but that won't matter: she had told him that you can't see where a stamp has been torn out. There was no scrap of paper even in his pockets, and in a sudden rush of jealousy he lifted up the little green image of George VI and wrote in ink beneath it: *I love you.* She can't take that out, he thought with cruelty and disappointment, that's indelible. For a moment he felt as though he had laid a mine for an enemy, but this was no enemy. Wasn't he clearing himself out of her path like a piece of dangerous wreckage? He shut the door behind him and walked slowly down the hill—she might yet come. Everything he did now was for the last time—an odd sensation. He would never come this way again, and five minutes later, taking a new bottle of gin from his cupboard, he thought: I shall never open another bottle. The actions which could be repeated became fewer and fewer. Presently there would be only one unrepeatable action left, the act of swallowing. He stood with the gin bottle poised and thought: Then hell will begin, and they'll be safe from me. Helen, Louise . . . and you.

At dinner he talked deliberately of the week to come: he blamed himself for accepting Fellowes' invitation and explained that dinner with the Commissioner the next day was unavoidable—there was much to discuss.

"Is there no hope, Ticki, that after a rest, a long rest . . . ?"

"It wouldn't be fair to carry on—to them or you. I might break down at any moment."

"It's really retirement?"

"Yes."

She began to discuss where they were to live: he felt tired to death: it needed all his will to show interest in this fictitious village or that: in the kind of house he knew they

234

would never inhabit. "I don't want a suburb," Louise said. "What I'd really like would be a weather-board house in Kent, so that one can get up to town quite easily."

He said, "Of course it will depend on what we can afford. My pension won't be very large."

"I shall work," Louise said. "It will be easy in war-time."

"I hope we shall be able to manage without that."

"I wouldn't mind."

Bed-time came, and he felt a terrible unwillingness to let her go. There was nothing to do when she had once gone but die. He didn't know how to keep her—they had talked about all the subjects they had in common. He said, "I shall sit here a while. Perhaps I shall feel sleepy if I stay up half an hour longer. I don't want to take the evipan if I can help it."

"I'm very tired after the beach. I'll be off."

When she's gone, he thought, I shall be alone for ever. His heart beat and he was held in the nausea of an awful unreality. I can't believe that I'm going to do this. Presently I shall get up and go to bed, and life will begin again. Nothing, nobody, can force me to die. Though the voice was no longer speaking from the cave of his belly, it was as though fingers, imploring fingers, touched him, signalled their mute messages of distress, tried to hold him. . . .

"What is it, Ticki? You look ill. Come to bed too."

"I wouldn't sleep," he said obstinately.

"Is there nothing I can do?" Louise asked. "My dear, I'd do anything . . ." Her love was like a death-sentence. He said to those scrabbling desperate fingers, O God, it's better that a millstone . . . I can't give her pain, or the other pain, and I can't go on giving you pain. O God, if you love me as I know you do, help me to leave you. Dear God, forget me. But the weak fingers kept their feeble pressure. He had never known before so clearly the weakness of God.

"There's nothing, dear," he said. "I mustn't keep you up." But so soon as she turned towards the stairs he spoke again. "Read me something," he said, "you got a new book today. Read me something."

"You wouldn't like it, Ticki. It's poetry."

"Never mind. It may send me to sleep." He hardly listened while she read: people said you couldn't love two women, but what was this emotion if it were not love? This hungry absorption of what he was never going to see again?

235

The greying hair, the line of nerves upon the face, the thickening body, held him as her beauty never had. She hadn't put on her mosquito boots, and her slippers were badly in need of mending. It isn't beauty that we love, he thought, it's failure—the failure to stay young for ever, the failure of nerves, the failure of the body. Beauty is like success: we can't love it for long. He felt a terrible desire to protect—but that's what I'm going to do, I am going to protect her from myself for ever. Some words she was reading momentarily caught at him:

We are all falling. This hand's falling too—
all have this falling sickness none withstands.

And yet there's always One whose gentle hands
this universal falling can't fall through.

They sounded like Truth, but he rejected them. Comfort can come too easily: he thought, Those hands will never hold my fall: I slip between the fingers, I am greased with falsehood, treachery: trust was a dead language of which he had forgotten the grammar.

"Dear, you are half asleep."

"For a moment."

"I'll go up now. Don't stay long. Perhaps you won't need your evipan tonight."

He watched her go: the lizard lay still upon the wall, but before she had reached the stairs he called her back. "Say good night, Louise, before you go. You may be asleep."

She kissed him perfunctorily on the forehead and he gave her hand a casual caress. There must be nothing strange on this last night, and nothing she would remember with regret. "Good night, Louise. You know I love you," he said with careful lightness.

"Of course, and I love you."

"Yes. Good night, Louise."

"Good night, Ticki."

It was the best he could do with safety.

As soon as he heard the door close above, he took out the cigarette carton in which he kept the ten doses of evipan. He added two more doses for greater certainty—to have exceeded by two doses in ten days could not, surely,

236

be regarded as suspicious. After that he took a long drink of whisky and sat still and waiting for courage with the tablets like seeds in the palm of his hand. Now, he thought, I am absolutely alone: this was freezing point.

But he was wrong. Solitude itself has a voice. It said to him, Throw away those tablets. You'll never be able to collect enough again. You'll be saved. Give up play-acting. Mount the stairs to bed and have a good night's sleep. In the morning you'll be woken by your boy, and you'll drive down to the police station for a day's ordinary work. The voice dwelt on the word "ordinary" as it might have dwelt on the word "happy" or "peaceful."

"No," Scobie said aloud, "no." He pushed the tablets in his mouth, six at a time, and drank them down in two draughts. Then he opened his diary and wrote against November 12: *Called on H.R. out; temperature at 2 p.m.* . . . and broke abruptly off as though at that moment he had been gripped by the final pain. Afterwards he sat bolt upright and waited what seemed a long while for any indication at all of approaching death: he had no idea how it would come to him. He tried to pray, but the Hail Mary evaded his memory, and he was aware of his heart-beats like a clock striking the hour. He tried out an Act of Contrition, but when he reached, "I am sorry and beg pardon," a cloud formed over the door and drifted down over the whole room and he couldn't remember what it was that he had to be sorry for. He had to hold himself upright with both hands, but he had forgotten the reason why he so held himself. Somewhere far away he thought he heard the sounds of pain. "A storm," he said aloud, "there's going to be a storm," as the cloud grew, and he tried to get up to close the windows. "Ali," he called, "Ali." It seemed to him as though someone outside the room were seeking him, calling him, and he made a last effort to indicate that he was here. He got on his feet and heard the hammer of his heart beating out a reply. He had a message to convey, but the darkness and the storm drove it back within the case of his breast, and all the time outside the house, outside the world that drummed like hammer blows within his ear, someone wandered, seeking to get in, someone appealing for help, someone in need of him. And automatically at the call of need, at the cry of a victim, Scobie strung himself to act. He dredged his consciousness up from an infinite distance in order to make some reply. He said aloud, "Dear God, I love . . ." but the effort was too great and he did not feel his body when it struck the floor or hear the small tinkle of the medal as it span like a coin under the ice-box—the saint whose name nobody could remember.

Part Three

WILSON SAID, "I HAVE KEPT AWAY AS LONG AS I could, but I thought perhaps I could be of some help."

"Everybody," Louise said, "has been very kind."

"I had no idea that he was so ill."

"Your spying didn't help you there, did it?"

"That was my job," Wilson said. "And I love you."

"How glibly you use that word, Wilson."

"You don't believe me?"

"I don't believe in anybody who says love, love, love. It means self, self, self."

"You won't marry me then?"

"It doesn't seem likely, does it, but I might, in time. I don't know what loneliness may do. But don't let's talk about love any more. It was *his* favourite lie."

"To both of you."

"How has she taken it, Wilson?"

"I saw her on the beach this afternoon with Bagster. And I hear she was a bit pickled last night at the Club."

"She hasn't any dignity."

"I never knew what he saw in her. I'd never betray you, Louise."

"You know he even went up to see her the day he died."

"How do you know?"

"It's all written there. In his diary. He never lied in his diary. He never said things he didn't mean—like love."

Three days had passed since Scobie had been hastily buried. Dr. Travis had signed the death certificate—*angina pectoris*: in that climate a post mortem was impracticable, and in any case unnecessary, though Dr. Travis had taken the precaution of checking up on the evipan.

"Do you know," Wilson said, "when my boy told me he had died suddenly in the night, I thought it was suicide?"

"It's odd how easily I can talk about him," Louise said, "now that he's gone. Yet I did love him, Wilson. I did love him, but he seems so very very gone."

It was as if he had left nothing behind him in the house but a few suits of clothes and a Mende grammar: at the police station a drawerful of odds and ends and a pair of rusting handcuffs. And yet the house was no different: the shelves were as full of books: it seemed to Wilson that it must always have been her house, not his. Was it just imagination then that made their voices ring a little hollowly as though the house were empty?

"Did you know all the time—about her?" Wilson asked.

"It's why I came home. Mrs. Carter wrote to me. She said everybody was talking. Of course he never realized that. He thought he'd been so clever. And he nearly convinced me—that it was finished. Going to Communion the way he did."

"How did he square that with his conscience?"

"Some Catholics do, I suppose. Go to Confession and start over again. I thought he was more honest, though. When a man's dead, one begins to find out."

"He took money from Yusef."

"I can believe it now."

Wilson put his hand on Louise's shoulder and said, "I'm straight, Louise. I love you."

"I really believe you do." They didn't kiss: it was too soon for that, but they sat in the hollow room, holding hands, listening to the vultures clambering on the iron roof.

"So that's his diary," Wilson said.

"He was writing in it when he died—oh, nothing interesting, just the temperatures. He always kept the temperatures. He wasn't romantic. God knows what she saw in him to make it worth while."

"Would you mind if I looked at it?"

"If you want to," she said. "Poor Ticki, he hasn't any secrets left."

"His secrets were never very secret." He turned a page and read and turned a page. He said, "Had he suffered from sleeplessness very long?"

"I always thought that he slept like a log whatever happened."

Wilson said, "Have you noticed that he's written in pieces about sleeplessness—afterwards?"

"How do you know?"

"You've only to compare the colour of the ink. And all these records of taking his evipan—it's very studied, very careful. But above all, the colour of the ink." He said, "It makes one think."

She interrupted him with horror: "Oh no, he couldn't have done that. After all, in spite of everything, he was a Catholic."

2

"Just let me come in for one little drink," Bagster pleaded.

"We had four at the beach."

"Just one little one more."

"All right," Helen said. There seemed to be no reason so far as she could see to deny anyone anything any more for ever.

Bagster said, "You know, it's the first time you've let me come in. Charming little place you've made of it. Who'd have thought a Nissen hut could be so homey?" Flushed and smelling of pink gin, both of us, we are a pair, she thought. Bagster kissed her wetly on her upper lip and looked around again. "Ha ha," he said, "the good old bottle." When they had drunk one more gin he took off his uniform jacket and hung it carefully on a chair. He said, "Let's take our back hair down and talk of love."

"Need we?" Helen said. "Yet?"

"Lighting-up time," Bagster said. "The dusk. So we'll let George take over the controls . . ."

"Who's George?"

"The automatic pilot, of course. You've got a lot to learn."

"For God's sake, teach me some other time."

"There's no time like the present for a prang," Bagster said, moving her firmly towards the bed. Why not? she thought: Why not . . . if he wants it? Bagster is as good

241

as anyone else. There's nobody in the world I love, and out of it doesn't count, so why not let them have their prangs (it was Bagster's phrase) if they want them enough. She lay back mutely on the bed and shut her eyes and was aware in the darkness of nothing at all. I'm alone, she thought without self-pity, stating it as a fact as an explorer might after his companions have died from exposure.

"By God, you aren't enthusiastic," Bagster said. "Don't you love me a bit, Helen?" and his ginny breath fanned through her darkness.

"No," she said, "I don't love anyone."

He said furiously, "You loved Scobie," and added quickly, "Sorry. Rotten thing to say."

"I don't love anyone," she repeated. "You can't love the dead, can you? They don't exist, do they? It would be like loving the dodo, wouldn't it?" questioning him as if she expected an answer, even from Bagster. She kept her eyes shut because in the dark she felt nearer to death, the death which had absorbed him. The bed trembled a little as Bagster shuffled his weight from off it, and the chair creaked as he took away his jacket. He said, "I'm not all that of a bastard, Helen. You aren't in the mood. See you tomorrow?"

"I expect so." There was no reason to deny anyone anything, but she felt an immense relief because nothing after all had been required.

"Good night, old girl," Bagster said, "I'll be seeing you."

She opened her eyes and saw a stranger in dusty blue pottering round the door. One can say anything to a stranger—they pass on and forget like beings from another world. She asked, "Do you believe in a God?"

"Oh, well, I suppose so," Bagster said, feeling at his moustache.

"I wish I did," she said, "I wish I did."

"Oh, well, you know," Bagster said, "a lot of people do. Must be off now. Good night."

She was alone again in the darkness behind her lids, and the wish struggled in her body like a child: her lips moved, but all she could think of to say was, "For ever and ever, Amen . . ." The rest she had forgotten. She put her hand out beside her and touched the other pillow, as though perhaps after all there was one chance in a thousand that

she was not alone, and if she were not alone now she would
never be alone again.

3

"I should never have noticed it, Mrs. Scobie," Father
Rank said.

"Wilson did."

"Somehow I can't like a man who's quite so observant."

"It's his job."

Father Rank took a quick look at her. "As an accountant."

She said drearily, "Father, haven't you any comfort to
give me?" Oh, the conversations, he thought, that go on in
a house after a death, the turnings over, the discussions, the
questions, the demands—so much noise round the edge of
silence.

"You've been given an awful lot of comfort in your life,
Mrs. Scobie. If what Wilson thinks is true, it's he who
needs our comfort."

"Do you know all that I know about him?"

"Of course I don't, Mrs. Scobie. You've been his wife,
haven't you, for fifteen years. A priest only knows the unimportant things."

"Unimportant?"

"Oh, I mean the sins," he said impatiently. "A man
doesn't come to us and confess his virtues."

"I expect you know about Mrs. Rolt. Most people did."

"Poor woman."

"I don't see why."

"I'm sorry for anyone happy and ignorant who gets
mixed up in that way with one of us."

"He was a bad Catholic."

"That's the silliest phrase in common use," Father Rank
said.

"And at the end, this—horror. He must have known
that he was damning himself."

"Yes, he knew that all right. He never had any trust in
mercy—except for other people."

"It's no good even praying . . ."

Father Rank clapped the cover of the diary to and said,
243

furiously, "For goodness' sake, Mrs. Scobie, don't imagine you—or I—know a thing about God's mercy."

"The Church says . . ."

"I know the Church says. The Church knows all the rules. But it doesn't know what goes on in a single human heart."

"You think there's some hope then?" she wearily asked.

"Are you so bitter against him?"

"I haven't any bitterness left."

"And do you think God's likely to be more bitter than a woman?" he said with harsh insistence, but she winced away from the arguments of hope.

"Oh why, why, did he have to make such a mess of things?"

Father Rank said, "It may seem an odd thing to say—when a man's as wrong as he was—but I think, from what I saw of him, that he really loved God."

She had denied just now that she felt any bitterness, but a little more of it drained out now like tears from exhausted ducts. "He certainly loved no one else," she said.

"And you may be in the right of it there, too," Father Rank replied.

ABOUT THE AUTHOR

GRAHAM GREENE was born in England in 1904. He served on the staff of the London *Times* and the *Spectator*. In World War II he was a member of the foreign office with special duties in West Africa. His first novel was *The Man Within*. He has written several thrillers, including *The Third Man* and *Our Man in Havana*. His more serious novels are notable for their subtle characterization and accomplished craftsmanship.

A number of Greene's novels and short stories have had successful motion picture adaptations, and two of his plays, *The Living Room* and *The Potting Shed,* were produced on Broadway. In 1952 Graham Greene was given the Catholic Literary Award for *The End of the Affair.*